YOUR
WONDERFUL
BABY

YOUR WONDERFUL BABY

a practical approach
to baby & child care

by **Willis J. Potts, M.D.**

RAND M^cNALLY & COMPANY
CHICAGO / NEW YORK / SAN FRANCISCO

To my wife,
HENRIETTA,
without whose help
this book could
not have been
written.

PREFACE

GROWING UP is a long, tedious process. Rearing children is a difficult task.

To promote understanding of the growing baby and his needs;

To furnish guidance in the prevention, recognition, and treatment of childhood diseases;

To point out practical methods for the treatment of accidents, poisonings, and other emergencies;

To assist in distinguishing serious from self-limited diseases;

To suggest sympathetic understanding of the eccentricities of normal children;

To emphasize again and again that the child sunned by love and security will be able to withstand the storms of illness and pain;

These are the objectives in writing this book.

ACKNOWLEDGMENTS

Acknowledgment of all the sources of information utilized in the writing of this book is impossible. For hundreds of years doctors and teachers have set forth their opinions on how to care for and rear children. Any book on child care is necessarily based upon an adaptation of what has been previously learned and upon an interpretation of what seems best today. The next generation may well call us stupid.

Such text books as Nelson's *Textbook of Pediatrics;* Gellis and Kagan's book on *Current Pediatric Therapy;* Bakwin's *Clinical Management of Behavioral Problems in Children;* Meyer's *Essentials of Infant Feeding;* such popular books as Emily Post's *Children are People;* Gruenberg, editor of *The Encyclopedia of Child Care and Guidance,* Volume 14 of *Childcraft, You and Your Child;* the "bible" of millions of mothers, Spock's book on *Baby and Child Care,* and innumerable pamphlets on all phases of child care have been read and reread.

To pediatricians, notably Doctors James H. Wallace, Alfred S. and Howard S. Traisman, Matthew M. Steiner, Pola Piotrowski, Eugene L. Slotkowski, L. Martin Hardy; Jerome L. Schulman, psychiatrist; the late Bert I. Beverly, author of *In Defense of Children;* William O. McQuiston, anaesthesiologist; and a host of other specialists in all branches of medicine, I am indebted and deeply grateful.

Through contact with thousands of mothers in private and clinic practice, I have found practical solutions to many minor problems. Letters of inquiry in response to my syndicated newspaper column, "The Doctor and Your Child," have given me an insight into the worries of harassed mothers. Interestingly enough, 60 percent of their questions pertain to psychological problems such as refusal to eat, thumb-sucking, stuttering, potty training, constipation, bed-wetting, etc.

To Lloyd Wendt, editor of *Chicago's American* newspaper, I am especially grateful for permission to use much of the material which originally appeared in my columns.

My most apt teachers have been the children themselves; observation of their uninhibited comments and uncamouflaged attitudes taught me much about the relationship of child to parent and doctor.

To Mary Alice Jones, Roy Porter, Bennet Harvey, and Shirley L. Warren of Rand McNally & Company, I am thankful for patience and help and faith that this book might be worth publishing.

Thanks to Viola Muffler, my secretary, for patiently typing and retyping the manuscript.

CONTENTS

Breakfast / Improper Dieting / Diet for Your Teen-Age Girl / Height is Inherited

YOUR
WONDERFUL
BABY

PART 1.

The First Two Years

FROM the moment a baby arrives, your way of life is changed. The task you have assumed is a complex one: a mixture of exquisite pleasure when the baby smiles and touches your cheek with his soft little hand; of unreasonable vexation when the rebellious nonconformist screams and kicks in a violent temper tantrum; of long, weary night hours spent at the bedside of the sick child; of merry days when in blooming health he again runs and plays.

The first two years are most important. You will provide him with food and care necessary for physical development. You and your husband will furnish an environment which will influence the basic pattern of his life. Nothing is more esential to a growing child than the feeling of being wanted and loved.

chapter One

THAT WONDERFUL
NEW BABY

YOU have been eagerly looking forward to the birth of your first baby and here he is. The doctor has told you that he is normal. The excitement and anxiety of delivery are forgotten and you are free to take a long and appraising look at this child you have brought into the world.

To you this little creature is the most adorable living thing you have ever seen; of course he is, he's yours.

We'll assume that he is of average weight, seven pounds and a few ounces and is about twenty inches long. He is as red as a broiled lobster, his skin is wrinkled and scaly. He sleeps most of the time but wakes up periodically to cry for no apparent reason. He is not hungry the first day.

Because he is still not accustomed to the change in temperature, his hands and feet are blue and his skin is mottled. For some days he will prefer to lie with his feet drawn up and his arms bent. His thumbs will be held inside clenched fingers but soon they will be brought outside to make a fighting fist.

All that fine downy hair on his face, shoulders, and back will slowly disappear and that adorable mop of hair on his head will surely fall out.

His head, as big around as his chest, may be misshapen due to molding during delivery. Swelling on one side of the head may give him a lopsided appearance. Time will erase these temporary and harmless irregularities.

You will be able to feel two soft spots (fontanelles) in the skull; the one in front is diamond shaped; the one in back, triangular. The notion that touching, pressure, or even mild bumps on these soft spots will injure the brain is false; there is a tough membrane in the fontanelle which gives ample protection.

Puffiness of the eyes is due to the silver nitrate which was put into them immediately after birth. Most of the time the baby will keep his eyes closed. If you catch a fleeting glimpse, you will see that his eyes are dark blue—newborn babies have dark blue eyes. Perhaps his eyes appear crossed; don't be alarmed. Until babies learn to focus their vision during the first few months of life, they all, at times, will have crossed or "wandering" eyes. During the first few weeks the baby will shed no tears when he cries.

Although long a part of you, he is now in this world as a brand new individual and vociferously will make that fact known in a few days. He probably will not conform to the pattern you are already cutting for him. Nor should he. All you can do from this day on is to give this little human being physical care plus love and security.

IS TWINS

"How wonderful to have twins." This remark is most apt to be made by those whose babies have come one at a time.

"It's almost as easy to take care of two babies as one," is a myth. Twins multiply work by two, in fact, slightly more because excessive fatigue decreases the mother's efficiency. If both babies would cry at the same time, be sick at the same time instead of passing colds back and forth, be satisfied with identical feedings and establish similar bowel habits, the doubled task would be lightened.

The mother of two children, two and four, is overwhelmed when her obstetrician tells her she is going to have twins. She will need all the help she can get from father, relatives, or from hired help if she can possibly afford it. Of course, twins are cute and as loved as single babies; nevertheless, my sympathy goes out to the woman who suddenly is confronted with twice the task she anticipated.

The chances of you, the average American woman, having twins is one in eighty-six pregnancies. Age is important; a woman nearing forty is three times as apt to have twins as a twenty year old. Father's age is of no significance.

Twins definitely run in families; the tendency toward having twins is passed on from one generation to another through both mother and father. A woman who has had twins is five times as apt to repeat as the average woman. If you are near forty and already have one set of twins, watch out.

Fraternal twins develop from two eggs; each fertilized at the same time by separate sperms. Fraternal twins are no more similar to each other than to other children in the family.

Identical twins—one-third as common as fraternal twins—come from one egg fertilized by one sperm. The fertilized egg instead of developing in the usual way splits into two. Identical twins, therefore, are always exactly alike, are of the same sex, have the same color of hair and eyes; one is a carbon copy of the other.

The long and deeply established custom of dressing twins alike seems inappropriate. Just because twins happen to be born at the same time and are alike physically is no reason to suppose that they will be alike emotionally. The reaction of each, especially fraternal twins, to environment is bound to be different. To try to pound twins into similar molds is unfair to both. Putting them in the same kind of clothes and giving them similar toys are psychological suggestions that they should be alike when the chances are great that they aren't and don't want to be.

IS BREAST FED

Nothing is better for a newborn baby than mother's milk. No one will dispute this statement; nevertheless, during the past twenty years the percentage of breast-fed babies has continued to fall until at present not more than 10 percent of suburban mothers nurse their babies. This trend toward artificial feeding has been brought about largely by the availability of excellent prepared baby foods and by changed customs. Bottle feeding allows more freedom and permits working mothers to return to their employment soon after delivery.

Whether this trend toward artificial feeding is good or bad is vigorously argued by doctors, and by prospective and experienced mothers. Certainly to nurse one's baby is to a mother as natural an instinct as breathing. It seems unfortunate that such an important and rewarding function of motherhood is slowly being eliminated from the pattern of modern living. Breast feeding furnishes two great essentials: perfect food for physical growth and close bodily contact for normal emotional development.

An expectant mother, with the advice of her doctor and experienced friends, has to decide whether the coming baby shall be breast or bottle fed. I believe the majority of women would enjoy the experience of nursing their babies for a few months but are dissuaded by reluctance to being tied to a rigid schedule. The woman whose sole reason for not nursing her baby is that she is involved in social and infant welfare work, is extending her activities in the wrong direction. Infant welfare begins at home.

If you as a healthy prospective mother are determined to nurse your baby, you have a 95 percent chance of being successful. Before your baby is due be sure to choose a doctor who is in accord with and enthusiastic about your decision. He will give you specific directions about diet, care of the nipples, nursing schedules, etc. Here are some of the benefits you and your baby will receive and some of the problems you will face.

In some mysterious way the stimulus of breast function furnishes a hormone or its equivalent which makes the uterus contract and quickly return to normal and makes you feel better all over. Emotional satisfaction will come from the knowledge that you are giving your child the best possible food and intimate personal contact, which the baby in his own way rightly interprets as being wanted and loved; nothing is more important for the foundation of a happy, well-adjusted life. Incidentally, you won't have to worry about formula preparation, bottle and nipple sterilization, or warming a bottle at night. You will even save some money.

Babies who are breast fed cry less, have fewer attacks of diarrhea, are less constipated, are less susceptible to colds, and are far less subject to infantile eczema and other allergies than bottle-fed babies.

The first day or two after the baby is born you will have little milk, only a small amount of what is called colostrum. The baby isn't hungry for at least two days after delivery. He has experienced an exhausting passage and is tired and sleepy. He will, when offered the breast twelve to eighteen hours after birth, do some sucking and will get only colostrum. It is said that this material has some special benefit for the child. By the third or fourth day the baby will be hungry and, as nature planned, that is the time milk begins to flow.

The fact that the baby does some crying frightens the mother of a first child into thinking that she has insufficient milk. Be patient. The hungrier the baby gets, the more vigorously he will nurse, thereby stimulating the breasts to produce more milk. Worry and panic tend to lessen milk flow. Trust Mother Nature to know what she is doing; she's been influential in keeping the animal kingdom going for a long, long time.

The first week you are home with the baby will be the most difficult. Newness of the situation, a crying baby, broken sleep, fear of failure—all join to lessen milk flow. Have faith, nap when the baby naps, and don't worry so much about the crying. Some crying is good; it expands his lungs.

Hopefully, you have chosen a good doctor who will patiently listen to your complaints and answer the most troubling question: "I wonder whether my baby is getting enough to eat." Examination of the baby by your doctor and reassurance that all is well will give you needed moral support to carry on.

Once in a while it will be good for you to go out for an evening of relaxation and fun. After all, you owe your husband some companionship away from home. Your doctor will wisely prescribe a bottle of supplementary formula for such occasions. No harm will come from having a baby sitter give a bottle provided you have previously demonstrated that the baby will take it. Some babies are mighty fussy about how they are fed and by whom.

The thrill, the sense of well being, and the feeling of having attained true motherhood by nursing your baby is best expressed—not by me, I'm biased—in a letter by Mrs. M.

"I am a mother of four sons ranging in age from fourteen years to four months. My first three children were bottle fed. I insisted on nursing the fourth and what a thrill it has been to enjoy the pleasure of being so close to him. I never felt better, and this baby is more content than my other children were. My only regret is that I didn't nurse the other boys. I think hospitals and nurses should encourage all mothers to nurse their children."

Here is the other side of the coin: A starry-eyed young mother, determined to nurse her baby, had visions of herself as the woman in "Madonna and Child." The evening before this mother anticipated leaving the hospital, the head nurse came into her room to find the mother sobbing because she thought she didn't have enough milk and because cracked nipples made nursing painful. The baby was screaming. Maybe the nurse had a point when she said, "Why don't you just put your baby on the bottle. Then you'll know exactly how much he is getting and you won't have to worry."

I don't believe the mother who can't or prefers not to nurse her baby should be troubled by a guilty feeling. The mother who herself takes time to feed her baby whenever possible, holding him in her arms while seated in a comfortable chair—preferably a rocking chair—is fulfilling her function as a mother. I'm sure that the baby who is artificially fed by a devoted mother will get as good a start in life as the breast-fed baby. Nursing is the frosting on the cake for mother and child.

OR IS BOTTLE FED

"What shall I feed my baby?" is one of the first questions that comes to your mind. In spite of the logical case just presented for breast feeding, the chances are at least five-to-one that you are going to bottle feed your baby.

Baby food manufacturing companies have been very successful in preparing formulas which are suitable for most infants. The ease with which these formulas are readied for feeding takes all the worry and most of the work out of food preparation.

By all means talk with your pediatrician or family doctor about food and feeding schedules. Of the dozens of excellent standard infant food preparations on the market, your doctor will most likely favor one and explain how to prepare it. Actually, preparation of baby food by the mother these days consists of following simple directions on the container. In spite of the fact that all you have to do is mix the formula with sterile water in sterilized bottles and put on sterilized nipples, it still is desirable to secure advice from your doctor about food for your baby. From the time of birth all babies are different and many require fine adjustment of formulas to meet their particular needs.

All baby foods contain protein, carbohydrates (sugars and starches), fat, and minerals properly balanced to meet the requirements of growth. Sugars are used during the early months; starches, in the form of cereals, are added to the diet later. Vitamins C and D are not normally present in cow's milk. Therefore, your doctor will prescribe these; often he will include vitamin A starting at about age one month. Although breast milk is the best baby food, it too contains insufficient vitamins. Whether breast or bottle fed, the baby will require these vitamins usually given with a marked medicine dropper and squirted directly onto his tongue. Five drops is an average daily dose.

Orange juice, usually started at about one month beginning with a teaspoonful diluted in a little water, is slowly increased to one ounce. Fresh and frozen orange juice contain approximately the same amount of vitamin C. Infants who are sensitive to orange juice get along perfectly well on daily doses of synthetic vitamin C. If you want to give your baby other kinds of juices, tomato or vegetable are good.

The average healthy baby requires fifty calories per pound per day for the first year. In standard formulas, one-third of these calories are derived from sugar, two-thirds from milk. An underweight child is given extra calories to bring him to the desired weight for his age.

Pay heed only to your doctor's directions, and disregard now and later the unasked-for advice handed out by grandma and Aunt Hattie. They brought up their children a generation ago, and since then, in fact, during the past ten years, the manner of infant feeding has changed remarkably.

Ready prepared liquid formulas to which nothing but sterile water is added are most popular because of simplicity of preparation. Powdered foods to which sterile water is added are just as good; they simply require a bit more time and a few added utensils.

If for economic reasons you wish to use a less expensive food, you may give your baby a formula made up of evaporated milk, sugar, and water. Evaporated milk, i.e., cow's milk from which most of the water has been removed, is a good, inexpensive food, available the world over and entirely satisfactory for the majority of healthy, full-term babies. The only possible drawback to its use is the time-consuming task of preparing and sterilizing the formula each day. Details of how to prepare such a formula are best obtained from your doctor or from a hospital nurse. For your first baby you will need a demonstration. A thousand words can't tell you exactly how to prepare a formula and how to sterilize it. You need to see it done.

For those who can afford it and for those who have to travel with a baby, there are now on the market ready-to-serve formulas. No refrigeration is necessary. All one has to do is take a bottle out of the container in which it was sold, take off the sterile cover, attach a nipple, feed the baby, and discard the empty bottle.

No matter how many books and pamphlets you may have read on formulas and baby feeding, you still will have a thousand unanswered questions to ask your doctor. That feeding schedules puzzle mothers is not surprising because babies differ in their reactions to schedules and so do doctors. Some pediatricians are emphatic about establishing a regular four-hour feeding schedule as early as possible and sticking to it rather religiously; others take exactly the opposite view and advise what is termed "demand feeding" or no schedule at all—simply letting the baby be nursed or bottle fed whenever he wishes.

Babies on a four-hour feeding program are sometimes hungry an hour ahead of schedule. It's poor judgment to let the baby howl for an hour while you watch the clock for the prescribed feeding time. When the baby finally gets his bottle, he is so tired and mad that he can't or won't eat. Schedules are fine but are made to be broken from time to time.

Demand feeding became popular about twenty-five years ago during the period when misguided psychiatrists said, "Don't frustrate the baby, let him develop his own schedule. Attempts at molding him to a routine against his wishes will warp his personality." Such nonsense! Babies like routine. In fact, they are much like old folks who want to eat on time, then relax and take a snooze.

This freewheeling attitude of demand feeding still wasn't as bad as the horrible one of absolutely rigid schedules imposed on babies during the twenties, Morbid-minded psychiatrists then advised mothers to feed strictly on a four-hour schedule and then leave the baby alone—no rocking, no loving, no cuddling. The natural reaction to such an abnormal, rigid regime was one of no schedule at all. Now, thank the Lord, parents and doctors have come to their senses in working toward an early reasonable schedule with just enough permissiveness to satisfy both parent and child.

Recently, a few pediatricians demonstrated that babies thrive just as well on cold formula taken directly from the refrigerator as on warmed formula. For millions of years mammals have suckled their young on body temperature milk and I doubt that we can suddenly .change the temperature of their food without some rebellion. I don't believe mothers will accept the idea of holding frosty bottles in their hands and sticking ice-cold nipples into their babies' mouths. It is good to know, however, that while traveling, for example, no harm will come from giving the baby a cold bottle. In general, I would continue to warm the baby's bottle. Even though he may tolerate cold drinks, it seems much more friendly to warm his milk.

AND HIS NIGHT FEEDING

"Will I be glad when my baby gives up that 2 A.M. feeding!" Quotation from every mother.

The average normal baby taking his food well and gaining weight will, with a little nudging, give up the 2 A.M. feeding when he is two to six weeks old. He doesn't need the extra calories. Of course, you don't suddenly snap off the 2 A.M. feeding, but gradually delay it until 3 to 4 and eventually to 6 A.M. Delaying the 10 P.M. feeding a bit the previous evening will help. Getting rid of that dead-hour night feeding is not difficult nor in any way harmful; time and a little patience will do it. The skinny baby who gains poorly and is not robust because of illness or some congenital deformity may need the 2 A.M. feeding for months.

The normal baby, steadily gaining in weight, can usually be induced to give up the 10 P.M. feeding between three and six months. The eagerness or indifference with which he takes the feeding in a measure indicates whether he is or is not ready to give it up. The only way to find out is by trying. Simply omit the feeding and see what happens. He may surprise you by sleeping through the night.

For a few nights he may wake up at midnight and demand a bottle. If one treats this midnight snack with as little attention as possible he may soon forget it and sleep through. One doesn't have to jump out of bed the instant the baby cries for a delayed 10 P.M. feeding. Wait a few minutes for him to go back to sleep. When unmistakable sounds of anger at delay pour forth, give him his bottle before he gets furious and really wide-awake. A little comforting after giving the bottle is OK but too much is surely going to lead to a demand for a bottle and attention sometime around midnight. Parents eventually have to make a choice between giving the one or two year old his beloved bottle or facing a showdown of not giving the bottle and listening for a few nights to some mighty loud crying.

One of my friends allowed her four-year-old daughter to have a bottle any night she wished when going to bed. There was nothing wrong with this child; she simply liked the bottle and her mother indulged her. If the truth were known, I'm sure many children are allowed the pleasure of this infantile habit far beyond the time it seems proper; mothers are bothered by it only because of what neighbors and friends say.

It's rather difficult to go wrong in feeding a healthy baby. All you have to do is give him as much as he wants, no more, no less. One day he'll eat voraciously, another he'll dawdle and eat only half his food. Let him be the judge of how much food is necessary for his physical wants. He'll get that by hollering for it.

Never force a bottle on a baby. If he refuses to eat, don't urge him; he isn't hungry. Let him get hungry; it's a feeling he should experience even though you have to listen to some crying. Coax your baby to take more of his bottle than he wants, or urge him to eat when he is not hungry, and you are sowing the seeds of a future feeding problem.

Water may be offered a baby any time you think he wants it. Keep a bottle of sterile water in the refrigerator. Some babies will enjoy an ounce or two of water between meals; others are infuriated by the very idea of being offered such an unpalatable substance.

The baby is the best judge of how much water he should take. During hot weather when he is perspiring freely or when his skin is dry and hot with a burning fever, give him as much water as he likes.

Following your baby's weight from day to day is an unnecessary pastime. So long as the baby acts as a baby should, takes his food with eagerness, cries with moderation, and sleeps peacefully, why worry about his weight? If you aren't happy unless you have actual evidence of gain in weight of five or six ounces a week, buy a baby scale.

For the baby who is skinny at birth or underweight because of poor feeding or chronic disease, it is well to have a scale. Weigh him twice a week, not every day. Sometimes even though you weigh him at the same time without clothing his weight may vary a few ounces one way or the other from the previous day; a loss will discourage you, an unusual gain mislead you.

Be sure the hole in the nipple is the right size before beginning a feeding; if too large throw the nipple away, if too small enlarge it with a hot needle. The hungry baby is annoyed if he can't get food as fast as he wants it; he chokes if it comes too fast. Babies love to suck, and for normal emotional development should be allowed to do as much of it as they wish. About twenty minutes is the proper time for taking a feeding.

Burping the baby is routinely done at the middle and at the end of a feeding. Some babies swallow so much air they have to be burped after each ounce. The prevalent notion that babies swallow air when sucking on an empty nipple or pacifier is wrong. Normal babies swallow air only with food or water.

A number of years ago an invention of the devil appeared on the market in the form of a bottle holder for nursing. All one had to do was stick the bottle in the holder and adjust it so the nipple reached the baby's mouth. The baby lay on his back—a most inappropriate position—and extracted nourishment from a heartless feeding mechanism. No baby, unless so ill that he cannot be picked up, should ever be fed while lying in his crib. There is only one position for feeding a baby and that is in a semireclining position in the crook of mother's or father's arm.

It seems an insignificant point to advise sitting in a comfortable chair while feeding the baby; yet it is more than a gesture. When you relax the baby relaxes and eats better, has less colic, and is in general more contented. For this purpose a rocking chair is unsurpassed. After the baby is through eating he loves that soothing to and fro motion of rocking and drifting away into sleep. I have no evidence but scattered observations to support this point, but I am convinced that a six-week-old infant knows whether he is being fed by someone who loves him or by someone whose duty it is to get some food into his stomach.

NEEDS SOLID FOODS

"At what age should my baby be started on solid foods?" is asked daily of every pediatrician. The answer is, at three months.

Stimulated by competitive spirit rather than scientific fact a few doctors have advised solid foods at unusually early ages. Mothers have accepted the advice and seem to enjoy the status afforded by being able to stop the conversation at a party with, "My baby was taking cereal at two weeks." "My baby was taking all kinds of solid foods at one month."

A baby is a baby for a long time. The fact that he can get away with solid foods at an early age is an indication of good digestion rather than precocity. One doesn't plant a tiny seedling in rich soil, neither does one give a two month old a hamburger.

If you want to feed your month old baby cereal, go ahead— it likely will not upset him for the simple reason that most of the cereal will go onto his bib. According to Dr. Harry Bakwin, a noted New York pediatrician, a very young infant merely pushes with his tongue against the spoon or food. Not until he is three to four months old does he get the idea of opening his lips and with his tongue propelling the food to the back of his mouth to swallow it.

The subject of when to start a baby on solid foods has been

so vigorously debated that the Committee on Nutrition of the American Academy of Pediatrics issued this special report. "Normal full-term infants can be expected to thrive for the first three months of life on human milk or a properly constituted cow's milk formula. On the basis of present knowledge the committee is in agreement that no nutritional superiority or psychological benefit results from introduction of solid foods into the infant's diet prior to two and one-half or three months of age."

Dr. G. James Fruthaler, a New Orleans pediatrician, says: "The infant needs nothing but milk and vitamins until about four months of age." Equally important is this added statement. "Early feeding of solid foods increases an infant's chances of becoming allergic to some of them for the simple reason that the immature gastrointestinal tract of many infants is unable to filter out complex substances in solid foods."

Most mothers start with one of the precooked cereals. Whether you use wheat, barley, oatmeal, or rice cereal, depends largely upon where you live and what the local custom is. The most acceptable time for trying to start the baby on cereal is in the morning before the 10 o'clock bottle, not because this time is more acceptable than any other from the baby's standpoint, but because it's the customary time and because the mother has more time and is less impatient with lack of cooperation in the forenoon.

"My baby won't take cereal, he spits it out and gets mad if I don't give him the bottle right away."

Very well, don't give him cereal for a couple of weeks. Give him a spoon to play with; he'll put one end or the other into his mouth. Some day when he seems to be in a cooperative mood, put a little highly sweetened cereal in the spoon; he may find he likes it.

Don't get "steamed up" if your baby flatly refuses to eat cereal. As long as he is taking a proper formula reinforced with iron and is getting vitamins C and D, he can grow up hale and hearty without ever eating a single dish of cereal.

Fruits are usually started two weeks or a month after cereal, but there is no reason why they can't be started in small quantities at the same time cereal is begun. In fact, some doctors feel that fruits are better tolerated than cereals and should be the first solid foods offered.

Pears, apples, apricots, and peaches, prepared by baby food manufacturers are almost universally used. These ready-to-serve fruits have the advantage of being strained, properly cooked, free from germs, and suitably sweetened. If economy is a factor, there is no reason why fruits for the baby cannot be prepared in the kitchen. Apples, pears, and mashed bananas are easiest to handle.

A few weeks after the baby has become accustomed to cereals and fruits, cooked vegetables are added at one feeding a day, and increased as it becomes apparent that he likes and assimilates them. All the fuss about making the baby learn to like all vegetables is silly. Many adults don't like certain vegetables and won't eat them. Why fight with the baby if he hates spinach or peas? Another vegetable is just as good.

Undigested particles of vegetables will appear in the stool. Don't be perturbed, that's normal. A woman, greatly concerned, called to say her baby had passed a large amount of blood. The baby seemed perfectly well and showed no signs of hemorrhage. She was told in case of recurrence to bring in the baby's diaper. The "hemorrhage" did recur and the diaper contained not blood but a mass of red, partially digested beets. She then confessed that the only vegetable the baby liked was beets and she gave him as much as he wanted.

A yellow tint to the skin in the baby's face, the palms of his hands, and the soles of his feet does not mean jaundice, but is simply the result of a diet high in carrots and disappears when the intake of carrots is lowered. The discoloration, due to carotene, is harmless.

Eggs, especially the yolks because they contain iron, are usually added to the diet at about six months. Some infants are allergic to eggs, some don't like them. The allergic child shouldn't eat eggs, and they shouldn't be forced on the child who doesn't like them; iron prescribed by the doctor will do just as well.

There is no specific age at which meats should be added to the diet. Feeding or nutritional problems at times require that a two-month-old baby be given meat. In general most babies accept meats any time after the fifth to eighth month. As with fruits, it is more satisfactory to buy prepared meats such as beef, liver, pork, lamb, etc., in cans or jars. Don't expect every baby to like them all. Start offering only tastes and cater to preferences. He will slowly learn to enjoy all foods if he is allowed to get used to one at a time and is not urged to take any.

Some babies accept any foods and, to the delight of the mother, placidly take from a spoon anything that is offered. Opinionated babies fight solid foods and in a manner that should be amusing rather than exasperating, hit the spoon from mother's hand. Give these rebellious little fighters time, patience, and indifference as you lead, not force, them into spoon feeding.

For the first year milk is the baby's basic food. Even though you add cereals, fruits, and vegetables between the third and sixth month and eggs, meats, and fish during the next six months, most of the calories are still derived from milk. Milk is the best food available for infants, but it lacks the essential building block for hemoglobin (red blood)—iron. The baby who lives exclusively on milk to the age of six to twelve months will become anemic—sometimes dangerously so. The amount of iron in one's blood is small but absolutely essential.

To avoid "milk anemia" babies are fed cereals high in iron and other iron rich foods, such as leafy vegetables, beans, peas, fruits, meats (fowl contains little iron), eggs, and liver. The infant who for some reason is not given or will not take solid foods and lives exclusively on milk, should be given iron in the absorbable form, ferrous sulfate, prescribed by your doctor.

REQUIRES VITAMINS

"What kind of vitamins should my children have and in which foods are they found?"

Four vitamins, A, B, C, and D are absolutely essential through-out life. Although there are many others and numerous subdivisions of vitamin B, you needn't be concerned about them because anyone eating a well-balanced diet containing the vitamins found in milk, cereals, enriched bread, fruits, vegetables, meat, and eggs will be getting sufficient quantities of the less common kinds and the neces-sary minerals.

During the first year, your baby will get sufficient vitamin A and B from breast or cow's milk, enriched cereals, and other foods, but will need supplemental doses of vitamin C and D—vitamin C to prevent scurvy, D to prevent rickets. When your baby is two to four weeks old, you should start vitamins C and D in whatever form your doctor advises. Since a few infants do not get sufficient vitamin A from milk, most doctors order a combination of A, C, and D and advise that they be continued until the baby is about one year old.

Don't give your baby more vitamins than the doctor orders on the theory that if a little is good, more is better. Too much vitamin A or B may cause indigestion and colic; excessive amounts of vita-min D may lessen appetite and actually cause slowing of bone growth, whereas the proper amount promotes sturdy growth.

Any child is getting enough of all the essential vitamins who each day is taking two glasses of fortified milk (A, B, and D), some fruit or fruit juice (C), enriched cereal and/or bread (A, B, and D), some egg in food or as a separate item (A, B, and D), any kind of vegetable including potatoes (A, B, and C), and some kind of meat—pork, beef, lamb, poultry—or fish (A and B).

After your baby is taking a general diet containing the above foods, there is no further need for drugstore vitamins. During pro-longed illnesses while food intake is greatly limited, it is well to give your child a daily dose of multivitamin preparations purchasable at any drug store.

Just as soon as health is restored and an adequate diet is again being taken, stop giving vitamins; you are wasting your money and good vitamins.

AND HIS ENVIRONMENT

Character and personality begin to develop immediately after birth. We know nothing about the thoughts, if any, which go through a baby's mind, but we do know that early impressions are recorded. Holding the baby, rocking, cuddling, feeding, playing with him and talking to him when he understands no word—all these activities are registered on a baby's mind.

A six-week-old infant with a broken femur (thigh bone) was brought to the hospital. To promote proper healing of the bone it was necessary to put the leg up in what is called traction. Consequently, the baby had to lie on his back twenty-four hours a day and had to be fed in that position. Family circumstances were such that the baby had no visitors. After about three weeks he lay in his crib in a constantly listless state, indifferent to food and people. He did not cry or fuss; he just lay there with eyes half-closed and, one might say, shut off from the world.

At this time a volunteer worker, a substitute mother from the "mother bank," was assigned to this baby for six to eight hours a day. She fed him while supporting his head and shoulders in the crook of her arm. During waking hours she played with and fondled him. In another three weeks, when ready to go home, he had gained weight and was again smiling, cooing, and acting as a three-month-old baby should.

This infant had not been neglected. He had been fed and bathed but that is not enough for babies, sick or well. They need personal contact and loving attention to give them pleasure in living. and healthy emotional development.

A child's mind is like an endless roll of unexposed photographic film. From moment to moment during infancy and childhood, in fact, throughout life, one film after another in endless succession is exposed. The quality of the film is inherited primarily from parents but also from grandparents and preceding generations; nothing but disease or injury will ever change it. No evidence has ever been found that a mother's thoughts during pregnancy have any effect upon the unborn child.

Each cell of this wonderful newborn baby inherits the elements of unalterable size, of future appearance, and of mental acuity. Whether one inherits blue eyes or brown eyes, big feet or little feet, white skin or black skin makes little difference. Of prime importance is the nature of the brain cells, that is, the speed and quality of the film which will receive and record all exposures.

During the early years of life, environment—the impulses which strike the film—is largely under control of parents, mostly mothers. From the moment of birth the baby begins to react to his environment. He hears but doesn't comprehend; he sees but doesn't recognize. He reacts only to the stimuli of bodily contact and through some mysterious power instinctively interprets that contact as one of being wanted and loved or as one of indifference or inattention.

The infant who is continuously exposed to an atmosphere of love and security will present the picture of a happy, well-adjusted child, and by the time he is six years old his emotional pattern of life will be fairly well-established.

We can't do much about the brains we bequeath to our children, but we can control the stimuli which reach them. Expose the film of your baby's inner self to love and acceptance of what he is, and even an inferior film will produce a picture of a personality with character and charm.

These high-sounding words give the impression that rearing a child is a simple matter of loving attention and nothing else. This loving attention at times is going to be displaced by annoyance and loss of temper when the four year old whines, the two year old throws his food on the floor, and the six months old indulges in an unreasonable bout of crying. Rare is the mother who hasn't at times screamed at her "impossible children." Such releases of pent-up emotion do no harm. On the contrary, peace and quiet are apt to follow the storm. So long as the relationship between parent and child is basically one of sincere and mutual devotion, the building blocks of a well-adjusted life will be securely laid.

CRIES

Every normal baby is born with a built-in, ready-to-use crying mechanism which functions perfectly from the moment of birth. The first cry is used to expand the lungs; thereafter, and for years to come, it is the child's only means of making his wishes known. Mothers listen attentively to their children's cries and soon learn to distinguish the cry for food from that of anger, the whimper of illness from that of boredom. Every mother, especially with her first baby, is concerned about her baby's crying and wonders how much is normal. She'd like to have the baby cry for each particular need and promptly stop after that need has been met. Babies aren't built that way. Some cry a lot; others are placid, "good"; each is different in his own reaction to the new way of life.

"How much should my baby cry?" has been asked innumerable times. Before reading on, how much do you think a normal four- to eight-week-old baby, one who is not sick, takes his food well, and is gaining weight, should cry each twenty-four hours? Guess.

To answer this question, Dr. T. Berry Brazelton had eighty mothers of perfectly normal newborn infants record hour by hour for three months exactly how many minutes their babies cried in twenty-four hours.

To keep crying to a minimum, the mothers were urged to be liberal with feeding demands, to change soiled diapers promptly, and to follow such standard procedures as frequent burping, giving a drink of water between feedings, playing with the baby, picking him up, turning him on his tummy, etc.

Now compare your estimate with these recorded averages.

At age two weeks, a normal, healthy infant cries an average of one hour and forty-five minutes each twenty-four hours.

At age six weeks, crying increases to two hours and forty-five minutes.

At ten weeks crying begins to taper off, and by three months drops to one hour.

Crying times vary from one-half hour more to one-half hour less than these averages.

Seven of the eighty children—even though not ill and gaining weight normally—cried four hours a day and that's a lot of pounding for anybody's eardrums to take. Much of the crying occurred during the evening hours from 6 to 12 P.M.

A comforting conclusion to be drawn from this study is that you can expect your baby to do some lusty crying. The reasons for crying are many; some known, some unknown. A baby cries because he is hungry; he wants his diaper changed; he has colic; a pin is sticking him; he's uncomfortable; or he wants some extra attention.

Hunger is the primary cause of crying. It is a source of great satisfaction to a mother to feed her hungry, crying baby and to watch him relax and fall asleep in perfect contentment. It's not always this simple because babies' appetites vary from time to time. One day a baby will take his feedings with alacrity; the next day, for no apparent reason, he'll decide he wants less. Such reactions are normal in everyone's life.

After a baby has been fed, he is laid in his crib. Instead of going to sleep he cries. What do you do? You pick him up, burp him again, make sure his clothing is comfortable, hold him in your arms or rock him for a few minutes, and then put him back in his crib. If he continues to cry, feel his forehead. If it isn't hot and he doesn't look sick, leave him alone. He may cry for as long as fifteen minutes. Then he will most likely fall asleep. As a general rule most babies like to be left alone after they have been fed. It isn't going to do the baby a bit of harm to cry for a while.

In your mind is always the recurring question, "Is he still hungry?" Sometimes babies are satisfied with a half-feeding, other times they want extra food. There is no reason why you should not again offer breast or bottle to the crying baby to find out if he is still hungry. If, after he has taken all the food he wants, he still cries, give him a pacifier. (See page 108.) The sucking instinct is strong and should be satisfied. Some mothers dip the pacifier in honey or granulated sugar. It seems to me that a pacifier sweetened a bit would be much more fun to suck on than a tasteless piece of rubber or plastic.

Colic is a common cause of excessive crying. (See page 66.)

Babies cry to get attention. During the first month or two they haven't learned the art, but at three months, and for years thereafter, they will be adept at trying to get what they want by crying. Your baby is repeatedly going to put you to the test. So long as you are not sure of the motive, you will do all the things you know of to stop the crying. If when you pick him up he smiles and coos with a sort of victorious look in his eye, you know that lesson number one is in order. Gently put him back in his crib. He'll cry and feel terribly abused. Leave him alone to cry and learn the first simple rule of discipline—conforming to the ways of the home.

Sometime that little angel of yours is going to put you to the test at night, most likely during the early morning hours when you and your husband are drugged with sleep. Someone gets up— usually mother—to see if anything is wrong. Again, if when you pick him up he favors you with one of those bewitching smiles, put him back in bed, close the door and your ears, or you will soon be in a position of the mother who wrote:

"I have a nine-month-old baby, Susie, who is driving me and my husband crazy. I put her to bed at 9 o'clock. For the past month she has been waking up between 2 and 4 A.M. every night. She screams until we come into her room. It takes an hour to calm her down. My mother says, 'Let her cry it out,' but my landlady is crabby and complains when the baby cries. I'm afraid if I let my baby cry, she'll lose her love for me. This is my first baby."

My answer was: "Your daughter has you buffaloed. Sometime in the near future, and it might as well be now, you and your baby are going to have a showdown to determine who is boss in the house. At seven o'clock, not nine, put Susie to bed. Before doing so, rock her, sing her a lullaby, play with and cuddle her. She must know that you love her. Kiss her goodnight and close the door. Explain your problem to the landlady over a cup of coffee and tell her that you are going to have to let the baby 'cry it out' for a few nights. When she puts on her early morning act, you will probably want to go into her room to see that she's all right. Give her a pacifier, put a toy or woolly animal in her arms—she will likely throw them out of her crib—and again sweetly say goodnight. Quietly, but firmly, close the door and go back to bed. Be deaf to her screaming. Be sure the windows are closed for the neighbors' sake. You are bound to have a few bad nights but don't get panicky and above all, don't weaken.

"If after a particularly bad night you feel that the strain on you and your husband is too great, call your doctor for a prescription for a mild sedative to be used for a week or two to break the waking habit. Remember, however, this sedative is a temporary measure. Basically, the problem is one of simple discipline. I don't mean spanking, just firmness and patience. Your baby will love you more and you will enjoy her more when she learns to conform."

After all the recognized reasons for crying have been eliminated, why do some babies still cry? I don't know. We have no idea, what thoughts if any, go through a baby's mind. I firmly believe that some infants cry for exercise and the fun of hearing their own voices. This supposition is based on the fact that adults with nothing to say use their voices in the same way. We have to listen politely to their pointless chatter. Why not take the same attitude toward the crying of babies?

SMILES

Nothing is more beautiful than a baby's smile; it signifies the outstanding difference between man and animal.

Between four and six weeks of age the first flickerings of human intelligence and personality appear. One day after the baby has been fed and is in a state of contentment while being played with, rocked, or chucked under the chin, he will suddenly for a brief moment stop moving his head, fix his eyes on his mother's face, and smile. It won't be much of a smile, but significant.

During the next few weeks he will repeat and improve the smile until finally along with that unmistakable look of recognition in his eyes, a smile will spread all over his face. He's in; he is now a bona fide member of the human race.

Mothers make sweeping claims to each other about the age at which their babies smiled. Doting grandmothers (they all dote) claim their babies smiled at three weeks and straight-facedly maintain that the first grandchild smiled at ten days. Sorry, baby smiles appearing before three or four weeks of age are only sardonic grimaces caused by spasm or colic.

Parents have heard so much about the importance of a smile as an indicator of a normal mind that they are distressed when the smile is slow in appearing. The baby who is born prematurely, is sickly, requires surgery shortly after birth, or adjusts poorly to his food will require some extra time before showing human characteristics. Don't worry, give the little fellow some time to catch up. As soon as he gets well and thrives he will make up for lost time and reward you with a smile.

Parents worry if their child doesn't conform to a set pattern and do all the things he is supposed to do at a specified age. The oft-quoted statement, "All babies are alike" is far from the truth. Some infants are born with quick reactions to stimuli; others are less responsive. The normal baby usually smiles before the sixth week—certainly before the eighth.

NEEDS LOTS OF SLEEP

Much needless worry would be avoided if mothers accepted the fact that healthy babies will instinctively get as much sleep as they require.

Children from earliest infancy through adult life differ in the amount of sleep required. The high-strung baby will grow and thrive on an hour or two less sleep than the placid infant, but rest assured each, in spite of what you do, will get the amount of sleep he needs. He may not sleep according to the schedule you would like, but during twenty-four hours he will piece together fragments of sleep sufficient for his needs.

Here are the average number of hours a healthy, normal baby sleeps each twenty-four hours:

First few months	18-20 hours
At 6 months	16-18 hours
At 1 Year	14-16 hours
At 2 Years	12-14 hours
After 5 Years	10-12 hours

Training in adjusting a baby's sleeping schedule—so necessary for the well-being of the entire family—begins early. During the first few months a baby spends practically all his time sleeping, crying, or eating. After a baby has eaten he normally sleeps. Expect him to sleep, and the chances are he will. A dry diaper, an extra burping, turning him on his side or tummy are appropriate, but then leave him alone.

"Shhh, you'll wake the baby," is your idea, not the baby's. He can sleep in a boiler factory unless you accustom him to sleeping in absolute quiet. I have seen babies sleep without wiggling or waking in a brilliantly lighted nursery where a half-dozen others were screaming at the tops of their lungs, and nurses and house staff were shouting to make themselves heard. A baby will take his nap in a carriage in the living room where other children are laughing, shouting, and banging things about.

I believe that the baby who from earliest infancy learns to sleep in an active, noisy household will grow up to be a sound sleeper, undisturbed by branches scratching against the window, hooting owls, or honking automobile horns.

Children disregard ordinary noises but are greatly disturbed by harsh and angry words. Even a six-month-old child has selective hearing. When parents quarrel and shout at each other children are frightened; somehow they get the idea that the love and security they have been enjoying is going to be lost. In other words, do your fighting in private.

The attitude toward fresh air at night has swung back and forth from the extreme of all windows open to none. Desirable day and night temperatures with adequate humidity are for most of us unattainable. We have to get along in overheated, dry apartments during the day and chilly bedrooms at night. A baby sleeps most restfully in a temperature of about 60 degrees. Common sense is the only guide to keeping the baby comfortable summer and winter. He will sleep better when a bit chilly than when perspiring in excessive or binding clothing.

Sleeping schedules are just as important as feeding schedules. It's easy for parents to allow the baby to set his own schedule and thereby upset the family. In the afternoon, for example, instead of taking a two-hour nap, he sleeps four hours. That evening he is unwilling to be put to bed at seven o'clock and remains bright-eyed until nine o'clock. The baby finds mother's attempts to get him to go to bed very pleasant attention. Repetition of these events a few nights in a row and you're in the situation of Mr. and Mrs. M. and their eight-month-old baby. They complained that the baby didn't sleep. The conversation went something like this:

"What time do you put your baby to bed?"

"At eight o'clock but that doesn't mean a thing. He just lies there, laughs, coos, shakes the bed—and cries. When he starts crying we can't stop it unless we pick him up and walk the floor. He finally goes to sleep about eleven o'clock. We're exhausted."

"What time does he wake up the next morning?"

"About nine o'clock."

"Any nap in the afternoon?"

"Yes, from 3 to about 6 P.M."

One doesn't need to be a doctor to answer that problem. This baby was getting plenty of sleep. He simply was doing his sleeping at inappropriate times and needed his schedule adjusted, a task requiring considerable firmness. These parents went astray in the first place by allowing the baby too long a nap in the late afternoon. For peace and harmony in the family, a well-established sleeping schedule is more important than an orderly feeding schedule.

From earliest infancy bedtime should be a quiet time. Holding the baby, rocking him, singing a lullaby—babies don't mind off-key singing—relax him and put him in the "going to bed" mood. This relaxed attitude continues to be important for years. Rough-housing with the baby or older child after dinner may seem like fine parent-child relationship to the father, but it is not conducive to going to sleep.

HAS A BATH

At the hospital the baby probably received no bath for several days; it is popular at present to leave undisturbed all the pasty, slightly oily stuff called *vernix caseosa* which covers a baby's skin at birth. The baby might look a bit more presentable if he had a bath with soap and water shortly after he was born, but it's much better for his skin to be protected by this greasy substance for a number of days.

Because the stump of the umbilical cord is not healed for a week, most doctors advise sponge baths until the cord is dried up. However, tub baths, if preferred, are safe.

It's the first bath that frightens every inexperienced mother with her first baby. Nothing more than common sense is necessary to give a baby a bath—even I could do it.

Most mothers bathe their babies some time during midmorning. There's nothing wrong with bathing in the evening before the six o'clock feeding except that it's an awkward time unless father's hours are such that he gets home from work early enough and has the inclination to perform this pleasant task while you get dinner. I'd suggest sticking to the midmorning hour and keeping father out of the baby-bathing picture.

First decide where you are going to perform this feat—at the kitchen sink, in a bathinette, in a dishpan, or in the bathtub. It will be much easier to give the bath seated or standing in a comfortable position. It is awkward to bathe a new baby in the family tub and too hard on your knees and back.

Gather every thing you'll need—clean clothes, towel, wash-cloth, soap, cotton balls, cotton applicators, powder, baby oil, and a plastic apron for yourself. Have all the essentials within reach. Draw water and test its temperature with your elbow or with a thermometer. The water should be near body temperature. With one hand under the back of the baby's head and the other hand under his buttocks or grasping his legs, lower him into the water. It is wise to have a towel in the water under the baby to keep him from sliding about.

Wash from the top down. Use any standard toilet soap. A soap containing hexachlorophene is excellent because of its anti-septic qualities. You may use a little soap on the baby's head but none on his face, and don't let it get into his eyes. In fact, be sparing with soap; too much takes oil out of the skin and makes it dry and scaly. Cotton applicators are used to clean the ears. Wipe the eyes from the inside out with wet (no soap) cotton balls, using a separate ball for each eye.

It isn't necessary to do anything to the nose but wipe it with a wet washcloth. Swabbing it inside with an applicator makes the baby mad; he wiggles his head vigorously and, unless you are quick, the applicator may be shoved up a nostril. The baby keeps his nose clean by sneezing.

Now proceed to wash neck, arms, tummy, legs, and bottom. Turn the baby and wash his back. Babies have lots of creases. Be sure to get them clean. Rinse off the soap well.

By this time you are wet, and the baby is probably crying. Don't let your anxiety to get the baby out of the water and have the bath over with make you hurry. A wet baby is as slippery as an eel. Place one hand under the baby's neck to support the head and, with the other hand, grasp the legs. Before boosting him out of the water lift him up a bit to make sure you have a good hold. Then lay him on a towel and dry him by patting rather than rubbing. Put some baby powder in the skin creases, a little extra here and there to make him smell nice or use some baby oil if the skin is dry.

Put on the clean clothes you have ready. The baby most likely will spit up on the clean clothes and again smell sour but at least for the moment he was clean.

Bath time is fun for both mother and child. Soon the baby will learn to splash and play in the water and have a heigh-ho time.

Before going on, I must emphasize: Never, but never, leave a baby unattended during his bath. As the baby gets older and smart enough to turn the faucets on and off, don't leave your child one minute. Let the telephone ring, leave the door bell unanswered, stay with your child, or take him out of the tub, wrap him in a towel and take him with you. The tragic burns I have seen from hot water turned on by an investigative child forces me to repeat— don't ever leave your child alone in a bathtub until he knows what hot water is and how to turn off a hot water faucet or jump out of the tub.

First babies are bathed every morning with meticulous attention to details. Second and third ones get along equally well with two or three baths a week provided the diaper region is kept clean.

I asked a mother of five children in our outpatient department how she bathed her baby. Her answer should be reassuring to every mother who bathes her baby the first time. "You mean how I bathe-a da baby? I jus-a put him in a pan and wash him." The look on her face suggested that only a man could ask such a stupid question.

HIS CLOTHING AND CRIB

In glowing anticipation of the coming baby, parents are inclined to spend more money than necessary for layettes. For those who can afford unlimited expenditures, it is simple to go to a large department store or a specialty shop and spend hundreds of dollars for essentials and luxuries. The majority of mothers, on a rather strict budget, buy what is absolutely necessary and save by taking advantage of "white sales" and special sales during "baby week."

To the baby it doesn't make a particle of difference whether he is robed in satin and silks and sleeps in a two-hundred-dollar crib or is clothed in shirt, diaper, and nightgown and sleeps in a wicker clothes basket. Of far greater importance to him than the finest wardrobe is the love with which the clothes are put on.

The items of clothing needed are:

Four to six dozen diapers. If a diaper service is used,
   it is still wise to buy a dozen diapers for emergency use.
Two to four packages of diaper liners are desirable
   but not essential.
Four cotton nightgowns.
Four shirts, long sleeves, size one.
Two rubber or plastic pants.
One diaper pail with cover (desirable).
Two sweaters.
Four flannel blankets.
Two dozen safety pins.

Let me digress for a moment with this warning. Whenever changing the baby's diaper, close the safety pin immediately. Never lay down an open safety pin within the baby's reach. In fact, don't leave an open safety pin anywhere; the baby or an older child may pick it up, put it in his mouth and swallow it. Open safety pins get stuck in the throat, stomach, or bowel and require emergency surgical removal. Closed safety pins, if swallowed, go down into the stomach and through the bowels without causing any trouble.

Diaper service is one of the finest luxuries, if such it is, that mothers can enjoy. Studies by the diaper industry have shown that the cost of washing diapers at home for the two years a baby needs them is $218.07 or $2.10 per week. This cost includes everything from the original cost of diapers to wear and tear on the washing machine. They estimate that diaper service costs only forty-two cents a week more. Relief from the boring task of washing diapers requiring about five hundred hours in two years and having this time for rest and enjoying the baby appears to justify the extra expenditure. One certainly should be able to squeeze forty-two cents out of the budget to be relieved of such a smelly, menial job.

Stockings are no longer considered an essential part of a baby's wardrobe. They still are useful for the active baby who lies on his tummy and does a lot of kicking. Tender skin on knees and toes may become red and irritated by rubbing on the sheets unless protected by stockings.

Coat, bonnet, bunting, and booties are nice to have, but why buy them? These articles have long been popular gifts by grandmothers, aunties, and friends.

For the baby's room a high-sided crib and firm mattress are essential. The baby can sleep anywhere on a firm surface but will eventually need a crib to keep him from "falling out of bed." If you can't afford to buy a new crib and mattress, watch the ads or place one in the local paper for used ones. Inquiry in the neighborhood is apt to remind people that they have these items stored away in an attic and would be glad to sell, lend, or give them to you.

Two waterproof mattress covers. Sheets of plastic are very inexpensive.

Two to four absorbent mattress pads.

Four sheets, contour or regular. If regular sheets are used, they must be large enough to be tucked firmly under the mattress so the wiggling baby doesn't get his bed all mussed up.

The number of cotton, wool, or synthetic blankets needed will depend upon climate. Babies hate to be hampered by too heavy coverings. No pillow. The baby doesn't need one.

NEEDS CIRCUMCISION?

Over the end of the penis is a circular sheath of skin called the foreskin. Removal of this piece of skin is a circumcision. Although this operation has been performed for thousands of years there still are differences of opinion about its advisability. The advantage of circumcision is that it prevents infection beneath the foreskin. The disadvantage is that the end of the baby's circumcised penis may get sore at the opening or meatus; this soreness may lead to narrowing of the opening and difficulty in urination.

Religion, local custom, and parental wishes usually decide for or against circumcision. I am inclined to advise circumcision during the newborn period before the baby leaves the hospital. Unless it is done then, I advise against it. A long foreskin is not responsible for masturbation. Circumcision will not stop bed wetting.

Care of the circumcision in a baby consists merely of placing a small piece of gauze well covered with vaseline over the end of the penis to keep the sensitive wound from rubbing on the diaper. Diaper rash appearing any time after circumcision must be promptly cleared up as it can be the cause of a sore on the end of the penis.

chapter Two

THE BABY HAS
TROUBLES

HOW TO TAKE A TEMPERATURE

Please don't think I'm insulting your intelligence when I explain
how to take a temperature and read a clinical thermometer. If
you are adept at this simple procedure, go play with your baby
while I explain to those who haven't learned.

In every family with children there should be two thermometers; one for taking rectal temperatures of babies and children
to age four or five years, the other for mouth temperatures of older
children and adults. The only difference between the two thermometers is in the shape of the mercury bulb.

Both thermometers are read alike. Mouth temperature normally is 98.6 degrees Fahrenheit. Rectal temperature is one degree
higher, 99.6 degrees Fahrenheit.

On each thermometer you will see an arrow which points to
normal temperature, 98.6 degrees. Notice that the cross lines above
this point are red and those below black. The numbers run 98—

100—102, etc. Each tiny mark between the longer marks represents two-tenths of a degree. Roll the thermometer in your fingers until you see the column of mercury; now with a quick flip of the wrist shake down the mercury to well below normal. Hold on to the thermometer tightly with dry fingers or you will throw it against the wall. A little gadget in the tube holds the column of mercury at whatever temperature is recorded. Cold water will not bring it down.

Experiment with the mouth thermometer; put it under your tongue and keep it there with your lips closed for two minutes. Read it. Shake it down and repeat until you understand this simple procedure. Your temperature may not be exactly 98.6 degrees. In the morning everybody's temperature is normally a degree or two below normal. In the afternoon it may be a degree above normal.

Even though your baby is not sick, why don't you practice on him with the rectal thermometer; he won't mind it. Lay the baby on his face or side in the crib or face down over your knee. Lubricate the thermometer. With your left forefinger and thumb separate the buttocks and with your right hand insert the thermometer about one inch into the rectum. Hold it there between your first finger and thumb while resting your palm on the baby's buttocks so that any sudden motion will not break the thermometer.

Many times in spite of precautions a thermometer in the rectum is broken by the mother or by a nurse in the hospital. Don't be alarmed; mercury in pure form is not absorbable therefore not poisonous. If the broken end cannot be seen, don't worry; with the next bowel movement it will be expelled.

No harm will come to a child who happens to bite off the end of a mouth thermometer and swallows a few pieces of glass and some mercury; the glass and mercury will go through the intestine without any difficulty.

Sometimes in case of chronic undiagnosed illnesses—more commonly seen in older children—your doctor may ask you to take your child's temperature repeatedly and report results to him. In such a case, take the child's temperature according to hospital routine at 8 A.M., 12 Noon, 4 P.M., and 8 P.M. Write down your findings properly dated. Often you can save days of hospitalization by having an accurately recorded daily temperature record.

FEVER

To the questions, "What is a normal temperature?" and "What is a fever?" we can't give specific answers. The temperature in some children is normally slightly below average; in some children slightly above. If the baby is chilled his temperature will be a bit below normal. On a hot summer day one expects the temperature to be at least a degree above normal.

As a rule of thumb, we say that mouth temperatures above 99.6 degrees or rectal temperatures over 100.6 degrees mean fever. The amount of elevation of temperature is not an index of the severity of infection because some children easily run a temperature of 104 degrees and are less ill than a child with similar trouble and a temperature of 101 or 102 degrees.

What causes a fever? We don't know what the physiological mechanism is but we do know that absorption of infection, or products of infection, toxic substances, and any foreign material, such as damaged cells from injury or burns, even severe sunburns, makes the temperature go up.

Preceding the development of severe infection in the bloodstream, such as blood poisoning or pneumonia, a chill occurs. Neither do we understand the mechanism of chills or chilly sensations. The more severe the chill, the higher the subsequent fever will be. Most people know that a chill is going to be followed by a fever but are fearful that warming the shivering child with blankets, hot water bottles, or a hot bath will later send the temperature higher. It will not. On the contrary, the longer a chill lasts the higher the temperature will go.

Fever is not a disease, but a protective mechanism called into action by nature to combat infection or neutralize toxic substances. Our concern is not with the fever but its cause. Even though fevers are protective, they should not be allowed to go too high. A mouth temperature of 104 degrees and up to 105 degrees is frightening but not in itself dangerous. However, when the temperature reaches this level it must be controlled because a sudden further rise might be disastrous. The brain can tolerate low temperatures but not 107 degrees or above; the overheated brain cells can't get enough oxygen to survive at this temperature.

Whenever your child's temperature has suddenly jumped up to 104 degrees or more, you have presumably called your doctor. While you are waiting for him to come, and in those rare instances when medical care is not immediately available, you will have to act as nurse and doctor.

Aspirin in appropriate doses and sponging are the best means of controlling fever.

An ordinary adult tablet of aspirin is five grains. A baby aspirin tablet is one and one-fourth grains. One-fourth of an adult aspirin tablet is exactly the same as a baby aspirin tablet. The proper dose of aspirin for a baby up to about one year of age is one baby-size tablet, 1¼ grains, repeated in two to four hours as seems necessary. A two-year-old child can have two baby aspirin tablets, a five-year-old child an adult size tablet.

Sponging is done with ordinary denatured alcohol or cool water. In the summertime remove all clothing from the feverish child and with a soaking wash cloth, wet the entire body. In the wintertime when rooms are apt to be chilly or drafty, cover the child with a light blanket and sponge one part of the body at a time. A piece of plastic or rubber sheeting on the bed will save a lot of mess.

Whenever a fever climbs to 105 degrees take the temperature every half-hour and continue with the sponging until it begins to fall, then stop; when started downward, temperature will continue to fall another degree or two.

For those instances in which the temperature reaches 106 degrees drastic measures are necessary; remove all clothing, wrap the child in sheets wrung out of ice water, and keep changing them until the temperature falls a degree or two. Needless to say, an emergency call has been put in for your doctor.

CALLING A DOCTOR

It's Saturday night and your baby suddenly becomes acutely ill. You have recently moved to a new locality from another city and have neglected to find a family doctor or pediatrician. What do you do? If you have moved to a large city, phone the central medical society calling-service which is open twenty-four hours a day for a list of reputable doctors in various sections of the city who are willing to make emergency calls. If you have moved to a small town, call the nearest community hospital and ask someone on duty to recommend a doctor.

The doctor, a total stranger, finally comes to your home. Supposing he says that your child is seriously ill. You feel uncertain and fearful. Frankness will serve you well. Tell the doctor that you are a stranger in town, that you are not questioning his diagnosis or treatment but would like to have another doctor's opinion. A good doctor never resents a request for consultation. Ask the doctor for the name of the man who takes care of his children, then have him call that doctor. You may be sure that a doctor will pick a capable pediatrician to care for his own children.

If the consultant confirms the diagnosis and agrees with the prescribed treatment, your faith in the doctor will have been established, and he will have added a loyal family to his practice.

In retrospect, you should have asked your former doctor to recommend a physician or two in the town to which you we're moving. There are available huge volumes listing every doctor in the United States with complete pedigree: age, medical school attended, postgraduate training, specialty, etc. It is possible to find out everything about any doctor except whether you will like him.

Having obtained the names of one or two doctors you can learn their reputations from newly formed friends and neighbors in the community to which you have moved.

After you have selected a doctor, make an appointment with him for a checkup examination of your baby. This visit will afford you and the doctor an opportunity for mutual appraisal. Inquire about routine fees and the most suitable time for telephone calls. Clarification of details helps avoid later misunderstandings.

Don't fail to find out whether the doctor will make home calls when necessary. I wouldn't have a baby doctor who wouldn't make a home call. The idea of wrapping a feverish, sick child in a blanket and taking him to a doctor's office seems totally improper and could well lead to the spread of contagion. You may not always be able to get your own doctor to make a home call. Today, three or four doctors often work together from one office and take each other's emergency calls. This arrangement must be accepted by parents; the doctor is entitled to some time that he may call his own.

WHEN TO CALL A DOCTOR

"I wonder whether my baby is sick enough to call the doctor?" is a question asked many times by every mother and ten times as often by mothers of first babies.

The baby has no language but a cry to tell you that he feels sick or has pain. You pick him up, rock him, he keeps on crying; you offer him food or water, he pushes it away. Don't panic. Listen to his cry. Does it sound different from the crying you are accustomed to? Try calmly to look at the baby and watch his expressions. Is he perspiring, is he pale or unusually flushed?

Before dashing to the telephone to call the doctor, take the baby's temperature. Be sure you have shaken down the thermometer before inserting it into the rectum and remember that a rectal temperature of 99.6 degrees is normal.

At least 90 percent of the worrisome upsets of babies and little children are due to upper-respiratory infections. Often the baby is fussy before any symptoms of an oncoming cold are obvious. If the baby has a fever of 100 to 102 degrees and signs of a cold, give him a tablet of baby aspirin or a quarter of an adult aspirin and repeat in two hours. Then take his temperature again and re-appraise the situation. If the temperature has returned to normal the chances are good that he will not need medical attention. Elevation of the temperature to 103 degrees, on the contrary, leaves no doubt that you should telephone the doctor. He will decide on the basis of your report and his knowledge of your desire for home visits whether a call is necessary or whether suggestions by phone are sufficient.

The baby who fusses, won't be comforted, can often be calmed by a dose or two of aspirin even though he has no fever.

Every conscientious mother is going to call her doctor more frequently than is necessary. The understanding doctor will not be critical of a mother's natural anxiety. Reassurance that the baby is not sick is worth the price of a home or office visit. It's far better that a few "wolf, wolf" calls are made than that a serious illness is overlooked.

VOMITING

All babies spit up or vomit from time to time. Overflow after eating and regurgitation of a few mouthfuls of food when burping are so commonplace as to be considered normal. Babies are apt to smell a bit sour most of the time. A father who doesn't have a stain or two on the shoulder of his coat simply doesn't hold and feed his baby often enough.

Mothers worry when their babies vomit—babies do not. They don't even make a wry face as they spit up a mouthful of curdled milk. Usually the amount of food lost is overestimated. It is not at all uncommon for a baby to spit up what appears to be an entire feeding. So long as the baby shows no other signs of illness and is gaining weight, there is nothing to worry about. Babies spit up food because the muscle guarding the opening of the esophagus or gullet into the stomach is lax; it will get stronger in time and, eventually, the "vomiting of infancy," as it is called, will stop well before the baby is a year old.

Infants and children vomit for many reasons: when ill with colds, sore throats, earaches, diarrhea, infections of any kind; following injury anywhere to the body—a stubbed toe may cause vomiting; to gain attention. Children learn early that vomiting is a useful tool to bend mothers to their wishes.

Persistent vomiting is an altogether different matter. A baby, not sick with a cold or any other kind of infection, who continues to vomit in spite of changes in formula, loses weight, looks peaked and unhappy, usually requires hospitalization and study to find the cause.

Pyloric stenosis (obstruction at the outlet of the stomach) is the most common cause of persistent vomiting during infancy. The story is usually something like this. The baby, most likely a boy, and often the first born, begins to vomit at about three weeks of age. He was normal at birth, lost a few ounces as all babies do, regained his birth weight and then within one to three days began to vomit all of his food and with great force. "Projectile vomiting" is the term used to describe the manner in which food literally shoots out of the baby's mouth. These babies in a few days easily vomit themselves into a state of dehydration (lack of water in the tissues).

A baby who vomits so strenuously should be seen by the doctor at once. Because the baby eats ravenously, mothers are apt to think little can be wrong and delay seeking medical attention until he is in serious condition.

Pyloric stenosis can be easily and accurately diagnosed by your doctor, and can be safely corrected by a simple but delicate operation in which the fibers constricting the opening of the stomach are cut. Within a week after operation, the baby will be taking and keeping down all his food.

You should know and remember this extremely important fact: Whenever a baby or young child vomits greenish material something is seriously wrong. Regurgitation of food eaten or of white curdled milk is of little significance, but vomiting of *green* material means that bile—green bile—has backed up from the intestine into the stomach. Get in touch with your doctor at once. Your child most likely has intestinal obstruction or blockage of the bowel.

CONSTIPATION

It is customary to speak of a baby's "footsies," "paddies," or "toofies," but when such baby talk is extended to a dissertation about the baby's "bowlies," and a detailed description of his little "movies," it is obvious that excessive attention is being focused upon a normal physiological function.

Misunderstanding of constipation and fear of its consequences cause mothers unnecessary worry and endless discussion of their babies' bowel habits. Constipation implies nothing but infrequent and/or difficult evacuation of feces. It is not a disease nor does it cause all the dire symptoms ascribed to it. In fact, a baby who moves his bowels once a day or every other day is just as healthy as the baby who moves his bowels three or four times a day. It is perfectly normal for a baby to strain and get red in the face when having a bowel movement.

Babies and children vary in their bowel habits just as adults do. The character and consistency of a baby's or older child's movements depend upon the amount and type of food eaten and upon whether the child and family are high strung or placid. Underfeeding, insufficient fruit and vegetables, and illness requiring bed rest promote constipation. Breast-fed babies are practically never constipated. Some healthy bottle-fed babies, for no apparent reason, pass "little marbles" once a day or every other day; others eating exactly the same food have three or more soft movements a day. Stools are hard or soft in direct relation to the speed with which the digested material goes through the intestine. The only difference between a hard and soft movement is its water content.

Rarely indeed is a baby below one year of age troubled with significant constipation. Infrequent bowel evacuation in a healthy, normal, thriving infant is no more abnormal than big ears or little ears.

If there is any question in your mind that your baby's constipation is due to a specific cause, take him to the doctor for a careful examination. Supposing the doctor finds nothing wrong—then what? He will most likely advise less white sugar, more dark sugar, or maltose in the formula, some prune juice instead of or in addition to orange juice, or a tablespoonful of strained prunes. Enemas and laxatives are rarely needed. Occasionally, a suppository may be helpful. If you don't have a glycerine suppository in the house you can easily carve one out of any toilet soap. Make it an inch long, tapered, and the thickness of a lead pencil. Lay the baby face down over your knee and insert it in the rectum; it will be effective.

For the occasional child who is truly constipated, has huge, hard passages causing pain, a lubricant to soften the stool is desirable. Mineral oil is most effective. When giving mineral oil to an infant it should be added to orange juice or formula. It is not advisable over a period of weeks to give mineral oil to an infant with a spoon; often the baby chokes and inhales a few drops of oil. Repeated inhalation of oil may cause trouble in the lungs—a disease called lipid or fatty pneumonia. Oil retention enemas are ineffective; they don't soften the stool and are usually expelled shortly after being given.

Parents have heard that mineral oil is bad because it interferes with absorption of vitamins. Theoretically, it is true that mineral oil prevents absorption of vitamins A and D, but from a practical standpoint no child who is getting only one or two teaspoons of mineral oil once a day will be robbed of necessary vitamins. To the occasional child who requires mineral oil for a long period of time, a daily tablet or capsule containing all the vitamins will offset any danger of vitamin deficiency.

If during an acute illness your baby becomes constipated, as so frequently happens, give him a dose of castoria or milk of magnesia. An occasional cathartic will do no harm but don't make it a habit.

The baby who cries when his bowels move may or may not be constipated, but almost certainly does have some trouble with his rectum. Take him to the doctor for a rectal examination. He may have a stricture (tightening) of the rectal opening or a fissure (crack) in the mucosa or lining of the rectum.

A stricture of the rectum must be treated, i.e., the tight opening must be dilated. Stretching the rectum should be done while the baby is below one year of age. The process is painful and all memory of the ordeal should have been forgotten before it's time for potty training. The doctor will dilate the tight rectum gently with his little finger and instruct you to do the same each day or every other day with your first finger covered with a lubricated finger cot. These dilatations are of the utmost importance early in life. Neither you nor the doctor should be satisfied until it is possible for the baby to have a normal-sized movement without pain.

You hear occasionally of stretching the tight rectum with an instrument while the baby is anesthetized. That's a mistake. Within a month or two after such forcible stretching, the rectum will be tighter than it was. Slow, patient stretching of a tight rectum with a finger is safer.

If your baby cries when he moves his bowels and at times you see a little blood on the outside of a stool, he most likely has a rectal fissure. This fissure is like a crack in the corner of the mouth. The doctor will touch up the fissure with a little medicine and prescribe liberal doses of mineral oil to be taken each day for a few weeks until the raw place is healed.

Constipation in children below one year of age is rare and in ninety-nine cases out of a hundred requires no treatment. True constipation, whatever the cause, should be corrected during early infancy, well before time for potty training. (See page 128.)

DIARRHEA

Diarrhea during infancy is extremely common. It is of more significance in babies below six months of age than in older children.

First of all, let's understand what is meant by diarrhea. A breast-fed baby during the first few weeks of life often has six to eight soft bowel movements in twenty-four hours. That's normal. By two to three months the number has fallen to two to four. The bottle-fed baby usually has two to four evacuations a day but may have more depending upon the type of sugar used in the formula.

An occasional watery movement is of no consequence so long as the infant takes his feedings with relish, doesn't act sick, or appear ill. By diarrhea we mean watery stools occurring with sufficient frequency to produce such general symptoms as loss of appetite and irritability and often a little fever.

Mild diarrhea in infants is most often due to infection in the intestinal tract following upper-respiratory infections (colds or sore throats). Overfeeding, especially of too rich a formula, is also causative. Contamination due to inadequate sterilization of formula, bottles, and nipples is a less common cause of diarrhea today since most mothers have learned the need of proper sterilization and refrigeration.

The baby who has diarrhea should be treated. Mothers of first babies will call a doctor but those more experienced may handle the problems themselves.

For breast-fed babies, incidentally, far less subject to diarrhea than bottle-fed babies, there is not much to do but omit a few feedings and offer the baby boiled water. It may be necessary to evacuate the breasts artificially for comfort and to avoid losing the milk. As the number of stools lessens, the baby should be allowed to nurse for a few minutes. He can slowly be brought back to full nursing periods, usually within forty-eight hours.

The bottle-fed baby likewise should skip a few feedings. Babies with diarrhea don't tolerate fat. Therefore boiled skim milk is good. Boil a pint of skim milk for ten minutes and skim off all the film which will get stuck in the nipple. Then add enough boiled water to again make a full pint. The baby probably won't take more than one or two ounces at a time. Don't urge him to eat—he knows how much he wants. Offer boiled water between times. Tea, sweetened with honey or a tablet of saccharine, is often taken eagerly. Babies with diarrhea lose a lot of water and are thirsty.

Your doctor will suggest by phone some simple medication which should control the diarrhea in a day or two. He may also prescribe small doses of paregoric for the baby who seems to have stomachache. Don't use paregoric, however, without specific instructions from your doctor.

Severe diarrhea, i.e., greenish, watery movements every hour or two in a baby below six months of age is quite another problem. After approximately twenty-four hours of persistent diarrhea responding not at all to simple measures, the baby will show signs of a rather serious condition called dehydration (excessive loss of fluid and essential body salts). You don't have to be a doctor or a nurse to detect the typical signs of dehydration. Such a baby will be pale and listless, his tongue will be dry (you can see that it's dry or feel the dryness with your finger); his eyes will be sunken and lusterless. He will likely have a fever of 102 degrees or more. Some babies vomit and that, of course, hastens the onset of dehydration.

The baby who is underweight and undernourished is more subject to infectious diarrhea and sicker than the vigorous full-weight infant. The younger the baby, the more serious is persistent diarrhea.

If you have not consulted a doctor during the beginning period of diarrhea, lose no time in doing so at the appearance of any of the signs listed above. Call your doctor and if he is not readily available drive to the nearest good hospital. As soon as possible after admission a tube will be placed in one of the baby's veins. He will be given the proper amount of salt and glucose (sugar) solutions to replace what he has lost. Almost like magic the alarming signs will disappear and his condition will improve.

I can't be too emphatic about getting prompt care for the baby ill with severe and persistent diarrhea. The neglected infant who has gone into a deep state of dehydration cannot always be brought back. Remember that on hot summer days a sick baby becomes dehydrated more rapidly because sweating adds to the loss of fluid and salts.

Less common is bloody diarrhea in babies during the first few weeks of life. The cause is unknown. The diarrhea is not severe but what is frightening to the mother is the appearance of blood and mucus in the stool. Such diarrheas usually appear a week or so after the baby has been taken home from the hospital. Should this happen to your baby, you will, of course, call your doctor, but be sure to do this: save the blood-stained diapers so that your doctor can see them and estimate the amount of blood lost; it will be far less than you think.

Blood and mucus will persist in the stool for a week or two. You will be anxious and often so will your doctor if by coincidence he has not seen such cases. Ordinary care and close observation is usually all that is needed. Occasionally, the loss of considerable blood for a number of days will suggest that an operation is necessary.

BREATHING DIFFICULTIES

From the moment the baby takes his first breath, life depends upon a constant stream of air (oxygen), and anything that interferes with its supply demands instant attention.

A baby breathes from thirty to fifty times a minute, more than twice as fast as an adult.

Shallow and irregular breathing from time to time is normal. Don't be alarmed.

Noisy rattling breathing is caused by vibration of the soft palate. Don't worry about that either; it will stop in the course of a few months.

Babies who snore do not need to have their adenoids removed. Disregard their snoring; it will stop in the course of time.

All babies hiccup, supposedly from overeating, or eating too fast. Hiccups are caused by sudden contractions of the diaphragm, the sheet of muscle that separates the chest from the abdominal cavity. Hiccups are of no consequence; burping may stop them— so will doing nothing.

Any time your baby develops difficulty in breathing or shows any signs of struggling for air, call your doctor. The two most common causes are: something stuck in the windpipe, discussed on page 264, and croup discussed on page 158.

When a baby chokes while eating and can't get up whatever is stuck in his throat, turn him upside down and give him a sharp slap on the back. Should he get blue and have to "fight for breath," take him to the nearest hospital as fast as you can. Artificial respiration, (mouth-to-mouth breathing, page 259) may be necessary.

Crowing respiration, a term used to describe just that—a squeaky noise as air is being inhaled—should be investigated by a specialist who is skilled in the diagnosis of breathing troubles. Such noisy breathing, caused by something inside the trachea, or windpipe, or something pressing on the outside, is usually of no significance when the baby is well. However, inflammation and swelling due to a cold added to the obstruction already there may be serious. Don't fail to get expert consultation about any difficulty with breathing.

THE NAVEL

Immediately after the baby was born the doctor closed the stump of the cord with a sterile ligature or a metal clamp. The cord heals better when it is allowed to dry in exposed air rather than under a dressing. It is well to sponge the cord with alcohol each day and any time it gets wet. Normally, the shriveled cord falls off within a week or ten days.

If, at any time, the skin about the cord is red or you see some pus, call your doctor immediately. Infection creeping up the cord into the abdomen may be serious.

Sometimes a bit of cord in the navel does not dry up and has to be touched with silver nitrate by your doctor. This little nubbin of cord, called a granuloma, is not serious and can be attended to at your first checkup appointment with the doctor.

When bathing the baby or changing his diaper you may, when

he cries, see a bulge in the navel. The moment he stops crying the bulge disappears. He has a rupture of the navel—an umbilical hernia.

Don't be alarmed about this common condition appearing usually about the second or third week. The next time you visit your doctor call his attention to it. Don't criticize the doctor who delivered the baby. How the cord was tied off has nothing to do with the development of an umbilical hernia; it is caused solely by a weakness in the abdominal wall where the blood vessels went through from mother to baby.

There is much difference of opinion about what to do for umbilical hernia; some doctors believe they will all close spontaneously. I don't. The little ones, yes; the big ones, no; the middle-sized ones, usually.

For years the accepted treatment has been taping or strapping the navel with a two-inch strip of adhesive tape put on tightly enough to hold the bulge down. Maybe such binding does some good; I doubt it. The adhesive band holds about three days, then slips, and is too loose to do any good. Another band is put on but after two or three applications the skin is so sore that taping has to be discontinued for a few weeks. I believe that umbilical hernias which close did so because of elapsed time and the normal tendency to close rather than because of any beneficial effect of strapping. I am convinced also that strapping will continue to be done for the simple reason that a mother is apt to feel that the doctor is neglecting her baby if he doesn't follow popular custom and stick some adhesive tape on the rupture.

A large navel hernia bulging far out through an opening an inch or more in diameter in the abdominal wall should be repaired surgically when the baby is about two years old—sooner or later depending upon the size of the hernia.

Having accepted the advice of the doctor for surgical repair, be sure to ask the surgeon whether he is going to take out the navel. If he says yes, get another surgeon. It is not necessary to remove the navel and is disfiguring to do so. When the child grows up he or she will be very self-conscious about the wide expanse of abdomen with no familiar landmark.

COLIC

Colic of infancy is not a disease but a condition, and a common and frustrating one it is. Of one hundred normal babies from one week to three months old, twenty-five have severe colic and another twenty-five have mild colic.

One can tell that a baby has colic or abdominal cramps by the way he jerks up his legs, thrashes about with his arms and cries and then cries some more. His tummy is often somewhat distended and he passes a great deal of gas.

The cause of colic is unknown. Improper digestion has been blamed but breast-fed babies, getting the best possible food, also have colic. Food allergy is rarely causative. High-strung infants of tense parents apparently are more subject to colic than placid ones.

After your doctor has ruled out intestinal disease or defects and has made a diagnosis of colic, what to do to muddle through the trying month or two ahead of you—that is the question.

So long as your baby is taking adequate food, gaining weight, and having more or less regular bowel movements, try not to worry or get nervous.

Keep in touch with your doctor for treatment and reassurance. He may change the formula from time to time; sometimes improvement follows but more commonly it does not. It will largely be up to you to carry on and soothe the unhappy child while you comfort yourself with the knowledge that colic rarely lasts more than three months.

Rocking the baby has been found more effective than any other treatment; it soothes him and, incidentally, you. If you don't have a rocking chair, get one with a high back and side arms. During the evening, the time when colic is at its worst, listen to the radio or watch television as you rock. You might as well rock, you can't read or knit when the baby is screaming. You and your husband will be happier and more companionable if the baby is kept quiet.

Give the baby a pacifier as often as he wishes; it's a wonderful soother and does no harm. He will not fill his stomach with air from sucking on a pacifier. It seems that colicky babies require more than average sucking satisfaction.

Burp the baby frequently during feedings and occasionally between feedings. Some infants force air in their stomachs with violent crying. In case of constipation or excessive distention of the abdomen with gas, an enema may be effective; two bulbs full of warm water are injected into the rectum with an ear syringe.

Fill a hot water bottle one-third full of warm water, express all air, cover it with a diaper and lay the baby face down with the bottle under his tummy. Heat and pressure often temporarily relieve cramps.

When home remedies fail and you find yourself getting overtired, nervous, and weepy, call your doctor for help. He will prescribe a mild sedative for the baby and one for you. You needn't apologize for temporarily using drugs; they help you both over the rough spots of total exhaustion.

For you mothers who have had to listen to seemingly endless crying of your colicky babies, here is a soothing ointment for your frayed nerves: the severely colicky baby is apt later in life to be a leader with better than average drive and ability.

THE BABY HAS TENDER SKIN

After floating in water for nine months it is little wonder that a newborn baby's skin is soft and tender. To prevent too rapid drying, the greasy, grayish-white material which coats the skin at birth is not washed off for a few days.

Eventually the baby is bathed, and is the most beautiful creature in creation with a skin as soft as rose petals. This tender skin, however, is subject to irritations, infections, and rashes which appear in spite of your best care.

Cradle Cap.   This is apt to appear during the first or second month. The scientific name for this condition is *seborrheic dermatitis* or inflammation of an excessively oily scalp.

The first sign of cradle cap is an accumulation of whitish flakes in the baby's scalp. If not treated these flakes enlarge and become yellowish, greasy, messy-looking crusts. Sometimes the infection spreads over the forehead and eyebrows and behind the ears. Unless the condition is badly neglected, the disease doesn't make the baby sick.

Cradle cap in the flaking stage is easily corrected in a few days by massaging the entire scalp with mineral oil each evening and giving a shampoo each morning with soap containing hexachlorophene.

For advanced cases with red, raw areas beneath and around the crusts, you'll need medical help unless the above treatment improves the condition greatly in three or four days.

Diaper Rash.   Almost every baby from time to time will have diaper rash. After a diaper has been left on a bit longer than usual and if covered with waterproof pants, the skin is apt to become red and irritated.

By giving special attention to washing, drying, and powdering the diaper area and the creases in groins and thighs, by changing the diaper more frequently, and by not using plastic pants, the skin irritation may quickly disappear. It is well to use medicated powder on the reddened skin but not too liberally. Excess powder in the creases absorbs urine, becomes caked, and causes irritation.

Some babies have especially tender skins and within a few days develop diaper rash so severe that the skin becomes fiery red and dotted with blisters. The entire diaper area looks as though it had been burned with too hot water.

This sort of rash is not caused by "strong urine" but by ammonia released from urea in the urine and by germs on the skin and in the diapers. You will notice the strong smell of ammonia when changing a diaper which has been left on overnight. The amount of ammonia in the urine has little to do with the baby's diet.

Treatment obviously is aimed at getting rid of the germs. Wash and boil the diapers, baby's clothes and shirts, and then soak them in an antiseptic solution—there are many on the market— which will kill the ammonia producing bacteria. If you use a diaper service you need do nothing to the returned diapers; they have been properly sterilized.

To get rid of all the germs, wash the mattress cover and plastic pants with plenty of soap and water and, if possible, let them dry in the sunshine.

Sponge the baby's sore bottom at each diaper change with a disinfectant in warm water. Dry the skin by patting and apply a protective ointment prescribed or suggested by your doctor.

If the rash doesn't clear up in a few days, keep the baby in a warm room and leave the diaper off during the day; just place a folded diaper under his buttocks. Exposure to air is healing. Don't use a plastic diaper covering at night. As the rash clears the skin will peel just as it does after severe sunburn. Baby oil will soften the skin.

Sore Bottom is the name given to redness and irritation around the rectum as a result of diarrhea; acid stools burn the baby's skin. Controlling the diarrhea will solve the problem. Changing diapers immediately after each movement and carefully sponging and drying the skin will help, but if the diarrhea persists nothing is quite as effective as laying the baby on his tummy on a diaper, exposing the buttocks to the air and giving local heat treatments with a heating lamp or an ordinary gooseneck reading lamp. Needless to say, be careful that the heat is not excessive. Putting a small pillow under the baby's tummy will elevate the buttocks, separate them, and allow better exposure to the warm air.

Prickly Heat. This appears not only during hot, humid weather but in any baby who is dressed so warmly that he perspires. Slightly elevated, pinpoint reddened areas appear around the neck and in folds of the skin wherever perspiration accumulates. Itching may make the baby very fussy. Since prickly heat is the result of too much heat, the treatment is obvious—cool the baby. Sponge the involved areas frequently, dry thoroughly, and apply powder; ordinary cornstarch is as good as any. Shake some cornstarch in your hand, rub your hands together, and apply a thin coating to the baby's skin. Treatment is summed up in this advice: Keep the baby clean, dry, and cool.

Rashes.   Reddish, scaly patches on babies' cheeks are common during the first three months. Some are caused by vigorous washing, most come and go for no apparent reason. Baby oil and time cure them all.

Rashes may result from contact with irritating substances such as wool, nylon, animal hair, soap, etc. Most standard toilet soaps are not irritating to babies' skins. The perfume in soap is more apt to be at fault than the soap itself. Instead of a rash the baby may have welts or hives from contact with something to which he is sensitive.

Impetigo.   A contagious skin disease of newborn infants, impetigo is characterized by small blisters which appear anywhere on the baby but mostly on the hands, face, and diaper region. The skin becomes slightly reddened, blisters form and are filled with pus. These blisters easily break and spread the infection. Call your doctor at once. It is important to stop this infection before it spreads all over the body. Impetigo can largely be prevented through cleanliness. No one who has any kind of infection, a boil, or even a minor infected hangnail, should handle the baby. Hands should be washed always before touching a baby; it takes time for the tender skin to become resistant to germs.

Any time your child has a rash which you don't recognize, call your doctor—the baby may have a contagious disease.

Infantile Eczema.   Eczema, although not a killing disease, drives baby, mother, and pediatrician to distraction.

Not much is known about the cause of infantile eczema except that some babies are sensitive to certain foods, notably cow's milk, eggs, wheat, orange juice, and/or to external irritants such as wool, cat fur, plastics, drugs, and even to wind and sunshine. What's confusing is that some infants tested and found sensitive to nothing still have eczema. In severe cases there is usually a history of eczema, hay fever, or asthma in the family.

Eczema rarely appears before the baby is two months old. It starts on the cheeks, spreads to the forehead and behind the ears. Little patches appear in the elbows and behind the knees. The skin gets red, dry and scaly, and itches. The baby scratches and opens the skin. These places "weep," ooze serum which dries and forms crusts.

So long as the eczema is mild—most cases are—simple methods of treatment will suffice. A minimum of soap and water should be used on the irritated skin. Clean and wipe away the crusts with cotton balls or a soft cloth soaked with mineral or baby oil. Your doctor will most likely prescribe a soothing ointment or advise you to buy one available at the drug store. It may be necessary to put tubular cardboard restraints on the baby's elbows to keep him from scratching. Drastic changes in diet and long series of skin tests are unnecessary in mild cases.

Eczema which suddenly spreads all over the baby's body is quite another problem. Prepare yourself for a long siege of living with a very unhappy infant. Find a doctor who is interested and sympathetic with your problem and stay with him. No doctor knows a magic cure and no pharmaceutical house has ever put out an ointment that will relieve all symptoms.

Elimination of the eczema-causing foods will be first on the list of instructions. Milk substitutes will replace cow's milk. Egg white is easily eliminated. Wheat cereals will be replaced by rice or corn products, and orange juice by synthetic vitamin C. Since fat babies are far more apt to have eczema than thin ones, the total diet will be adjusted downward.

Some doctors advise complete dietary changes at once, others eliminate one food at a time in an attempt to find the culprit. The latter approach seems more sensible.

It is well not only to keep a detailed record of all foods taken by the baby but also to make notes of everything with which he comes in contact. The chances of finding the offending substance are few. However, stay with it; success in identifying and eliminating it may promptly clear up the eczema.

The saddest, most pitiable creature is the infant who has eczema from head to foot. Hospitalization is necessary for the child's care and for preservation of the exhausted mother's sanity. In spite of the best medical nursing care, it may take weeks to clear up severe cases.

While the baby is continuously scratching and crying, it is poor comfort to the mother to be assured that in time he will again be well. Just when you think that the battle has been won flare-ups occur. Eventually, however, the last red spot will disappear and he will be healthy, happy, and unscarred.

Birth Marks. A mother brought in her three-months-old baby with a "strawberry mark" on his shoulder. The birth mark was a typical, fiery red capillary hemangioma, meaning, a nest of tiny blood vessels heaped up in a mass; it was the size of a quarter and looked exactly like a slice of ripe strawberry.

With considerable heat the mother said, "I took my baby to one doctor who said I should do nothing about the birth mark and then to another who wanted to cut it out. What shall I do?"

Both doctors were right. Most "strawberry marks" slowly fade and completely disappear in about two years. If you can be patient, nature will perform a cure and leave only a round small scar. If you can't bear the sight of the blemish, go to the second doctor and have it removed. An operation has the advantage of quickly accomplishing what nature does slowly, but the disadvantage of requiring admission to the hospital, anesthesia, and some added expense. I'd be inclined to let nature perform her cure; the decision is up to you.

A word of warning is necessary about the strawberry marks in babies below three months of age. Occasionally, for no reason, the mark suddenly—that is within a week or two—begins to grow. Should this happen, consult a skin specialist who will freeze the surface with dry ice (carbon dioxide snow) and stop the growth.

Bluish red lumps called cavernous hemangiomas, nests of enlarged veins, do not go away spontaneously and have to be surgically removed, if unsightly.

These birth marks are not cancers and never turn into cancers. Don't believe any opinion to the contrary.

The cause of birth marks is unknown. The old superstition that seeing something frightening or being startled by an insect or a mouse or being jolted in an accident during pregnancy causes birth marks is pure nonsense.

Moles. Moles come in assorted sizes and shapes and in a variety of colors, but mostly brown. Look your baby over and you'll probably see one or more tiny moles. During the years they will grow very little. I doubt if there is an adult who doesn't have a mole somewhere. Then why all the fuss about moles? Because occasionally a certain type of mole, the blue mole, turns into a cancer, but not during childhood.

Black, hairy moles are unsightly and should be removed; small ones are simply excised, large ones are removed and the surface covered with skin grafts. Moles, unlike strawberry marks, do not disappear spontaneously and when large and unsightly should be removed. An ugly mole on a child's face should be taken off before he goes to school and is exposed to thoughtlessly unkind remarks by schoolmates. The answer to a simple mole is easy—leave it alone. Pictures of Abraham Lincoln wouldn't look right without that mole on his right cheek.

Albinism. Albinism means absence of pigment in the skin. There are two kinds of albinism, complete and partial.

Total absence of pigment in the skin is extremely rare. Such children, called albinos, have milk-white skins, pure white hair and eyelashes. Their eyes instead of being brown or blue are pink like rabbit's eyes and constantly waver from side to side.

Partial albinos, people with white spots, are very common. The streak of white hair called a "white forelock," so commonly seen, is due to absence of pigment in that portion of the scalp from which the white hair grows. It can't be unsightly or so many young girls wouldn't have a white streak bleached in their hair.

Nothing can be done about albinism. Girls can cover such white patches on their faces with makeup. During the summer the white patches will be more noticeable because they do not tan.

LESS COMMON TROUBLES

Enlarged Thymus.   Parents are frightened when it is suggested that their baby may have an enlarged thymus. This fear stems from old teaching which claimed that an enlarged thymus could cause sudden death. Well, it does not cause sudden death, or difficulty in breathing, or any other symptoms.

The thymus is a mass of tissue in the chest behind the upper part of the breastbone. After years of research we still don't know what, if anything, is its function. Why is it there? you ask, and my answer is, "I don't know." The thymus may be as big and thick as the palm of a woman's hand or as small as a lima bean. The only way one can find out about the size of the thymus is by taking an x-ray picture.

In spite of the fact that the thymus, large or small, has been proven innocent and harmless, some doctors are still afraid of it and prescribe x-ray treatment when it is larger than average.

Now hear this: X-ray treatments of the thymus are wrong for three reasons. One, they are unnecessary; two, x-ray irradiation is a powerful force not to be used indiscriminately; three, x-ray treatments to the region of the thymus during infancy may cause cancer of the thyroid during adolescence.

An enlarged thymus is harmless—leave it alone.

Thrush. Babies on a milk diet normally have a coated tongue, but when baby's tongue and the inside of his cheeks and lips are covered with white patches, he most likely has thrush.

This fungus infection, often contracted from the birth canal during delivery, is common during the first few weeks of life. An older infant who is being treated with antibiotics for some serious infection may suddenly develop thrush because the drugs destroy the mouth germs which normally keep the fungus in check.

Thrush is not a serious ailment. The only symptoms are mild soreness of the mouth during nursing and sometimes a little diarrhea.

The treatment is simple. Your doctor will most likely prescribe 2 percent Gentian Violet in water to be swabbed on the white patches with a cotton applicator two or three times a day. When using this medication, put old sheets on the crib and the least fancy nightgown on the baby because Gentian Violet stains linen. The advantage of this treatment, usually effective in a few days, is that it is cheap.

In severe cases, a new drug called Nystatin given in the baby's formula, is effective and will stop the infection in forty-eight hours. This drug is rather expensive.

Sudden Severe Stomachache. One of the strangest, yet not at all unusual, affliction of infants is in-tus-sus-cep'-tion, or telescoping of one portion of the bowel into another. The last part of the small intestine forces itself into the beginning of the large intestine and by so doing causes intestinal obstruction—complete blockage of the bowel.

We do not know the cause of this odd mechanical difficulty. The mystery of intussusception is that it most commonly strikes infants four to eight months old. Equally mysterious is the fact that the healthy "never been sick a day in his life" baby is more susceptible than the child who has battled his way through feeding problems, colic, and poor weight gain.

So typical are the symptoms that the doctor can make a diagnosis by telephone. The mother reports, "This morning (it may be any time of the day or night) my baby cried as I have never heard him cry before. All of a sudden he screamed. A few minutes later he quieted down, then got pale and limp and just lay in his bed as though completely exhausted. I watched him for a few minutes and offered him a bottle. He took a little bit and then screamed again just as before and vomited. He's never been sick before. He sure looks knocked out. I wish you would come right away."

The doctor recognizes the symptoms and saves time by advising immediate hospitalization. By the time the baby has been admitted to the hospital, he probably has passed some blood and mucous, a so-called "current jelly" stool.

If the symptoms have been of short duration the doctor may advise reduction, (correction of the intussusception) with a barium enema given in the x-ray department. Most doctors, however, advise correction by operation.

Other causes of stomachache will be discussed on page 172.

THE PREMATURE BABY

A premature baby is one who weighs less than five pounds eight ounces at birth.

The old method of labeling a baby born three or four weeks early as premature is unsatisfactory for the simple reason that women often cannot know the time of conception. Many full-term babies are born a few weeks before or after the expected date. For this reason the medical profession has established the five pound eight ounce birth weight as a dividing line between full term and prematurity. It is recognized that many babies weighing approximately five pounds are actually full term and require no special care. Some women normally have small babies.

Approximately one baby in ten is born prematurely. The percentage is higher in first-born babies of mothers less than twenty years old and in those born after the fourth pregnancy.

The baby weighing two to four pounds at birth is in for a rough time. His digestive system is inadequate, he is extremely vulnerable to infection, and he is in constant danger of hypoxia (insufficient oxygen) because his lungs are underdeveloped. He will have to live in an incubator for weeks, preferably in a hospital especially equipped for the care of "preemies." These tiny mites of humanity require special food, constantly humidified air at a temperature of 89 degrees Fahrenheit and exactly the proper amount of oxygen.

When the baby's weight reaches about five and one-half pounds, he is ready to go home. After this his care is the same as that of any full-term baby except that he still must be guarded against infection for another month or so, meaning absolutely no visitors.

In about two years most "preemies" will have caught up with the physical and mental level of the average two year old.

In case the premature baby is an only child, parents must be warned against the natural tendency toward overprotection and excessive coddling. After the baby is well on his way to normal development, the past should be forgotten and he should be treated as a normal child.

THE RH BABY

About 85 percent of the people have Rh positive blood and 15 percent Rh negative. The term, Rh, comes from the Rhesus monkey on which research was done in discovery of this strange substance in blood, of no significance except during pregnancy.

If a man and woman are both Rh positive or negative, or if the woman is Rh positive and the man is Rh negative, there is no danger of this couple having what is called an "Rh baby." However, when an Rh negative woman, married to an Rh positive man, carries an Rh positive baby, some of the baby's Rh positive blood cells may escape into the mother's blood through the placenta and stimulate the formation of an antibody, i.e., a substance antagonistic to Rh positive cells.

Seepage of these antibodies back into the baby from the

mother tends to destroy the baby's blood cells. The amount of antibody escaping through the placenta determines the amount of damage to the baby; a small amount may be harmless or cause mild anemia, a large amount will cause miscarriage, stillbirth or jaundice and brain damage in a full-term baby.

The chances of an Rh negative woman and Rh positive man having an "Rh baby" are about one in two hundred. The first baby of such matings is rarely affected unless the mother has through some error or in an emergency received a transfusion of Rh positive blood. It usually requires two or three pregnancies to build up enough antibodies in the mother to injure the baby before or at birth.

Most couples don't know whether they are Rh positive or negative. When pregnancy occurs, it is customary for the obstetrician to have blood tests made to determine this factor. Should the tests show an Rh negative mother and an Rh positive father, tests will be made during pregnancy to determine the level of antibodies in the mother's blood.

When tests show that the antibody level is dangerously high, arrangements are made for an exchange or massive blood transfusion of the baby as soon after birth as possible. The transfusion gives the baby fresh blood and washes away the perilous antibodies. The importance of an exchange transfusion to protect the baby against brain damage cannot be overemphasized.

Rh negative mothers who have had one or two normal babies and then an Rh baby—fortunately normal after an exchange transfusion—often ask whether it is safe to have more children. I think it is hazardous. An exchange transfusion at birth does not always prevent serious complications. Be satisfied with two or three normal children.

It has been suggested by scientific enthusiasts that boys and girls have blood tests before falling seriously in love. Some go so far as to say that an Rh positive boy should not marry an Rh negative girl. Anybody who thinks that such advice will alter the course of true love should read more love stories and less science.

WRY NECK

About two to four weeks after delivery, a mother one day discovers that her baby has a hard lump in the muscle in the side of his neck. She also will have noticed that the baby always holds his head to one side. If the lump is in the right side of the neck the baby will hold his head turned to the left, and when sleeping on his tummy will insist on lying on the right side of his face. The constant pressure of lying on one side of his face will make his head look lopsided.

Wry neck, not an uncommon condition, is presumably due to a tear in one of the muscles in the side of the neck. Many cases follow breech delivery. It is not the obstetrician's fault. Some babies have wry neck after easy deliveries.

How to treat wry neck in a baby is a matter of dispute. Some surgeons advocate operation, others advise conservative treatment. I cast my vote against operation.

Conservative treatment consists of gently turning the baby's head at least fifteen times a day in the opposite direction to which he holds it to stretch the shortened muscle with the lump in it. Forceful turning, enough to make the baby cry, will further injure the muscle and make the condition worse.

As soon as the baby is old enough to recognize you and turn his head at your approach, lay him in his crib in such a position that to see you he will have to turn his face and thereby make a slight pull on the shortened muscle. When the baby is fast asleep on his tummy, gently turn his head to the opposite side. In the course of a few months the lump will disappear, the muscle will stretch, and the baby will hold his head straight.

Such treatment will be effective in almost all cases. I have never seen wry neck in a baby that needed operation. Cases of wry neck unrecognized and untreated during infancy may later require surgical correction.

chapter Three

INOCULATIONS

WHAT FOR AND WHEN

If your children haven't received the usual immunizations, lay down this book, go to the telephone right now, and make an appointment with your doctor. It should not be necessary to urge parents to protect their children against disease. Yet 20 percent of infants and children in some localities remain unprotected. The only reason sweeping epidemics of diphtheria, for example, no longer appear is that a sufficiently large majority of children have been immunized against the infection and, therefore, cannot spread it. Ask grandma to tell you about the terrifying epidemics of contagious diseases she lived through and you won't long remain in the group of mothers who puts off shots for her children.

DTP and Polio Vaccine. The name of the vaccine, DTP, is derived from the first letters of three diseases—Diphtheria, Tetanus (lockjaw), and Pertussis (whooping cough). The first injection against these three diseases is given at about age two months. At the same time a dose of Sabin polio vaccine, Type I, is given orally (by mouth). At age three months the second injection of DTP is given along with a dose of oral polio vaccine, Type III, and at four months the third injection of DTP and oral polio vaccine, Type II, are given.

A booster dose of DTP and a combined oral dose of all three types of polio vaccine (Sabin) are given at age fifteen months and again at four years. (See schedule of inoculations, page 89.)

Approximately one month after the third injection of DTP and three doses of polio vaccine, immunity has become established. The booster shots and repeated doses of combined types of polio vaccine are given to maintain a high level of protection. Although it is desirable to have inoculations at specific times as advised, the schedule cannot always be adhered to because of illness or moving to another community. Some doctors begin inoculations when a baby is six weeks old and repeat them each six weeks; others don't advise starting until the baby is three months old and allow two month intervals between inoculations. Rules are not rigid; the vaccines will be effective even though the intervals between administrations are irregularly spaced. Needless to say, these inoculations are effective at any age.

That's all there is to this important matter of protecting your child against the dangers of strangulation from diphtheria, death from lockjaw, pneumonia following whooping cough, and crippling by polio. Failure to get these inoculations cannot be excused on the basis of expense because those who cannot afford to pay can get them free at city, state, or county health departments.

A few children react to DTP injections with slight fever and sickishness for a day or two and in some the site of injection gets sore and red. A tablet or two of aspirin is all that is needed in the way of treatment. The doctor should be told about the reactions; he may wish to alter the size of the next dose.

Lockjaw. A serious, greatly feared complication of open wounds of any kind is tetanus or lockjaw. Any person who has had the usual three doses of tetanus toxoid and booster shots will not get lockjaw. During my tour of duty in the South Pacific in World War II and observation of thousands of soldiers with horrible, jagged wounds, open fractures contaminated with dirt, bits of clothing, and shell fragments, not a single case of lockjaw was seen. These men had all been immunized against lockjaw during basic training and were given booster doses of toxoid as soon as possible after being wounded.

Rest assured, your child, inoculated against lockjaw during infancy and given a booster shot of toxoid following injury of any kind, such as stepping on a nail in a barnyard where tetanus germs thrive, is safe.

Unfortunately, a person who has not previously had inoculations against lockjaw is not benefitted by a dose of toxoid at the time of injury. That person, child or adult, will require an injection of 15,000–30,000 units of tetanus antitoxin. Doctors hate to give this antitoxin derived from horse serum because of the severe reactions it often causes; fear of tetanus leaves little choice.*

Polio.   It appears that polio has been added to the list of preventable diseases. The debate about which type of vaccine is better—Salk or Sabin—has been pretty well settled in favor of Sabin.

Salk vaccine, the first to be released for general use, is made of all three strains of killed polio viruses and is given only by injection. It has been instrumental in reducing the incidence of polio, but because the viruses are killed, immunity is not permanent and injections have to be repeated every two years indefinitely.

Sabin vaccine is made of live polio viruses greatly weakened (attenuated), but still able to produce the disease in very mild form, thereby conferring immunity. Another advantage, attractive to children, is the fact that Sabin vaccine can be taken by mouth on a lump of sugar.

To the question: "Shall my child who has had three or four

---

*A nonallergic, antitetanic serum has just become available.

shots of Salk vaccine be given the Sabin vaccine?"—the answer is, yes, for the reason stated above; a mild attack of the disease affords lifetime immunity.

The vaccine may be given at any time of the year but preferably during the months from October to May. No precautions are necessary, except that it is not given during a febrile illness of any kind. The vaccine is safe for all children including the allergic and for adults up to thirty years of age, including pregnant women.

When Salk vaccine was first released, some improperly prepared vaccine caused a number of cases of polio. Because of this misfortune parents are still a bit shy about the use of "live" Sabin vaccine which actually gives the child a mild case of polio. Millions of doses of Sabin vaccine have been given to children all over the world without any authenticated misfortune. Furthermore, the vaccine causes no signs of illness of any kind. Investigation of complaints that children were sick following doses of Sabin vaccine has proven that the illnesses were nothing more than coincidental colds, flu, stomach upsets, etc.

Measles. The most contagious of all children's diseases is now preventable. Unless protected by vaccine, 95 percent of children will at some time contract measles. The idea that this disease is a harmless contagion—just part of growing up—is decidedly wrong. Measles is dangerous; in 1962 before vaccine was available, measles caused more deaths in the United States than any other common childhood disease. The danger of measles lies in complications, the greatest of which is encephalitis, or inflammation of the brain. Approximately one child in a thousand with measles will get encephalitis. Fortunately, the majority of cases recover but those who do not either die or become permanently mentally defective. There is no specific treatment for measles encephalitis; it can be prevented.

Every child between nine months and sixteen years who has not had measles should be vaccinated. As with polio there are two types of vaccine; that made from killed viruses and that made from the weakened or attentuated viruses. The "live" vaccine is favored because it gives the child a mild attack of actual measles and thereby confers lifetime immunity.

To lessen the symptoms produced by the vaccine—some children will be moderately sick for a day or two with fever of 102 degrees or more—a dose of gamma globulin is given at the same time. Even this precaution does not prevent minor symptoms of illness and discomfort. Lifetime protection against the treachery of measles in exchange for two shots at one visit to your doctor and a slightly sickish and irritable child for a few days is a priceless bargain. No booster shots are needed. To the oft asked question: "Is there any danger of complications such as encephalitis from giving a child a mild case of measles?"—the answer is, no.

German Measles.   This is also known as the three day measles, and is altogether different from regular measles; each is caused by a separate and distinct virus.

German measles, appearing fourteen to twenty-one days after exposure, is the mildest and most harmless communicable disease of children and adults, yet treacherous because it may cause serious deformities of the baby if contracted by a woman during early months of pregnancy. The virus in the mother's blood goes through the placenta and strikes the tiny fetus. The consequent deformities follow a rather set pattern of mental deficiency, blindness, deafness, and heart defects; the baby may have one or all of these deformities.

A woman who contracts measles during her first month of pregnancy has a 50 percent chance of giving birth to a deformed child; during her second month, a 25 percent chance; and during her third month, a 10 percent chance. Apparently, the virus has no ill effects upon the fetus after the third month of pregnancy.

These rather frightening statistics make it desirable that our daughters contract the disease early in childhood. One attack confers lifetime immunity. Deliberately exposing grade school girls to German measles would be advisable were it not for the possibility of thereby transmitting the disease to women in the first months of pregnancy. The German measles virus has been isolated and it is anticipated that a vaccine will be perfected for immunization of all little girls.

Supposing a woman, one or two months pregnant (we'll omit the less hazardous third month), has unmistakable German measles, or supposing the disease is suspected and later proven to be such by laboratory tests, then what?

My answer to this question, a personal viewpoint, is influenced by the large number of pitiable German measles babies I have seen. If religious or moral scruples do not interfere, I advise therapeutic abortion for pregnant women in their twenties who have unmistakable German measles during the first two months of pregnancy. I don't believe a loving God wants parents to be burdened with a defective child. Childless parents in their late thirties usually decide to take the chance and go through with the pregnancy. Hopefully, in the near future a vaccine against German measles will be available to the public.

Mumps. Primarily a childhood disease, mumps rarely appears in children below one year of age; it may affect adults.

From eighteen to twenty-one days after exposure, swelling appears in one or both parotid salivary glands lying just below and slightly in front of the ears and over the back of the lower jaw. The infection may occur on one side and in a few days spread to the other side.

The typical swelling leaves little doubt of the diagnosis, but it is wise to consult your doctor to be sure.

There is no specific treatment for this mild disease. The affected child is kept in bed if feverish and out of school for about a week. Mumps is not very contagious. Often only one child of three or more in the family will have it at one time.

After puberty mumps is not a joke as pictured in cartoons, but a serious disease. For some unexplained reason, adolescent boys and men are apt to have inflammation of one or both testicles as a complication of mumps. Such inflammation often leads to atrophy (shrinkage) of the testicles and, in rare cases, to sterility. Therefore, when the children have mumps father should stay away from them if he hasn't had it. He should not touch "mumpsy" children nor any of their playthings and should thoroughly wash his hands immediately before eating. Dishes used by the ill child should be boiled.

Some doctors advise deliberate exposure of little boys to mumps.

Chicken pox. About two weeks, often to the day, after exposure, chicken pox, an extremely contagious disease of childhood appears with little red spots that look like mosquito bites or beginning pimples on the chest or back. In less than twenty-four hours a small blister appears on the top of each pimple. New spots keep coming out for three or four days, most on the body, a few on the face.

While the pocks are coming out the child may have some fever and feel sick. It is very unusual for a child to be seriously ill with chicken pox or to have any serious complications. By the fifth to seventh day, the blisters have all dried up and by the tenth day most of the brownish scabs will have fallen off.

Parents are most concerned about scarring on the face. Chicken pox itches and children scratch; in so doing they open and infect the blisters and that's what causes scarring. You can't keep children from scratching itchy places but you can lessen the chances of secondary infection by cutting their nails short and by washing their hands three or four times a day with soap or a germicidal solution. Itching can be relieved somewhat by applying calamine lotion with menthol. Baths in soda or starch solutions are soothing for severe cases; use one cup of soda or cornstarch in a bathtub one-third filled with warm water. As soon as the blisters have dried up and scabs have formed the danger of contagion is past. However, a child with a visible scab or two sent back to school will almost certainly be sent home by the school nurse.

The occasional adult who gets chicken pox is apt to be very sick and will not consider the wisecracks about his reversion to childhood as very funny.

Smallpox. In 1798, Edward Jenner of Scotland discovered that cowpox, a mild disease of cattle, will, when transferred to man, protect him against the deadly and disfiguring disease, smallpox. Cowpox vaccine is still used today.

Your child should be vaccinated between age six and twelve months when he is in good health and free from a cold. Vaccination should be performed preferably during cool weather because secondary infection in the pock is less apt to occur if the skin remains dry.

A child with eczema or open skin wounds of any kind should not be vaccinated until his skin is clear. Neither should a child with clear skin be vaccinated if another child in the family has open skin lesions. These precautions are taken to avoid transference of the virus from one child to another and consequent production of numerous vaccination sites (Vaccinia).

The most common and desirable site for vaccination is the outer surface of the left upper arm. Some parents prefer that their daughter be vaccinated on the left upper thigh.

A few days after vaccination, appearance of a red, itchy pimple indicates a "take." When the usual blister forms on top of the pimple the area should be protected against scratching fingers to prevent transference of the virus to eyes or to some tiny scratch anywhere on the body. Since the vaccination or pock dries up more rapidly when exposed to air, put on a light gauze dressing fixed with adhesive strips far from the site of the pock or pin a piece of gauze inside the clothing over the upper arm or thigh. Keep out probing fingers. Give the baby sponge baths until the scab is dry. The scab will fall off in about three weeks.

It is not unusual at the height of the reaction for the baby to be rather sick for two or three days with a fever of 101 to 102 degrees. The only treatment necessary is aspirin and cool sponging in case the fever goes high. Don't be alarmed if the lymph glands in the armpit or groin enlarge and are painful. Leave them alone. Don't rub or put on hot packs; they will get well sooner without treatment.

Practically no one is naturally immune to smallpox. Therefore, if vaccination does not take the first time, repeat until it does. Vaccination should be repeated every six years, and at any time exposure to smallpox may have occurred. Reactions to revaccination are usually minimal.

Tuberculin Tests.   These tests are used to determine whether a person has or has had tuberculosis. A tiny amount of tuberculin, an extract of killed tubercle bacilli, is injected into the skin in the forearm. No redness around the site of injection a few days later means a negative test, a sign one does not have and has not had tuberculosis; a certain degree of redness means the person is tuberculin positive—has tuberculosis in some form, active or inactive. Now don't go into a panic. Unless a child is ill, shows definite signs and symptoms of tuberculosis, and the doctor finds an active lesion somewhere in the body, a positive tuberculin test simply means that the child sometime has had a mild case of tuberculosis—so mild that it produced no symptoms. Well-cared-for children below school age living in a healthy community are rarely tuberculin positive. However, during the course of years almost everybody is at some time exposed to tuberculosis. The few germs which enter the body lodge somewhere and produce a tiny focus of infection which acts as a "vaccination" against tuberculosis. The majority of people above forty years are tuberculin positive.

Tuberculin tests are important in children as a means of finding the occasional child who has unsuspected tuberculosis. In such a case, tests are made of all members of the family and those with whom the child has been closely associated in an effort to find the source of the infection. The child is carefully examined, x-ray pictures of the chest are taken, and laboratory tests made. The earlier tuberculosis is found, the easier it is to cure. Don't be alarmed when your doctor suggests a tuberculin test. It's easy, harmless, and relatively painless. If negative you relax; if positive, be grateful that the test was made and that measures can be taken to determine what treatment is necessary.

SCHEDULE OF INOCULATIONS

AGE	IMMUNIZING MATERIAL
2 months*	DTP—Diphtheria, Tetanus (lockjaw), Pertussis (whooping cough), and Type I Sabin oral polio vaccine.
3 months	DTP and Type III Sabin vaccine.
4 months	DTP and Type II Sabin vaccine.
9 months	Measles vaccine.
12 months	Smallpox vaccination. Tuberculin test. Repeat as necessary.
15 months	Booster dose of DTP and a combined dose of Types I, II, and III oral polio vaccine.

The above inoculations are mandatory.

Those below are advisable.

4 years	Booster dose of DTP.
6 years	Repeat vaccination against smallpox. Repeat tuberculin test.
8 years	Booster dose of DT (diphtheria and tetanus). No further need for protection against whooping cough.
12 years	Booster dose DT and revaccination against smallpox.
16 years	Booster dose of DT.

*This schedule is not rigid.
It may be modified to suit parent and doctor.

Parents at times are inclined to feel that their children are, as they say, "being 'shot' to death." Actually, the contrary is true, they are being shot to live. Look over the schedule of inoculations and you will see that more than half of the shots are given before the baby is eighteen months old and capable of retaining any permanent memory of unpleasantness. As soon as children are old enough to recognize a needle, they usually cry and object to its use; some make a terrible fuss. You can make it easier for the doctor to give an injection of any kind and lessen the psychic shock to your child if instead of telling him not to cry and to be a big boy, you take a nonchalant attitude toward the procedure; admit that it will hurt for a minute, that you don't care if he cries but wouldn't it be fun to surprise the doctor by not crying.

Five-year-old Kathy didn't utter a peep when she had an injection. I asked her, "Did it hurt?" She said, "Yes, a little." When I asked her, "Then why didn't you cry?" she looked at me with great pride and said, "We Jacksons don't cry." A child with an attitude like that is already immunized against the knocks of life.

HEALTH RECORDS ARE IMPORTANT

One reads and hears much about health records but few people keep them, primarily because they are too complicated. The few facts important to know are these: Against what diseases have you been immunized; have you had booster doses against lockjaw; was your tuberculin test positive or negative five to ten years ago? Are you sensitive to any antibiotics or foods? Do you have diseases such as diabetes, congenital heart disease, epilepsy, etc.?

This situation has arisen innumerable times: A person sustains a severe injury, open fracture, or just a puncture wound of the foot. The doctor, concerned about lockjaw, asks, "Did you have shots against lockjaw when a child?" Often the answer is, "I don't know." The parents, if available by telephone, are called but remember only that some shots were given but they can't recall what kind. If the record of immunization were available a dose of toxoid

CHILD'S HEALTH RECORD

Full Name_____Date of Birth_____

Address_____

Physician_____

Address_____

Immunizations

DTP Injections   Dates _____   _____   _____

Polio Vaccine—Salk, Sabin   Dates _____   _____   _____

Booster doses DTP   Dates _____   _____   _____

Booster doses Polio   Dates _____   _____   _____

Measles vaccine   Date _____

Tuberculin test   Date _____   Positive   Negative

                                Date _____   Positive   Negative

Smallpox vaccination   Dates _____   _____   _____

Booster dose of DT   Dates _____   _____   _____

Sensitive to

Foods_____

Drugs_____

Allergies_____

Other_____

Important Illnesses

Nature_____

Nature_____

would suffice. Without a record the doctor is forced to give tetanus antitoxin so likely to cause serious reactions. (See footnote page 82.)

A few people are sensitive to certain antibiotics but they don't remember which one. In case of severe infection valuable time is lost while the doctor goes through a series of sensitivity tests.

The solution is simple. Write down in the blank form provided in this book the immunization record of your first child. Don't put off recording type and date of shot the day it was given. For future children make a copy of this form and paste it in the book. A better suggestion is to buy a book for each child. The book with the complete immunization record can be taken along by the young adult when leaving home. A book is less apt to be lost than a copy made from the inoculation record, folded and carried in a wallet.

chapter Four

GROWTH & DEVELOPMENT

FROM the moment of conception when the egg and sperm unite, the growing process starts and continues until the late teens. Every mother wants her baby to grow fast. Actually, she can do nothing about this growing process except furnish essential foods and vitamins. Each child is born with a growth potential which cannot be hastened or retarded. The genes, inherited from parents and preceding generations, contain the factors which determine physical stature.

A chart listing how much the average boy and girl should weigh each month during infancy and each year until full growth has been attained is a source of worry to mothers whose boys are slow growers and whose daughters seem to be growing too fast. So long as your baby is well, takes his food with relish, has a bright eye, and is full of energy, relax in the knowledge that growth will take care of itself.

The rate of growth varies greatly from time to time: for a year or more it may appear to have stopped, then a sudden spurt follows. Boys may be average or below normal size at twelve or thirteen years, then all of a sudden grow as much as three inches a year for a year or two. Girls grow more rapidly than boys, often attaining their full height by the time of adolescence.

Let your doctor keep a record of your baby's weight, height, circumference of the head, state of nutrition: you feed him and enjoy him. Too soon he will have outgrown babyhood. Measure your children from time to time if you wish, making a distinctive mark for each on a bedroom wall. Of course, when the room is redecorated all the marks will be covered but it will have been fun. Every child has to hear from relatives and friends the monotonous repetition, "My, how you've grown."

BABY'S BEHAVIOR

At eight weeks, the baby is completely helpless. His eyes follow light and moving objects; from time to time they stop roving and focus on a person's face in what seems to be a look of recognition. He lies on his back or tummy as he is placed but is apt to show preference for one position. Once in a while he coos; it won't be much of a coo but music to mother's ears. About all the baby does is eat, sleep, cry, and get daily exercise by kicking and waving his arms. The first feature distinguishing your baby as an intelligent human being appeared at about five or six weeks when he smiled.

At three to four months, although still completely helpless, the baby can raise his head and move it from side to side. He will try to and sometimes succeed in grasping objects and bringing them to his mouth. He will take hold of fingers and hold on tightly enough to be pulled to a sitting position. By pushing with his feet and stiffening his legs he will be indicating that he knows what legs are for. He likes to be held in a propped-up position. Personal attention has become a distinct pleasure and in response to it he will laugh out loud. His coos will be more emphatic and will be interspersed with some ahs and gurgles.

At six months the baby can roll over by himself and, with or without support, can sit up. He now reaches for and grasps objects and likes to hold them. Everything he can hold in his hand he tries to put into his mouth. He will contentedly lie on his back, strike at, and grab hold of a string of spools or buttons tied across his crib.

At this age he is not afraid of strangers. Although he loves attention, he also enjoys privacy, time just to lie in his crib and amuse himself by cooing and playing with his hands or easily handled toys. In response to play or the sight of food, he will bounce up and down in his high chair.

At nine months the baby will sit up unsupported, creep, crawl, or, in some odd fashion, work his way over the floor. He will try to pull himself up to a standing position by hanging on to the side of his playpen. He will enjoy sitting on the floor, rustling papers, or pounding on a pan. He'll be able to transfer an object from one hand to the other. He may be able to say what sounds to parents like "mama" or "dada." He will wave bye-bye—but usually not when requested—will play pat-a-cake and will put up his arms when asked, "How big is baby?" Fear of strangers appears at about this age.

When a birthday cake with one candle is brought in and the baby realizes that he is the center of attention, he will shout with glee. He may be able to walk to the table unaided but likely will need some help.

The one year old is usually shy, clings to mother or members of the family, and hides his face when strangers come near. He is just beginning to know what he wants and doesn't want and emphatically makes those wishes known. He enjoys trying to eat with a spoon but gets most of the food all over his face, in his hair, and on the floor.

At eighteen months the average child can walk and run but still falls frequently. He can climb on furniture and crawl up stairs. He will say a few words and point to things he wants. He is on the threshold of the "no, no" age. He has absolutely no sense of self-protection, gets into things, puts everything he can into his mouth. He is totally selfish, having not the slightest interest in social behavior. If left to his messiness, he can feed himself, wants to hold the cup himself and is apt to raise a howl if someone interferes. Food not liked is picked up in a little fist and thrown on the floor.

Two years—that's the age that tries mothers' souls. One minute the little angel is all sweetness and light; the next he is a rip-roaring demon. The ability to walk, run, climb is far ahead of the slightest sense of self-protection. He may speak in short sentences but emphasizes one word over and over again and that is, "no."

Mothers read about what their babies should do at various ages, worry if they don't measure up to certain standards, and brag if they are ahead of schedule. All babies are different. Some talk, using short sentences at fifteen months; others don't say more than a few words before age two. Yet the intelligence quotient of both groups may be the same. A first child talks earlier than a third or fourth for the simple reason that the mother spends more time playing and talking with him.

Sally, a third child, seemed normal in every respect but didn't use even simple sentences until she was three. She got what she wanted with gestures. She understood everything and would follow directions such as, "Will you bring mommy the spool of thread that lies on my dresser upstairs?" All of a sudden she discovered the advantages of language and hasn't stopped talking since. Her I.Q. is above average.

Children may walk at nine months—three months ahead of standard schedule—or not until they are fifteen months.

You should be concerned if your baby, otherwise apparently normal, hasn't smiled at age two months, can't hold up his head at three months, or makes no attempt to stand at age one year. Instead of worrying yourself sick, consult your doctor or a specialist; either you have been needlessly anxious or you face the fact that your baby has a handicap which you now begin to deal with intelligently.

The famous child behaviorist, Arnold Gesell, and his associates in their books on child development and child behavior, outline in detail what average infants and children do from babyhood to ten years, but emphasize again and again the tremendous variations in rate of development. So long as your baby is healthy, active, and emotionally responsive, don't worry if he seems a bit slow or conclude that you have an All-American football player or an Einstein if he is ahead of schedule.

WEANING

To the common question, "At what age shall I wean my baby?" the answer is: when he decides that the proper time has arrived. Naturally, a bit of common sense and guidance will be necessary.

When your baby is approximately six months old—four months or eight months, if you prefer—he should be introduced to a cup. At this age he already has some definite feelings of preference for bottles or cups. If he gets the idea that drinking from a cup is being forced upon him, he probably will balk. (It is amazing how mulish attitudes begin during infancy and persist throughout life.) Give him a cup, tin or plastic, plain or colored, to play with. Let it be apparent that this is his cup to do with as he likes. Some day put a half-ounce of formula in it and offer him a sip. Most of it will go on his bib. In a month or two he may enjoy drinking from the cup. Some infants take to cup feeding; others despise it. Between nine and twelve months most children are weaned from the bottle. It is not a sign of precociousness if a baby weans himself before nine months nor a sign of retardation if he hangs on to his beloved bottle until he is fifteen months old.

As a general rule as the baby shows signs of enjoying milk from a cup, the midday or morning bottle is omitted. Hard and fast rules won't work. Let the baby decide whether he wants all his milk from a cup or would like to finish up with a bottle. The evening bottle is given up last, and should be because it gives relaxation and comfort at the close of day, especially if taken while being held in mother's arms.

How long that evening bottle is continued is a matter for

baby and mother to decide—not neighbors, friends, or medical columnists. There is nothing wrong with continuing the night bottle until age two or three. A little discipline has to be exercised if the baby decides to have a bottle or two during the night. That sort of impulse has to be curbed early or some violent bouts of crying and temper will have to be dealt with.

Mothers are mistaken who are concerned that their babies six to nine months old, taking three cups of milk a day—about fifteen ounces—won't get enough milk unless they are urged to take some more from a bottle. A baby who is eating cereal, prepared baby foods, and table foods, doesn't need more than fifteen ounces of milk a day. In fact, better nutrition is maintained with an intake of a moderate amount of milk plus plenty of solid foods. The nine- to twelve-month-old child who is allowed as much as two quarts of milk a day will refuse solid foods and will likely develop "milk anemia." Milk contains no iron.

Weaning from the breast is usually begun between six and nine months. Milk in a bottle or cup is offered instead of a breast feeding. As the breast feeding is slowly discontinued, the flow lessens and within a month or two the baby is weaned.

If this discussion of weaning appears too simplified, look at it from the baby's viewpoint. Babies who need the satisfaction obtained from sucking should be indulged. Give them time and eventually they will wean themselves. Gloating with pride over the baby who at six or eight months discards the bottle is unjustified. All babies are different and especially so in their eating habits. One baby will hold a cup by himself at ten or twelve months and enjoy it. Another won't touch it until he is fifteen months old and will take fiendish pleasure in knocking the cup out of mother's hand. I repeat, time and patience, liberally sprinkled with indifference, will accomplish weaning without battles.

THE BABY'S TEETH

The reader who looks only at the illustration on the next page will get the idea that baby's teeth should appear at a specific time. All the numbers of months are average and may vary from three to six months either way.

Many normal children don't cut any teeth until they are eight to ten months old. However, if no teeth have appeared at the end of a year, suspicion arises that some disease is retarding the baby's development.

UPPER TEETH

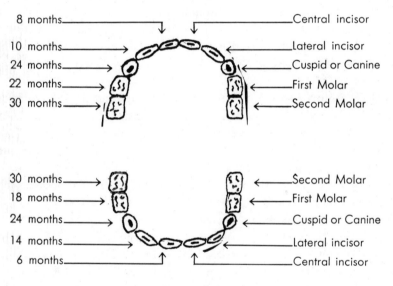

8 months	Central incisor
10 months	Lateral incisor
24 months	Cuspid or Canine
22 months	First Molar
30 months	Second Molar

30 months	Second Molar
18 months	First Molar
24 months	Cuspid or Canine
14 months	Lateral incisor
6 months	Central incisor

LOWER TEETH

Teeth begin to develop at least six months before the baby is born. At birth every tiny deciduous (milk) and permanent tooth has already formed and begun to harden. For this reason, it is important that the prospective mother's diet contain, besides standard foods, plenty of fruit and vegetables and two glasses of milk daily. Skim milk contains just as much calcium as whole milk and is preferred because of the tendency to gain weight during pregnancy. A proper diet, plus fluoride during pregnancy, will usually assure normal teeth for the baby and negate the old wives tale that with each baby the mother loses one tooth. A tendency toward good or bad teeth is an inherited characteristic. A few lucky people can disregard all rules of dental care and have perfect teeth; others fight a losing battle with their teeth in spite of all precautions.

Once in a long while a baby will have a tooth at birth. All sorts of happy omens are ascribed to this phenomenon, but I'm afraid the occurrence is nothing but a variation from normal. Most dentists advise leaving the tooth alone.

It is always a thrill to parents when their baby cuts his first lower tooth at about six months. Don't worry about delay in dentition; when your baby is two and a half to three years old he will have twenty teeth.

The Teething Problem. "My baby is teething. I'm sure that's why he is so fussy and irritable." The assumption that teething is a cause of fretfulness is so deeply ingrained in the minds of mothers and so unquestionable to grandmothers that I would not dare refute it. Maybe it's a good idea to have a scapegoat.

Years ago teething was blamed for all sorts of illnesses, such as convulsions, vomiting, diarrhea, fever, etc. Today, the causes of children's diseases are known and teething is not one of them. However, it is still convenient, rightly or wrongly, to ascribe changes in temperament to teething. Most healthy, happy infants have no trouble with teething, nor should they because it is a physiological process no different from growth of any other part of the body. However, some children have distress as each tooth comes through; the gums swell and occasionally black and blue spots are seen. I'm sure those gums hurt.

The desire to chew on something hard is nature's attempt to assist eruption of teeth, so give the baby a teething ring, or anything solid but unbreakable. A good way of introducing him to table foods and at the same time satisfying his desire to bite on something hard is to give him crusts, zweibach, or drumsticks. He will gnaw on and be happy with a drumstick for a long time.

The overhygienic mother is distressed when her drooling baby drops his saliva-covered teething ring or drumstick on the floor and puts it back in his mouth. When a child is old enough to handle objects he is well immunized against germs on furniture, floors, and kitty's tail. Let him have fun and don't annoy him by washing his messy hands and face every hour.

Prevention of Tooth Decay. It has been established beyond the shadow of a doubt that fluoridation of water helps prevent tooth decay. Fluoride is not a medicine; it is a mineral which, in small quantities, should be present in all drinking water but in some localities is not. As calcium is necessary to harden bones, so is fluoride necessary to harden the shell of enamel covering every tooth. Water should contain approximately one part per million for prevention of tooth decay.

To assist this process of hardening enamel, every woman throughout her pregnancy should drink water containing the proper amount of fluoride. In localities where water is not fluoridated, the doctor should prescribe the proper amount of fluoride.

Since practically all tooth decay begins during the development of baby teeth and permanent teeth, it is essential that the child continue the intake of fluoride until all the permanent teeth are formed at about age eighteen. Fluoride is most effective during the first few years of life. In later childhood when the enamel has become so hardened that insufficient fluoride reaches it by way of the blood stream, most dentists swab the teeth with fluoride. Fluoridation of water in many cities in this country and abroad has reduced the incidence of tooth decay by as much as 50 to 75 percent.

The Sweet Tooth. Children aren't going to like this statement: Sweets cause dental caries (tooth decay). Acids result from the action of germs, always present in the mouth, on bits of sugar stuck to the teeth. These acids attack and make holes in the enamel.

Children love sweets, so what are parents to do? They cannot deny their children candy without fighting a losing battle. Insofar as possible, candy and sweets should be eaten at mealtime. Hard candies sucked on between meals are as bad as they are delicious. Nothing will destroy baby teeth faster than trying to stop thumb sucking or restlessness at night by giving the child candy to suck on.

Ideally, teeth should be brushed after each meal. That ideal will rarely be reached in the average family. It should be a firm rule, however, that children brush their teeth after breakfast and as soon after the evening meal as possible.

Nothing, of course, is better for children's teeth than a well-balanced diet with plenty of fruits and vegetables. The best between-meals snack is an apple; chewing it cleans the teeth and the juice neutralizes acids.

Even though the baby is going to lose all his baby teeth, they should be kept as free from cavities as possible and existing cavities should be filled to avoid mouth infections, to keep proper space for, and to prevent damage to, the permanent teeth.

If you, the mother, have taken fluoride during your pregnancy, if you limit to reasonable amounts the sweets your children eat, if you insist that they brush their teeth twice a day, they will have few cavities. Observation of these rules is a small price to pay for a beautiful set of teeth.

FLAT FEET

All babies have what appear to be flat feet; most of them aren't— they just look that way because a baby's foot is soft and has a lot of fat at the instep.

Don't be concerned about flat feet during early childhood, but do insist that the shoes he wears are sturdy and well-fitting. At the age of rapid growth a too short or too tight shoe may deform the foot. Pass up that tempting shoe bargain unless the shoes fit well.

The foot is a complicated mechanism containing twenty-six bones, muscles, tendons, and ligaments all beautifully fashioned to serve one purpose—body support. So long as feet fulfill their function without pain, it doesn't make any difference whether the arches are high or low. Negroes are inclined to have very flat feet, yet they have no more foot trouble than white people.

The teen-ager who complains of tired, aching feet and pain in the calf muscles should be seen first by your doctor or pediatrician. Such symptoms may be due to illness or malnourishment or to a sudden spurt in weight and growth which puts undue strain on the feet. Many times all that is needed to relieve the trouble is time and patience. It's amazing how many minor ailments disappear spontaneously if not overtreated.

The youngster who continues to have aching flat feet should be seen by an orthopedist who will order a fitted pad along the inner side of the shoe or a wedge in the inner side of the heel to turn the foot inward and thereby remove the strain from ligaments and tendons supporting the arch. Such corrective shoes will have to be worn until the feet are molded into proper position for painless weight bearing.

BOWLEGS

One expects the average healthy child to be somewhat bowlegged when he starts to walk. Before the baby was born he was enclosed in a tight compartment which kept his legs folded up over his abdomen with knees bent outward and feet inward. It stands to reason that it requires time for bowlegs to straighten out.

Parents have heard that bowlegs are caused by rickets and up to thirty to forty years ago, before vitamin D was universally given to children, they would have been right. In these days of reinforcement of milk, bread, and cereals with vitamin D, rickets is extremely rare.

The few cases of bowlegs due to congenital deformities of the bones or joints are usually so severe—often affecting only one leg— that they are easily recognized. If you are worried about your child's bowlegs, take him to the doctor who will have x-ray pictures taken and, in some cases, a photograph for comparison with the condition in a few years.

Very few children with bowlegs require treatment with drugs, casts, or operations. When one of your friends or neighbors says, "Your child is bowlegged, isn't he?" you nonchalantly answer, "Yes," with full knowledge that the condition will correct itself. I asked Dr. Harold A. Sofield, Head of a Shriners Hospital for Crippled Children, whether bowlegs ever require operative correction. His answer was, "Practically never. A child with bowlegs, even if severe, requires no treatment. Time will effect a better cure than operation."

IS MY BABY DEAF?

While the baby is lying in his crib with his face turned away from the observer and all is quiet, smartly bang two pans together about five feet from the crib. A "startle reflex" in response to the sound indicates normal hearing.

At three months a baby should turn his head toward the source of familiar sounds. Failure to do so suggests deafness if the child is otherwise normally responsive, i.e., smiles, coos, gurgles, and looks his mother "straight in the eye."

A nine- to twelve-month-old baby should be suspected of hearing loss if he does not turn his head in response to a rattle, a loud whisper, or the noise of stirring a spoon in a cup; the noises should be made behind the baby while he is sitting in a chair or being held by another person.

A two year old who is bright appearing and responsive, who doesn't say a single word, doesn't identify any object when it is named, and makes his wishes known by gestures, is probably deaf.

"How could you be so stupid?" This incriminating question, asked by me of myself, would have stung more had it not also been appropriate for a few other doctors and nurses in the hospital.

Henry, a bright, attractive, two-year-old boy, while a patient in the hospital for ten days didn't say a word. He paid no attention to anybody's remarks, responded to no questions, but got what he wanted by pointing and gestures.

At a return checkup examination, all of a sudden a sadly delayed observation struck me. I said to the mother, "Do you think your boy might be deaf?" Her answer was, "I've been wondering about that; my husband thinks Henry is stubborn and inattentive, but I think he doesn't hear. I have a sister who was born deaf."

Henry was sent to an audiology (hearing) clinic where it was demonstrated that his hearing was so impaired that he could catch only the most violent sounds. This poor little fellow had been spanked for inattention and had been considered backward. Of course, he spoke no word; he had never heard a human voice. Henry, at age three, attending a preschool clinic for the deaf and wearing a hearing aid, is learning to talk.

Partial hearing is often overlooked because we take good hearing for granted. It is estimated that between 5 and 10 percent of children have some degree of hearing loss. Many children are considered backward or psychological problems simply because they don't hear. Not until the child is tested in school is the hearing loss discovered. Don't let anybody put a "backward" label on your child until his hearing has been tested by an ear specialist.

Do you have a deaf child? Write to The Alexander Graham Bell Associates, 1537 – 35th Street, N.W., Washington, D.C., or to the American Hearing Society, 919 – 18th Street, N.W., Washington, D.C., for educational material and for the address of a center in or near your community to which you can take your child for special training.

CROSSED EYES

The statement, "Most babies are cross-eyed during the first two months" requires clarification. It is more accurate to say that all babies' eyes "drift"; one or the other turns in from time to time. If one eye is constantly turned the baby is truly cross-eyed or has a squint. There are two kinds of squint, convergent, by far the most common, in which one eye turns inward, and divergent, in which one eye turns outward.

Early examination of a cross-eyed child by an eye doctor interested in eye defects in children is important because crossing is often due to some less obvious defect inside the eye. The majority of crossed eyes, however, are due to imbalance of the muscles attached to the eyeball. An eye turns in because the outer muscles are weak or the inner muscles too strong.

Patching, that is, covering the straight eye with a black patch, is begun at age three to six months. When eyes are crossed they do not focus, and to avoid the annoyance of double vision, the child soon learns to disregard the image in the crossed eye. An eye which is not used weakens and eventually loses its sight. By patching the good eye, the crossed eye is stimulated to develop normal vision.

Slightly crossed eyes may be corrected with glasses and muscle exercises. Severely crossed eyes require surgical correction, preferably between one and two years. The surgeon loosens and tightens muscles to bring the affected eye in line with the normal one. A perfect result cannot always be obtained at the first operation because it is difficult to gauge exactly how much a muscle should be loosened or tightened.

If your baby is cross-eyed or you fear he is, consult an eye specialist interested in such eye problems. For those who cannot afford private care, excellent free eye clinics are available in all medical schools. Your doctor will direct you.

Watering Eye.   Our eyes are constantly kept moist by secretion of tears from a lacrimal (tear) gland above each eye. Excess fluid drains through an opening in the edge of the lower eyelid into the nose. The duct should be open at birth; if not, the eye waters. Usually only one eye is affected. In the majority of cases nothing needs to be done. The tear duct opens spontaneously some time before the baby is six months old.

During the waiting time a swelling due to distention of the upper end of the duct may develop just below the inner side of the lower lid. Gentle massage from above downward, but only upon the advice of your doctor, may relieve this swelling and help open the duct. The baby's eye will get red from time to time because of infection (conjunctivitis). Such infections are not serious but should be treated with an eye wash, or some medication prescribed by your doctor.

In case the watering persists beyond approximately six months, the duct will have to be probed. This procedure, performed by an eye specialist and consisting of running a tiny probe through the duct into the nose, is relatively simple but must be done in a hospital under anesthesia because a baby will not hold still while the tiny duct is being opened and stretched.

chapter Five

WORRISOME
HABITS

EVERY normal baby loves to suck. Whether breast fed or bottle fed he is going to do a lot more sucking than is necessary to obtain food. Exercise of this sucking instinct is essential for the baby's happiness. He is going to suck on anything he can get to his mouth—fist, bed sheets, clothing—so why not recognize his wishes and give him a pacifier?

Pacifiers.   Fifty years ago pacifiers were standard equipment enjoyed by babies until they got tired of them. Then we went through that horrible period in the twenties, thirties, and forties, when infants were denied such pleasant activities as rocking, cuddling, and pacifiers. In those days it was "disgusting" to see a baby with a pacifier in his mouth; it was considered unhygienic, actually almost dirty. At that time a pacifier was not allowed in the Children's Hospital where I worked. I used to help the infant find his thumb; he needed what comfort he could get in those medieval days when hospital visiting hours were limited to an hour a day.

The cycle is complete and the pacifier is back in its rightful place—the baby's mouth. Many a tired mother's nerves have a chance to rest while her baby contentedly works on his pacifier. There are those who feel that by sucking on a pacifier the baby will fill his stomach with air and later have colic. Nonsense! A baby swallows air only when taking food or water. We proved this point by x-ray studies. After a half-hour of sucking on a pacifier the amount of air in the stomach was not increased.

Let your baby have a pacifier as he wishes; it will do him no harm and will stop a lot of crying. Many years ago I learned that examination of a fussy baby's abdomen was made possible by wetting a pacifier and sticking it in sugar. The fine tasting pacifier was effective in relaxing the baby and allowing a satisfactory examination. Some mothers when dealing with those trying times when the baby is superirritable, put a drop of honey on the pacifier to make it more acceptable; it sounds like a good idea.

When the baby is six to nine months old he usually gives up the pacifier in favor of his thumb.

Thumb Sucking.   It is unofficially reported that while the pyramids were being built children stood by watching and sucking their thumbs. Children haven't changed. The inborn desire to suck has not been outgrown when the baby gives up the pacifier. The thumb, so conveniently set on the hand as to be readily available, is universally enjoyed by infants and children as a source of comfort until they are two to three years old; not a few children continue the practice until age four or five.

Thumb sucking per se is harmless; it does not cause buck teeth nor does it deform the mouth. By the time permanent teeth are erupting practically all children have given up the habit. Because of custom and social attitudes, parents so hate to see their child suck his thumb that, to break the habit, they resort to putting splints on the elbows so the child's hand can't reach his mouth, bandaging the thumb to the hand, anointing it with some foul-tasting material, or actual punishment. Restraints and punishment are of no avail and lead only to frustration.

A mother should be concerned about a three year old who would rather sit alone and suck his thumb than play with other children. Such a child is unhappy, insecure, and must be coaxed out of his mood by more attention, interest in toys, and little activities he can do well. Instead of jerking his thumb out of his mouth, sit down on the floor and play with him until he forgets about the thumb. It's not the thumb sucking you should worry about but the reason for excessive thumb sucking.

For the well-adjusted three or four year old who is still sucking his thumb a few heart to heart—not heat to heat—talks may be beneficial. "You are a big boy (girl) now and will soon be going to school. Don't you think it's kind of babyish to suck your thumb?" Don't expect too much cooperation, and don't be impatient. During illness or upsetting experiences, a child may temporarily revert to his thumb. For some time after quitting the habit during the day he will still use his thumb for comfort when going to sleep.

Don't be concerned. In time every mentally normal child discards the habit. Some men substitute for thumb sucking the habit of chewing on the stump of a burned-out cigar. No one openly criticizes them. Why not give a child the same consideration?

Blanket Sniffing.   A baby in the second half of his first year is apt to single out a particular blanket, woolly animal, teddy bear, or fuzzy object which, for some strange reason, he insists on holding to his lips and nose when distressed or unhappy, and routinely demands when going to sleep. Blankets are the most popular and a woolly one with satin edges rates first. The older and more disreputable the objects, the dearer they become. Children hate to have them washed.

When blanket sniffing continues until age three or four, as it usually does, mothers are distressed; they feel that this babyish tendency should be curbed, that the "filthy" teddy bear carries germs; a few complain that the "baby gets a sexy look on his face when sniffing his blanket." Stuff and nonsense! Familiar objects provide a feeling of security. I don't know why mothers are so apologetic about blanket sniffing. Let them sniff to their heart's content. When going to a strange place, above all when going to a hospital, let them take along their little idols for what comfort they will afford. If at five or six they still want the "comforter" when going to bed, indulge them. A woman admitted in a "confessional" to me that her fifteen-year-old daughter still found comfort in her teddy bear at night after a frustrating day. A sign of maladjustment? I doubt it.

Breath-holding. A few high-strung children at about age one year or even younger discover the power of breath-holding as a means of obtaining their wishes. After a fit of rage, temper, fright, or injury, the child starts to cry. As his crying increases he holds his breath sometimes until his lips become blue. For a minute or less—it seems interminable to mother—he holds his breath and makes no sound. Then he suddenly begins to breathe and the episode is over. However, if mother shows unusual alarm and goes all out to comfort and soothe the child, memory of the episode is stored away to be recalled when occasion demands. It doesn't take long for a baby to learn where his power lies.

The best treatment for a breath-holder is to disregard completely his demonstrations of temperament. It's not easy but, insofar as possible, be deaf, dumb, and blind to his antics. Don't throw cold water in his face or slap him to bring him out of a spell. A little extra loving attention when he is not putting on a scene will be helpful. Letting the first breath-holding performance influence you to give in to unusual demands will only strengthen the power of the child's weapon.

A child may hold his breath until he becomes unconscious and at times has a convulsion. Nothing is more frightening than a convulsion and the fear that it may have been an epileptic seizure. Dr. Samuel Livingston of Johns Hopkins University, an authority on convulsive disorders, has pointed out that breath-holding convulsions are precipitated by fright, anger, pain, and mostly by temper tantrums. They are always preceded by vigorous crying. An epileptic seizure, on the contrary, comes on at any time and is rarely initiated by emotional upsets or crying. (See chapter Ten.)

Naturally, a convulsion will prompt you to seek medical advice. A diagnosis of convulsions as a result of breath-holding should relieve your anxieties. Your child will eventually quit the habit, his brain won't be damaged, and he will most likely grow up to be a well-adjusted citizen with no more serious characteristics than throwing a club after a poor golf shot or kicking the car when it won't start.

Voluntary vomiting like breath-holding is a child's means of obtaining his wishes. Infants and children vomit easily; a few learn to gag and vomit at will to show their objection to certain foods, to gain attention, to avoid going to a doctor's office, to get out of going to school. In an otherwise healthy child it is not difficult to recognize voluntary vomiting. The less attention paid to it, the sooner the practice is given up.

Head-banging and Rocking.   Why babies enjoy banging their heads and rocking back and forth on hands and knees is known only to them. Usually the actions are combined; as they rock they knock their heads against the end of the crib. Mothers aren't concerned about the rocking but are fearful that the child will damage his brain by butting his head against solid objects. He may raise welts and blue spots on his scalp but is smart enough not to crack his skull.

Most likely the reason that babies give up rocking before head-banging is that no one is concerned about it nor tries to stop it. Scolding or punishing for head-banging is a sure way of letting the child know he has a means of obtaining his wishes.

Combined rocking and head-banging in the crib are annoying because of the noise. One can hear all over the house the rhythmic shaking of the baby's crib usually before he goes to sleep and the first thing after he wakes in the morning. On an uncarpeted floor the crib will creep until it bumps against a wall. To stop the noise the crib can be set on a thick rug or some padding can be tied to the four casters. A folded quilt securely fastened to the end or side of the crib, whenever the head bumping is carried on, will not only stop the noise but also keep the child from bruising his head. By the time the child can walk he will likely discontinue these practices.

THE SPOILED CHILD

Spoiling is difficult to define. Some parents consider their child's unpleasant antics and unusual demands as normal, to be expected and tolerated. That they may be spoiling their child with excessive indulgence never enters their minds and if it does it is crowded out by the greater fear of frustrating him. Others make severe demands of their children and allow no deviation from the rules and standards which they, the parents, have set up. They fear spoiling. Both are wrong.

As usual, a middle-of-the-road attitude is most acceptable. How can one love a child and provide security without from time to time indulging him? I think a little so-called spoiling is good for every child. A baby wants to feel that he is an important member of the family. He gets this feeling of importance by having some of his simple wishes fulfilled. Of course, one must try to be consistent. A child becomes confused if one day he is allowed to do anything he wishes, and the next day is punished for the same behavior.

A baby, meaning a child below two years of age, who completely dominates the home and everybody in it is spoiled. His slightest wish is gratified. He enjoys getting his mother up at all hours of the night to walk him, play with him, or give him a bottle or two. He screams when he wants something and puts on a temper tantrum when responses are not immediate. He cries and fusses more than average.

Such a child in the usual meaning of the word is spoiled. Indulgent parents may consider such behavior normal even cute; friends secretly say, "the spoiled brat."

Children are spoiled for many reasons. One can predict that an only child of parents near their forties will be spoiled. Many children are spoiled because parents don't get along and contemplate divorce. Each parent, hoping to court favor with the child, tries to outdo the other in indulgences and presents. Spoiling that follows prolonged illness is to be expected. It is natural to cater to the whims of a sick child. Upon recovery it is not difficult to reestablish the rules of conformity which were accepted before illness occurred.

Children, even babies, enjoy orderly living. They actually want to be taught what they may and may not do. It doesn't require nagging or slapping to mold a little child into a happy routine of eating on schedule, sleeping through the night, playing contentedly with toys. At this point, I can hear a mother of a vigorous, self-willed eighteen-month-old child, say, "If you had to take care of my baby for a few days you would sing another song." You are right; I know I would. It requires superb judgment and limitless patience to deal with the daily problems of being fair, firm, but not too harsh. Overindulging a child leads to later maladjustment; too harsh conformity breaks a child's spirit. Most mothers using plain common sense manage nobly in steering a course between the two.

Sad but true, the spoiled child is an unhappy child. Being accustomed from babyhood to do whatever he wishes, he expects such treatment to continue.

All goes well until he begins to mix with children in the neighborhood. As he insists on being first all the time and refuses to take his turn at play, he gets his first shock—the kids don't like him. Upon being too demanding one of the neighborhood boys gives him a sock in the face; he runs home to mother crying for sympathy and gets it in huge measure plus a comment that the neighborhood boys are mean and that if this ever happens again she will call their parents. Such an attitude, if continued, leads to tragedy. The poor boy hasn't been taught that this is a give-and-take world. Thus far to him it has been all take.

Public school may be his salvation. Either he will learn the hard way by knocks and rebuffs that he must conform to the rigid rules of unsympathetic grade school youngsters or be ostracized from play.

Without malice, children can be very cruel in making life miserable for the spoiled mamma's boy. Hopefully they will teach him the error of his ways.

chapter Six

BABY SITTERS

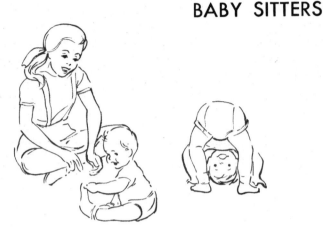

BABY SITTING is big business conducted largely on personal arrangements between parent and sitter.

While trying to prepare a list of practical instructions for baby sitters, I asked a number of mothers, "What instructions do you give your baby sitters?" The wide variety of answers prompted me to ask readers of *Chicago's American* newspaper to give their opinion on such controversial points as:

Do you expect a sitter to do extra work such as washing a sink full of dishes without extra pay?

May the telephone be used for personal calls?

How about raiding the refrigerator?

Shall the doorbell be answered?

May the sitter sleep after the children are asleep?

Shall a young woman be allowed to have her "date" come to your home?

Shall high school girls be allowed to have their girl friends in and, if so, how many?

Answers were many and varied.

Parents and baby sitters—professional and neighborhood high-school girls—were all emphatic that baby sitting is a business and should be conducted on an employer-employee relationship. Baby sitters called to my attention the overlooked need for a list of instructions to parents, offered their suggestions, and emphasized that these were just as important as instructions to baby sitters; where there were differences of opinion, the majority ruled in making these lists.

INSTRUCTIONS FOR BABY SITTERS

You can reach us at telephone number _____

If there is a change in plans we will call you.

We will be unavailable.

If you can't reach us, call relative, neighbor, friend.
   Tel. No. _____

Our doctor's name is _____. *Tel. No.* _____

If the doorbell rings, ask who is there and do not open the door unless you are positive that you know the caller.

Sorry, no boy friend visitors. You may have one girl friend with you, if you wish.

Use the telephone only for emergency calls.

Incoming calls are to be limited to three minutes.

Give the baby a bottle at _____

Put the other children to bed at _____

Please clean up the children's supper dishes.

If the baby cries change his diaper; give him another bottle if he wants it. Give no medicine, not even aspirin.

If any question arises don't hesitate to call us.

There are _____ *in the refrigerator for you.*

You will be paid _____ *an hour.*

Fire Department Tel. No. _____

Police Dept. Tel. No. _____

Obviously, this list does not cover a variety of details pertinent to varying circumstances. Leaving a baby with a neighborhood girl for an hour or two in the afternoon is quite different from leaving three vigorous young children with a baby sitter on a long Saturday night. Until you have a known and trusted baby sitter, take time before dashing out to a party to go over these instructions, modify them as you see fit and emphasize what you think is pertinent. They are meant only to serve as a guide. You wouldn't think of handing your fur coat to a stranger in a railroad station while you went around the corner to buy a newspaper. Neither should you leave your children with a baby sitter about whom you know nothing. Baby sitting is more than a job—it's a trust.

A devoted professional baby sitter sent in what she called her "Baby Sitter's Creed," worthy of being framed and hung on a wall.

May love of children unfailingly guide me.

Let me always be patient, kind and thoughtful.

Give me a sense of humor tempered with good judgment.

May I act wisely when unexpected emergencies arise.

With God's help I shall care for and protect these children.

INSTRUCTIONS FOR PARENTS

Never hire a baby sitter unless you know her or have unquestionable character references; it's safer to stay home or take the children with you.

A baby sitter who has never been in your home before should come at least a half-hour before you leave.

It's your responsibility to allow sufficient time to explain your wishes about:

What to feed the children.

When they shall go to bed.

Bed clothes, night lights, ventilation.

The children's idiosyncrasies.

Tell the children they are to mind the sitter as they mind you.

Provide favorite story books and toys.

You have chosen a baby sitter. Now trust her and go out and have fun.

Come home at the time you've promised.

Be sure to have money with proper change to pay the sitter; no charge accounts allowed.

Pay for each hour and fraction of an hour at the agreed price; more if asked to wash dishes, tidy the house, do ironing.

It's your responsibility to see that the sitter gets home safely.

Kindness and consideration will get you interest and cooperation from the sitter.

Of course, grandma is the best baby sitter in the world. She knows the children, is available at a moment's notice and, a not unimportant consideration, she makes no charge. Often she's a widow with lots of time on her hands.

Requests by mothers for newspaper columns on what grandma's attitude should be when coming into their homes and staying with the grandchildren, prompt me to write what married sons and daughters don't dare say without fear of hurting grandma's feelings.

Grandma, when your children left home, married, and established their own home, they formed a new pattern of living often quite different from yours. When going to their home to baby sit or help out with a new baby, go as a guest. Follow your children's pattern of disciplining the grandchildren. Bite your tongue instead of letting it wag with advice about how to feed the baby (customs have changed), what the children should wear, how to keep house and, above all, what church to attend and how often. This is a tough assignment. We grandmas and grandpas think we know all the answers. We don't. Therefore, give advice only when asked and then sparingly. Be liberal with praise for the things you like. Praise the grandchildren instead of criticizing them and they will think you are the best grandma anyone ever had. Bring along little presents and remember birthdays with a coin or a bill for them to spend as they wish.

You, the widowed grandmother, are lonely, terribly lonely, but don't let your children find out and make them feel that they have to take pity on you and invite you to dinner every Sunday noon. Your children owe you nothing. Expect nothing and through the strange workings of psychology you will receive much. Once in a while when invited, have a previous date even though it's a trumped-up one. When invited to spend a month with children in a distant town cut the time to a week—you'll get more invitations. During visits a serene face and a motionless tongue when family crises arise, tolerance of the children's antics, interest in the things they are doing, willingness to read stories over and over again will bring forth these comments when you leave. "Isn't grandma wonderful? It's fun to have her come. Let's ask her again soon."

chapter Seven

THE TERRIBLE TWO'S

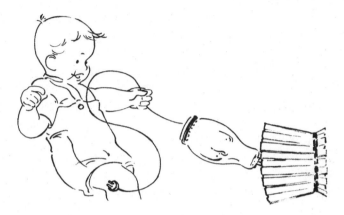

THE LITTLE INVESTIGATOR

Not the great scientist but the two-year-old child is the world's most tireless investigator. After learning to walk, he goes from one fascinating problem to another. Without fear he tastes everything he can get to his mouth. He dashes about testing the breaking point of every object within reach. The law of gravity is confirmed by taking an egg from the refrigerator and dropping it on the floor. He studies balance by tilting his glass of milk and by swinging a floor lamp back and forth. He works on the laws of combustion with a package of matches picked up in the living room. He instinctively knows better than many professors that the best way to learn is by trying. The toddler is a most industrious student, practicing coordination, learning a language, exploring all the attractive avenues of his little world.

This active youngster from one and a half to three years old is truly a "bull in a china shop." He has absolutely no sense of values nor any thought of self-protection. The only way he can be

121

kept from breaking things, prying the lids from boxes, tearing pages from books, is to put them out of reach, and the only way he can be kept from hurting himself is by constant supervision and repeated warnings.

It's not fair after a child has innocently broken some prized object to call him a naughty boy; he isn't naughty, he's just experimenting. "You bad boy!" a mother shouted and slapped her two-year-old's hand. What the little fellow had done was to reach up and knock an ash tray from my office desk. It fell on the floor and broke. So what! It was only an ash tray. Anyway it was my fault; if I didn't want the ash tray knocked from my desk I had no business letting it stand where investigative fingers could reach it. I felt so sorry for the crying youngster I did what probably was wrong— I gave him a lollipop. (The previous day I likely had told some mother that candy is bad for children's teeth.)

After these folks left the office, I got to thinking about this mother's outburst, "You bad boy." I'm sure she didn't mean the expression as it sounded because there is no such thing as a bad child. Little children may be stubborn and opinionated—it's their way of developing an individual personality—but they are never "bad."

A child between eighteen months and three years is in what is appropriately called the "No, No," age. Mother says, "no" many times each day as her child approaches the stove, blows in ash trays, puts his greasy hands on furniture, bites the dog's tail, eats lipstick, empties bureau drawers, etc., ad infinitum. The child, exposed to a barrage of No, No, answers in like manner. No becomes a favorite word. A certain amount of No is necessary, but too much generates rebellion. Children in this respect resemble adults who likewise resent being told they can't do something. What can one expect from a child?

It requires infinite patience and cool-tempered judgment to balance No, No, with permission to learn by experience. No mother would deliberately allow her defiant child to burn himself on a hot stove and, yet, when mother's back is turned, a little self-inflicted burn on a testing finger is powerfully instructive. Pulling kitty's tail stops far more promptly after kitty uses her claws than after repeated warnings.

For a child's protection some emphatic No, No, is absolutely essential. For example: Your child runs across the street even though you have warned him that if he does it again he will be punished. He does it again; he is testing your authority. At exactly that moment quick punishment is due. A few spanks on his bottom or confinement to his room for a time will convince him that you mean what you say. Of course, he'll cry, feel and look terribly abused. Remain firm. After he calms down, not with aid of cookie or candy, take him on your lap and tell him you are sorry you had to punish him, but that he has to obey mommy. He'll love and respect you more for being firm with him.

Destructiveness about the house calls more for repeated, patient instruction than for punishment. Some children are destructive, others are not. Supposing your youngster gets hold of a book and is about to tear out pages. Instead of snatching it or slapping his hand, take the book and explain that it belongs to mommy and must not be torn. He will be confused because he has been allowed to tear up old magazines. Give him one of his books, preferably with fabric pages which won't easily tear, and tell him that this is his book.

Children are quick to sense attitudes. Knowing that you are particularly fond of some object, such as a vase, your child will take the first opportunity to handle it. He proudly carries it to you in the kitchen. While you guard against its falling, let him hold the vase as you admire it with him. Explain that this is not a plaything and put it out of reach. Even though you have been gentle with him, he'll likely cry. Forbidden things hold great fascination. That's where substitution is in order. Give a child with destructive tendencies playthings he can abuse to his heart's content, pans he can pound on, a toy with pegs he can pound with a hammer. Sit down on the floor and play with him until his interest has been deflected from a No, No item and focused upon his own playthings.

Praise for doing the things you approve of, for building a house of blocks, coloring a picture, plus a minimum of criticism for errors will pay big dividends in happy relationships. For a few weeks cut down No, No, 75 percent, raise approvals by a similar margin and you will be surprised at the change from rebellion to co-operation. Application of this basic principle of psychology applies to a two year old just as effectively as to a sixteen year old, or to mother and father.

FOR FATHERS

This little boy of yours is two years old. Remember how thrilled you were when the doctor announced that you had a son. As a baby he didn't cry too much, smiled readily, and was the apple of your eye.

Now you are worried because he is so uncooperative and negativistic. Cheer up, you needn't be. All youngsters with individuality and drive go through this phase. A two year old is totally selfish, follows no code of ethics, is interested only in his own pleasure, and has an uncamouflaged desire to be the center of attention.

Your boy, mine, in fact, all normal boys between eighteen months and about three and a half are alike: they are little animals with animal instincts. From this status they grow into young savages. You might as well make up your mind that until your boy is about seven years old he will continue to show all the characteristics of primitive man. Without training, he would remain so. Social consciousness, fair play, kindness, consideration for others, honesty, in fact, all virtues are products of civilization slowly instilled by word and example—mostly by example.

Don't expect too much from this little boy of yours. Give him time, be patient, try not to get mad when he breaks things and acts like an impossible little monster. Take an interest in his spirit of research. Make it fun for him to learn. Slowly—too soon—he will grow up and, in spite of what you say or do, will mimic you in manners, attitude, speech, and all the faults and virtues you may have, or not be conscious of having. Patience with his problems, praise for his little successes, sympathy with his failures and, as he gets older, trust in his judgment will produce a son of whom you'll be proud.

MY CHILD WON'T EAT

Imagine the look of utter disbelief that would come over the face of a Chinese peasant woman if she heard an American mother say, "My child won't eat."

Eating is a basic instinct. In the presence of food, no child, physically and mentally normal, ever starved. What's more, children old enough to feed themselves will, if given the opportunity, choose a well-balanced diet. Years ago, Dr. Clara Davis proved this statement. A group of fifteen children, recently weaned, were allowed to choose their diet. At each meal simple, basic foods such as milk, eggs, cereals, bread, meats, fruits, vegetables, and sugar in its natural state, were set before these children. Each child was allowed to eat with hands or spoon as he wished. As one item of food was eaten, another similar one was unceremoniously set before him. Amazing things happened.

At one meal a child might eat nothing but meat, at the next only fruits or vegetables. Some children ate cereal, milk, and sugar separately rather than in standard fashion. One child at one meal ate seven eggs!—nothing else. No, he didn't get sick. Another day this same child concentrated on vegetables. Over a period of some months these fifteen children actually exceeded the average in health and weight gain.

The "poor eater" problem usually arises between twelve and twenty-four months and for one reason: parents don't know or have forgotten that a normal baby's growth rate at this age slows down. The baby refuses food because he is not hungry. He doesn't need and doesn't want as many calories as he took during the period of rapid growth. A baby doubles his birth weight in six months and triples it in a year. If that rate of growth continued, children would soon be giants. In the matter of food intake, these infants are smarter than their parents. Solicitous mothers use every conceivable method of wheedling, coaxing, bribing their babies to eat as much food as they think they should eat. An occasional youngster with an affable disposition and a powerful digestion succumbs to the forced feeding regime and at two or three is greatly overweight.

The majority of children rebel against overfeeding; they close their lips, knock the spoon out of the zealous feeder's hand, or throw food on the floor. They are smart; they know when they have had enough to eat and make that fact known in no uncertain terms.

Avoidance of the no-eating problem is easier than its correction. At the age when a child can sit at the table in a highchair, place before him bits of food—cracker, zweibach, pieces of soft fruit, and tiny pieces of ground meat. Then leave him alone to learn the texture and flavor of foods. When he is old enough to feed himself and is eating three meals a day serve him small portions of the same food the family eats. He'll like some foods better than others; who doesn't? Maybe he hates a certain vegetable. Don't get into a fight trying to make him eat that specific vegetable before he can have dessert; you'll weaken and lose the battle. Many children, especially boys, are meat and potato eaters; they hate all vegetables. Potatoes contain just as many vitamins as spinach.

The less attention paid to the amount of food the child eats the better. You think he isn't eating enough to "keep a bird alive." So long as he is active and healthy he will eat as much as he needs. Supposing he skips a meal, takes nothing but a glass of milk. Think nothing of it, he'll be hungry at the next meal. Remember, your child will not starve nor will he get sick if he eats less than you think he should. More children are ill from overeating than undereating.

While attending an international conference on "Growth and Nutrition," distinguished scientists spoke long and fervently about proper diets for children. When the session was thrown open for general discussion, a doctor from Mexico rose and said, "I practice in the extreme southern part of my country amongst the poorest people. Down my way our only concern is getting enough food of any kind for the children. From my observations—no scientific studies—I have found that children thrive on just four foods: powdered milk, meat, beans, and potatoes." Applause following this short speech exceeded that of all the other speakers.

To transform a confirmed, temperamental, poor eater into an affable child who eats three square meals a day is impossible. Cutting down on between-meal snacks and allowing the child to eat what he wants at mealtime will improve the eating problem, but not correct it. Some high strung, skinny children require five or six small meals a day. To trim them down by force to three would likely make the child still more irritable. Best results toward peace at mealtime and reasonable selection of an adequate diet will be obtained by following a strict rule of serving the child what the family is having and letting nature take its course. Pay no attention to his eating foibles; part of the reason for his nonconformance is to gain attention.

Stop worrying about the skinny youngster who doesn't eat as much as you think he should. So long as he is active and healthy, relax. The more relaxed you are, the better your child will eat. In a few years a growth spurt will whet his appetite and dissolve the "my child won't eat" problem.

Milk.   "My baby is twelve months old. At about age eight months he took a liking for all kinds of baby foods and practically eliminated milk. Even with lots of coaxing I can't get him to take more than two cups of milk a day, sometimes less. He seems healthy to me. Is there anything to worry about?"

You just don't know what a smart baby you have. In fact, your boy is two jumps ahead of the child who presents exactly the opposite and more serious problem—refusal to take solid foods in preference to milk. No, you needn't worry.

Milk is one of the finest foods in the world, absolutely essential to the newborn. However, after a few months a diet consisting of nothing but milk is inadequate. (See page 98.)

Pampered children, poor eaters, and those who have had prolonged illnesses are inclined to live on practically nothing but milk. Because these milk-guzzling babies are fat, there is a false feeling of assurance that they are well fed. They get plenty of calories—often too many—but insufficient iron. Between six and nine months these children become pale with a condition known as nutritional or iron deficiency anemia. Fortunately, iron deficiency anemia is easily corrected by giving the baby large doses of iron, but substitution of cereals, fruit, vegetables, and meat for excess milk is necessary for a permanent cure.

If your baby, six to fifteen months old, a heavy milk drinker, appears pale, flabby, and more irritable than you think he should be, take him to your doctor for a checkup and blood examination. He may need iron.

TOILET TRAINING

We parents expect too much of our children too early in life. We press the baby to advance too rapidly. Nowhere is this desire for advancement beyond ability more forcefully manifested than in the matter of toilet training. Mothers feel that their babies should be toilet trained at eighteen months, are upset when they are not, and what is worse, are in open conflict with their nonconforming children.

The age at which toilet training should be started varies with children. A few—very few—can be toilet trained at approximately twenty months. The long struggle of trying to toilet train a baby between age twelve and twenty months is not worth the effort. Furthermore, too zealous early attempts are apt to lead to balkiness and delayed training.

At about age two years, set the baby on either a small potty of his own or on a "toidy" seat on a standard toilet at a time when he is most apt to have a bowel movement. If he is successful, a few words of praise are appropriate. "You are a big boy. Pretty soon you won't have to wear diapers any more." At this age he likely talks some and understands your words and facial expressions. Grunting conveys an idea to the child's mind.

Let him look at the movement and comment about it. Children have an odd interest in bowel movements. If the child is seated on a regular toilet, don't flush until he gets off the seat and can watch it flow away. Many children are frightened by the flushing, some even are afraid they may be carried away by the water.

Failure to have a bowel movement on the toilet after sitting there a reasonable time calls for no comment nor any semblance of irritation. Curb the natural tendency to be cross when, immediately after removing him from the potty, he soils his pants. He simply hasn't caught on. Outburst of temper and "you naughty, dirty boy" will lead to future trouble. The child can't understand why you are angry. He has done no wrong and is left with the impression that something connected with the sitting on the potty has led to your displeasure. His simple conclusion is, "I hate potties."

One of the surest ways of delaying potty training, making it a pitched battle between you and your child, is to force training beyond the speed at which he wishes to be trained.

Think it over. Isn't changing and washing a few diapers less trouble and easier on your nerves than a daily battle on the "toidy" seat? Time and patience will yield far better results than annoyance and scolding. Place toilet training in the child's hands. Let him decide when he wants to be trained. After a few successes put him in training pants. Often this gesture of trust in his judgment brings success.

For no apparent reason a child who has been trained may slip back to soiling and wetting his pants. Don't get ruffled or scold. It is a bit annoying to have a child old enough to know what's proper come to you with a fresh diaper immediately after soiling himself. Total indifference will come to the rescue. All of a sudden some day, and again for no apparent reason except that the child probably wishes to please you or has decided he doesn't like the feel of diapers, he will tell you when he needs to go potty.

A bright little girl was totally indifferent to potty training at two years. She would contentedly sit on her potty for fifteen–twenty minutes but do nothing. Her mother, a sensible, even-tempered person, made no fuss and remarked, "I've decided to give up and let her roommate in college teach Helen toilet training." At age twenty-six months, one day Helen came to her mother and said, "Go potty." In less than a week she was toilet trained.

Prolonged obstruction to toilet training presents a tough problem. Here is a letter, typical of many, written by mothers who are at "their wits end."

"My daughter is almost four years old and is still not toilet trained. I started her when she was fourteen months old (I realize now that was too early) because I was expecting another baby. The second child, a boy, now two years old, was trained in two weeks but I can't train my daughter. She's a smart little girl and cooperative in every other way.

"Two doctors have examined her and had x-ray pictures made of her bowels. They say there is nothing physically wrong.

"She wets her pants all the time and refuses to move her bowels. After a few days the movement is so hard she can't get rid of it. My husband and I have had to give her enemas and that's a real battle. Twice we've had to take her to the hospital to have impactions removed.

"I've tried everything; ignoring, giving her fancy pants to wear, punishing, bribing—nothing does any good. I'm at my wits end. What shall I do?"

Such a problem is not easily solved. Of course, this mother, as she admits, went astray in trying to force toilet training at a too early age, but that's past history.

To remodel a stubborn obstructionist who has made up her mind not to conform to mother's wishes requires time and the patience of a saint. A four year old knows she'd be happier if toilet trained, but prefers the attention she is taking away from the baby in her daily struggle with mother. A strong-willed child hates to give in.

Don't fuss about her diet. You can't force enough fruit and

vegetables into her to do any good. She is not truly constipated, just willfully constipated. The only way to prevent hard movements (impactions) is by giving each day sufficient mineral oil or other lubricating substance prescribed by your doctor. The oil is a must; it will do no harm if given for a number of months.

Patiently repeat again and again how much you love her, what a pretty girl she is, how cute she looks in her clothes. Buy her a dress with panties to match. When she soils herself make no comment. It's far better to have her change panties herself; you won't be able to do it without showing annoyance.

Send her to a nursery school, and explain your problem to the supervisor. Nothing is more effective than having one of her playmates say, "I don't want to play with you. You stink."

From time to time, preferably in the morning after breakfast before anybody is cross and tired, gently suggest going to the bathroom. Disregard refusals. Eventually—it will be a long time—the problem will be solved. I haven't suggested the help of a psychiatrist; usually parents can handle these problems themselves.

Those of you who have little babies benefit by this mother's experience and don't start toilet training until your child is about two years old. Let it proceed as a natural and not a forced process.

GOING TO BED

To put a child to bed in the evening is easy; to make him stay there all night is quite another matter. The active, high strung two to four year old should be tired at the end of a day and is, but to convince him that sleep is necessary as well as pleasant and will make him bright and cheerful the next morning is about as easy as making him eat when he doesn't want to.

No one can live without sleep, yet the amount of sleep required by children and adults varies greatly. A two- to four-year-old child normally sleeps from ten to eleven hours at night and usually takes a nap in the afternoon.

Youngsters who fight going to bed think up all sorts of delaying tactics. "I want a drink," "I have to go to the bathroom," "Mommy, I want to tell you something," "My bed isn't comfy," "My dolly fell on the floor." When two children close to each other in age sleep in the same room, you add to these delaying tactics: talking, occasional fighting, messing each other's beds, and "I can't go to sleep because Eddy is always turning on the light." After all of these have been repeated a few times, it's nine o'clock, you are ready to scream and father is threatening in no uncertain terms to come upstairs and put an end to this nonsense. Objections to going to bed persist for years; only the reasons for not wanting to do so change.

If any parents have found a satisfactory answer on how to stop such goings on and get their children to go to sleep quietly in a reasonable time after going to bed, I'd like to know the secret.

Going-to-bed habits are established during infancy by putting the baby to bed routinely at a reasonable time. If the afternoon nap has been longer than usual, bedtime may be extended a bit.

A little rocking—again I repeat, there should be a rocking chair in every home—is soothing to child as well as mother. Babies are quick to sense a relaxed attitude. Sleep is coaxed; it can't be forced.

Somewhere between eighteen months and two and a half years children begin to love stories. Nothing is more conducive to relaxation than sitting on mommy's or daddy's lap before bedtime and listening to a simple story which the child follows by looking at the pictures on each page. Of course, there have to be limits to, "Read it again" and "Another story." Story reading is doubly valuable; it soothes by distracting the child's mind from wanting to play or roughhouse, and it subtly teaches the pleasure of books and reading.

Bad going-to-bed habits and night prowling arise from allowing repeated exceptions to routine. A mother wrote, "My three-year-old daughter won't go to sleep at night unless I lie on the bed with her until she falls asleep. At times it's very inconvenient to spend an hour waiting for her to go to sleep. If I get up before she's asleep she screams and has a temper tantrum. What shall I do?"

It's not the child's fault that she is so demanding; she tried something, it worked, got the attention she wanted, and she won't easily give up. Tell her a story, sing a song, whatever she likes before bedtime, then sit, not lie, on her bed for a few minutes, tell her what a good little girl she is, kiss her good night, close the door and leave it closed. It won't be easy to disregard her tantrums. After a few unpleasant evenings, she'll comply and you'll both be on better terms.

Night prowling children usually begin this annoying activity after they have learned to crawl out of their cribs. They get up at all hours of the night, wander about the house, turn on lights, play with things they shouldn't, and disturb the family's sleep.

I don't go along with the idea that night prowling should be allowed lest the child feel inhibited and frustrated. Far better that the child experiences a bit of frustration rather than upset the entire family. Night prowling is difficult to control.

Upon the first occurrence, the child should be told firmly that such action is not allowable, that daddy and mommy need their sleep. The second time more firmness is needed. Some parents take everything breakable out of the child's room and lock the door. Locking the door is not too satisfactory because it makes the child angry. Far better to try persuasion and trust that he will cooperate. Praise and some little award for a quiet night will accomplish more than punishment.

As a final resort, a fish net can be tied over the child's crib. Instead of putting on the net at bedtime with an attitude of "Now try to get out of bed, you little devil," practice a little justifiable deception. While tying the net over the bed, make up some sort of a story about nets over beds. Your story won't be accepted if you have previously threatened to use it if he didn't stay in bed. A mother reported that her son reminded her to put the net over the crib when she put him to bed; he thought it was some kind of a special cover.

Getting in bed with mommy and daddy is another one of those activities which is pleasant for child and parent occasionally, but a real annoyance when repeated at odd hours during the night. Balanced judgment will have to be exercised. Such an excuse as "I don't feel good," "I'm scared," may justify getting in mommy's bed, but be judicious; your child will soon learn that conjured-up illness and fear is effective; soon that little toddler is at your bedside every night. The instant you feel that getting in your bed is becoming a habit, be firm and stop it. Children should sleep in their own beds. Give the child a special toy or coloring book to play with as a reward for staying in his own bed.

Night Fears.   "Mommy, I'm afraid in the dark." Your youngsters have said it and so have mine. In fact, most children some time or other have become frightened in the dark. It's not the darkness itself they fear, but the unknown, distorted in their imaginations.

A creak in the stairs, a howling wind, the scraping of a branch against the window, or the hoot of a screech owl is transformed in childish minds into fearful monsters or threatening villains. Of course, such frightened children cry in terror.

So what do you do? Turn on a light and chase away the fears. Remember, you were afraid of the dark when you were a child and, admit it, you're still scared once in a while when you are awakened by a bad dream.

When a child in the dark is frightened, it is no time to say, "Don't be silly, there's nothing in your room. Don't be a baby. Now go back to sleep." He can't go to sleep; he's still scared.

Sit on his bed or pick him up and hold him in your arms until he himself sees that his fears are groundless. You won't be "making a baby of him" by being sympathetic and understanding. Reassure him of your loving protection. Tell him a simple story. Far better to banish fear by substitution than useless argument. You'll be teaching him to displace needless anxiety by good judgment.

Be practical. Get one of those small bulb night lights and let it burn in his room all night. The cost is minimal; the returns in contented children are high.

JEALOUSY

Jealousy is an inborn characteristic of man and animal. Pet the cat and the dog will show signs of resentment. Admire the newborn baby and the two to three year old will be green with envy.

Jealousy appears early in almost every family with two or more children and persists in some form throughout life. Keen, high-strung children are far more apt to be jealous than the easygoing and placid. It is quite understandable that children are jealous of each other. A two-year-old child, totally self-centered, wants to be important, another characteristic that persists throughout life, and any intruder who detracts from that status rouses envy. Maybe a little jealousy later in life is a good thing—a stimulant to greater efforts; uncurbed it is a devastating trait.

The first wave of jealousy is seen in the toddler when a new baby is brought home. To lessen the coming blow of having to share his position in the family, he is told that he is going to have a baby brother or sister and "won't it be fun to have someone to play with." Then mother goes to the hospital and even though warned that this is going to happen, he feels deserted. Leaving him at home with grandma or a well-liked baby sitter is usually better, if it can be done, than farming him out to a relative in strange surroundings. A daily telephone conversation with mother in the hospital—just hearing her voice—will be a comfort. At this time father can play an important role by lavishing extra attention on the bewildered child and bringing home little presents sent by his new brother or sister. Under the circumstances, a little stretching of the truth will do no harm.

The day mother comes home, he looks at the new baby, sees everybody admiring it, and forgets all the sweet talk about how grand it would be to have a brother or sister. A snappy three-year-old girl said, when she saw her baby sister the first time, "Mommy, why don't you take her back to the hospital?"

To keep jealousy from getting out of hand and leading to

open warfare between children requires, first of all, recognition of the older child's line of reasoning. He was king of the household and here is a little imposter trying to snatch his crown. Of course, he resents the baby. This resentment will be softened somewhat by having the older child take part in caring for the baby, changing diapers, and giving baths. He will be very proud to be allowed, under supervision, of course, to hold the baby and give him his bottle. Tell him often what a big boy he is when he helps mommy. The mother instinct of a three- or four-year-old sister responds to the privilege of being asked to play with and watch the baby. Build up the older child's ego. Make him feel that he is just as important to you as ever. If the children are of the same sex and the older one is about eighteen months, all attempts at interesting him in the baby will likely fail.

Friends and relatives spoil your efforts at a truce when they come in and "oh" and "ah" over the baby and pay no attention to the older child. He then resorts to all sorts of maneuvers like trying to stand on his head, running around the room, shouting, throwing toys, anything to regain the center of the stage. Why can't friends and relatives realize that undue attention only to the baby stirs up jealousy in an unnoticed child? On such occasions, try not to scold or show annoyance with these silly antics—a difficult task— but rather emphasize what a big boy he is, how he helps take care of the baby. If remarks are made about the baby's adorable blue eyes, and the older child's are brown, counterattack by saying that the older child's eyes are a beautiful brown just like his daddy's.

Nothing counteracts jealousy so effectively as diverting attention to the jealous child. As the baby grows older and snatches toys, take them away from the baby and give them back to the rightful owner. He will see that you are playing fair. By dividing your time and attention equally, he will slowly learn that he has not lost your love. When the baby learns to walk and everybody watches and praises those few steps, the older child may go up to him and push him over. Instead of losing your temper—a quite normal thing to do—take the little offender on your lap and explain, "You're a big boy, your brother is only a baby. Maybe you can help teach him to walk so that he can run and play with you."

Don't expect too much cooperation; it comes hard for a child to have to share his position of importance in the family. When the two year old slaps the baby, pulls his hair, or sticks him with a pin, he is not being naughty; he is simply giving expression to resentment. At such occasions the impulse to spank is overpowering. However, firm commands that he can't do such things, separating the children, and interesting the older child in some other activity will be fairer treatment.

Rare is the family that doesn't battle with the problem of jealousy; rarer still is the family that completely solves it. As children grow up, don't expect the problem of jealousy, (sibling rivalry) to disappear.

BITERS AND SLAPPERS

Biting and slapping in early childhood are largely natural tendencies; only when excessive or persistent do they require correction.

I have absolutely no evidence to support this statement, but I believe biting is an instinct inherited from our animal ancestry. Certainly an eighteen-month-old child with no older brothers or sisters has had no opportunity to learn by imitation. The same may be said for slapping—the equivalent of puppies cuffing each other—except that this act may be learned from elders. If this assumption is correct, one may anticipate that the average child, without malice, will occasionally bite or slap. Such actions in little children are best ignored. It is startling and annoying to have a child suddenly sink his teeth into your arm or give you a quick slap. The natural impulse to "bite back" or "slap back" is not the way to handle this problem.

The older child who bites or slaps his playmates or the baby usually does so as an expression of jealousy, frustration, or resentment; these can be counteracted by giving the belligerent child more attention and diverting his activities to more peaceful pursuits. By giving him lots of praise when he cooperates you will convince him that he is loved. Tell him often that he is a good boy. Don't expect a sudden change; children are as stubborn as adults.

At times firm discipline is necessary. When in defiance he deliberately hurts someone, hold your temper and gently but firmly put the child in his room and say, "You may not hurt other children. When you decide to play nicely you may come back." He'll howl. Be firm, not belligerent, and that's not easy. After peace is restored, a little award for deciding to behave is not out of order. As he learns that cooperation with your wishes pays higher dividends in loving attention than misbehaving, he will slowly change.

THE DIFFICULT CHILD

Why, when children are born of the same parents and grow up in the same environment, aren't they all alike? The answer is that certain traits or tendencies are inherited from countless generations.

For years it has been emphasized that environment is the all-important factor in development of personality. Dr. Alexander Thomas and associates in a book on *Behavioral Individuality in Early Childhood* do not agree. They say, "The assumption that all children will react to the same environment has resulted in a search for the right set of rules for bringing up baby. If all children were alike how easy their rearing would be. Mothers would simply follow the rule book and have no problems." What a dull life that would be.

Children born with certain willful tendencies—objecting to everything you want them to do and wanting to do everything their way—have to be recognized as nonconformists. This doesn't mean that all rules of discipline have to be scrapped. But it does mean that the sooner certain eccentricities of eating, sleeping, and acting are accepted as variations from what is supposed to be normal, the happier everybody will be. You don't need a psychiatrist to analyze your nonconforming little fighter. Roll with his punches. A smile instead of a frown at harmless stunts he thinks up will take some of the fun out of doing things that annoy you. Be firm yet gentle with discipline and who knows, he may grow up to be the individualist who is a leader instead of a follower.

MOTHER'S BOILING POINT

"I think I'm the worst mother in the world," my next door neighbor blurted out. Knowing this normally even-tempered mother and her four lively children, I asked her, "What brings you to this inappropriate conclusion?"

"Last night," she said, "I was exhausted after a day of listening to complaints about lost toys, the rainy weather, and of settling quarrels. My husband was away on a trip. At the dinner table a fight started over nothing and when Jimmy (he was four years old) said, 'I think you're just a mean old mama,' that was the last straw. Like a fishwife I screamed at the quarreling children and shook Jimmy until his teeth rattled.

"I sent all the kids to bed, slammed the door, and said, 'If I hear another peep out of any of you, I'll whale the tar out of all of you.' It was awful, the way I lost my temper. When I went to bed, I peeked into their rooms. All were sleeping peacefully like little angels. Their relaxed innocent faces made me feel so ashamed, I went to bed and did some crying all by myself."

I patted her on the shoulder and said, "It's a pleasure to meet an honest woman. I think your children are wonderful. Of course, they act up once in a while; all children do. Every mother gets mad at her kids occasionally. I know you as a kind, patient, understanding mother, but I also know that every woman has a boiling point and you hit yours at dinner time.

"Forget the episode of last night. The children probably have already forgotten. All children have a terrific sense of justice. They know they were impossible brats and had some stern discipline coming.

"This afternoon, without comment, bake a batch of the children's favorite cookies."

PART 2.

Real Troubles *&* Needless Anxieties

FEAR of losing a child haunts every parent. Even though we know that full recovery follows the great majority of illnesses of infants and children, still we can't help but be fearful that this or that ailment may fall in the category of fatal.

In the following chapters the symptoms and a few basic facts about treatment of the more common diseases of children will be discussed, not with the idea of teaching you to be a doctor, but to lessen your normal concern about illness, to guide you in methods of home treatment, and to help you in deciding when to ask for medical aid. You need not apologize for calling a doctor no matter how busy you think he may be. When your child is sick or when you think he is sick and are worried, you are entitled to expert opinion. Often an answer is available by telephone. A considerate doctor will not scold you for calling him for what proves to be an inconsequential ailment. To see the cloud of worry lift from a mother's face when she is told that her child is not seriously ill is one of the great rewards of the practice of medicine.

chapter Eight

RESPIRATORY
DISEASES

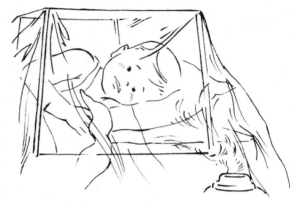

THE COMMON COLD

Colds, ordinary, miserable colds, with runny noses, cough, normal temperature or a degree or two of fever, pester children throughout the winter months. It is estimated that school children have an average of five colds a year. The lucky child may escape with only two or three; the susceptible child may have six or eight.

We know little about the common cold except that it is caused by viruses so tiny they can be seen only with the most powerful microscope and so light they can long hang suspended in the air. More than a hundred different viruses have been identified. Wet feet, drafts, chilling, undereating, and malnourishment do not cause colds; they just increase susceptibility to a virus already in the nose or throat.

The medical profession has no curative treatment. For the ordinary cold associated with little or no fever, there's no use calling your doctor; he can do little more for a cold than you can. However, when your child has a fever of 102 degrees or more, at least telephone him. He will decide from your description of symptoms whether the illness is more than a cold and whether a call is necessary. The best thing you can do for your child with a cold is make him as comfortable as possible while nature effects a cure. No drug is more useful than aspirin for relief of fever, aches, pains, fretfulness, and irritability. Be liberal with aspirin; an appropriate dose may be repeated every two to four hours. (See page 53.) Sensitivity to aspirin in proper doses is extremely rare.

Let your child's wishes be the controlling factor in the matter of food and drink. If he is hungry, let him eat; if he is not, don't urge him. Let him have fruit juices, carbonated drinks, or just plain water, if he prefers. Forcing fluids has long been popular, but useless; excessive quantities of orange juice, lemonade, or any other liquid will not wash away a cold.

You may rub the youngster's chest with this or that remedy, if you wish. The widely advertised ointments scented with pine, camphor, eucalyptus, or menthol don't kill germs or relieve congestion, but they do seem to make the child more comfortable. I am inclined to think the beneficial effects come from the clean smell of the ointment and from personal attention.

The dictum that a child with fever must stay in bed until his temperature has remained normal for twenty-four hours, is a bit too rigid and difficult to enforce. The normally active child who doesn't feel very sick and has a fever of only one or two degrees chafes at the restraint of lying in bed. I don't believe it does any harm to let him be up and about in the house, provided he is relatively inactive, keeps warm, and stays off drafty floors. He will be happier and much easier to care for if he is allowed in the living room on the sofa or in a comfortable chair where he can read, nap, and watch television. The youngster with a fever of 102 degrees or more should remain abed. In fact, he will be willing to do so because he finds that he doesn't feel well enough to get up except to go to the bathroom.

The stuffed-up nose presents a problem in infants who are breast or bottle fed. You stand by helplessly wishing the baby could blow his nose. Some pediatricians advise trying to suck mucus from the nostrils with an ear syringe. A baby doesn't like this procedure; in fact, he cries furiously at having the syringe tip stuck in his nose. I'm inclined to believe that the extra flow of tears draining through the nose and the sneezing stimulated by the suction tip are more effective than aspiration.

Nose drops containing a drug that shrinks the mucous membrane and dries secretions are most popular. To reach the congestion in the recesses of the upper part of the nose, the drops must be put in while the baby lies on his back on your lap with his head held far backward. Nose drops put in a nostril while the child is sitting up promptly run out; if put in when the child is lying flat on his back the drops run straight back to the throat and do no good.

Don't expect cooperation from a baby when inserting nose drops. You'll have to hold his head very firmly with one hand while you try to put the end of a medicine dropper in a tiny nostril. He'll wiggle his head and most of the solution will run over his face but you'll probably get in a few drops. Anyway, the battle will have given him considerable exercise, also effective in promoting a flow of nasal secretions. Fortunately, infants below one year of age have fewer than average colds and rarely have severe colds; in a few days they are again moderately comfortable.

Coughing is almost always associated with a cold. The infection from the nose or throat spreads downward into the bronchial tubes where it produces irritation and collections of mucus. Some coughing is necessary to bring up these secretions. For the ordinary cough, simple cough medicines are satisfactory; they don't kill any germs but they do relieve the tickle. Years ago a teaspoonful of honey or a piece of rock candy were standard treatment for simple coughs. Naturally, the cough persisted until the second or third treatment was given. They still are effective.

Persistent coughing is very exhausting. Keep the bedroom windows closed. Get a humidifier to moisten the air; cold dry air irritates the bronchial tubes. (See Croup, page 158.) You may be sure that a dry persistent cough will be worse during the night, often uncontrollable. Get a prescription from your doctor during the daytime to be prepared for a bad night. Such prescriptions usually contain codeine and must be used strictly according to directions.

To the question: "Should our children be given penicillin every time they have a cold?" the answer is, no. Penicillin, or any of the other antibiotics, has little or no effect upon the viruses which cause colds. It has been shown again and again that children given nothing but aspirin and routine care recover from colds just as rapidly as those who also receive penicillin. Cold viruses in the nose and throat weaken tissues and allow other germs to gain a foothold. These secondary infections are treated with antibiotic drugs. The oftener penicillin is given the less effective it eventually becomes. Therefore, its use should be avoided unless definitely indicated.

Vitamins are useless for prevention and treatment of colds. Any child eating a regular diet each day consisting of meat, potatoes, vegetables, fruit, eggs, fortified bread, cereal, and milk is getting all the vitamins his body can absorb. Extra vitamins are simply excreted. However, the child who is sick for two or more weeks during which he is on a self-imposed or necessarily limited diet should be given a daily dose of multivitamins to maintain his vitamin balance.

Immunization against colds has been disappointing. It seems so reasonable to suppose that vaccines, "cold shots," made from viruses found in the nose and throat of people with colds would be effective as are vaccines against whooping cough, measles, or polio, but they are not because the cold viruses are many and change their form and characteristics from year to year. Cold vaccines made from a mixture of the most common viruses are available. One season they seem to be effective in preventing colds; the next they are useless. It is difficult to distinguish benefit from coincidence. I do not recommend them. The slim chance of benefit does not justify the discomfort of injections nor the expense. Some parents, convinced that the vaccine has greatly lessened the number of colds in the family, demand it year after year. Then all of a sudden the vaccine fails, the family is riddled with colds, and their faith is shaken. You have about as much chance of getting protection against ordinary colds from vaccines as a hunter has of hitting a duck when shooting from a blind with his eyes closed whenever he hears quacking overhead.

Isolation as a preventive against colds is impossible. Try as you may you cannot avoid exposure to colds. When one or more children in a family go to school, exposure to cold viruses is almost constant. Even an only child of preschool age kept at home catches colds from parents and playmates who are seemingly perfectly well. For some hours before symptoms are apparent, a child coming down with a cold is already spreading germs. A sneeze or a cough by an infected person sends thousands of viruses floating in the air. Wearing a mask over mouth and nose to prevent spread of infection is useless; the tiny, invisible germs go right through the ordinary mask.

Should a child with a simple upper-respiratory infection, feeling fine, having no fever, and with a good appetite be kept home from school because of a runny nose? Some parents emphatically say, "Yes, I don't want my child to spread infection and I don't want other children to infect mine." Less dogmatic parents who tend to disregard their own colds as they carry on at work are inclined to let their children with minor colds go to school. They say with some justification, "We don't want our children to get the notion that every cold or minor illness justifies time off from school and later from work." In a classroom of twenty-five to thirty pupils there will constantly be some children who have obvious or unrecognized colds. I'd be inclined to let the child go to school. Unbroken school attendance records through four years of high school, so highly praised, are attained not because these children were fortunate enough to escape colds, but because they took their colds along to school.

The Nobel prize awaits the person who discovers how to prevent the common cold. Sainthood will be added, if not by the Pope, certainly by the mothers of the world.

Persistent Colds.   After a long, dreary winter, mothers crowd doctors' offices with variations of this story: "We have all had a lot of colds this winter but this child of mine (boy or girl of grade or high school age) has had a cold for at least a month and can't shake it off. He still coughs and his nose runs every day. He's cross and irritable and his appetite is finicky."

In the doctor's mind these children fit into one of two categories; either the child has nothing more than a chronic cold or some complication has arisen.

Before taking your child to the doctor you will greatly assist him by taking the youngster's temperature four times a day, at about 8, 12, 4, and 8 o'clock each day, for two or three days. Be sure to write down all temperature readings; it's so easy to forget. Naturally, any fever is of great significance.

Category One: You bring in a normal temperature record. The doctor gives your child a complete physical examination and, except for a little congestion in the nose and a mild degree of anemia, finds nothing wrong. The urine is negative.

In such cases the doctor says, "I don't believe your child has anything more than a nasty cold. See that he gets a little more rest by going to bed earlier. Cater to his appetite for a couple of weeks. Limit outdoor play to nice days—if there are any. Don't let him get chilled or overtired. Here is a prescription for an iron tonic, enough for ten days. Don't worry, he'll be all right." The majority of persistent colds fall in this category.

Category Two: The history of a prolonged cold is largely the same but the symptoms in general are more pronounced. The youngster looks run down, probably has lost a little weight, has no appetite, is listless, and lacks energy. Again, you have taken his temperature for a few days. If you have found the temperature a degree or so above normal, most likely at 4 P.M., there is reason for concern. Even though the temperature has been normal but the youngster looks and acts sick a more extensive medical examination will be necessary than for the child in Category One. Appropriate x-ray examinations and detailed laboratory studies will be made in a search for smoldering infection somewhere in the body. See following chapters.

TUBERCULOSIS

Parents are apt to think of tuberculosis in children as it is seen in adults with cavities in the lung, cough, fever, wasting away, and hemorrhages. While it is possible for a child to have this form of tuberculosis it is more likely to appear in lymph glands in the neck and at the root of the lung in children below adolescence. Tuberculosis of the spine (Pott's disease) causing the well-known hunchback, has become a rarity in this country. In communities where children are well-fed, well-housed, and well cared for, tuberculosis in all forms is definitely on the wane. Nevertheless, when a child has a chronic cough or is run down, he should have an x-ray picture of the lungs and a tuberculin test. (See tuberculin tests page 88.) The treatment of early tuberculosis is so effective that one can almost guarantee a cure.

Remember, tuberculosis is no respecter of persons. Exposure to tuberculosis may occur any time, anywhere. The tubercle bacillus is fighting a losing battle but has not been conquered.

BRONCHIECTASIS

Supposing your child, seven to fifteen years old, has a chronic cough which hangs on and on after every cold. X-ray pictures show a little congestion at the base (the bottom part) of the lung on one side, occasionally both sides. The youngster feels well, or only slightly below par, but each morning upon arising coughs up considerable thick phlegm; the same thing happens after violent exercise. Your doctor may suggest the possibility of bronchiectasis (little blowouts or pockets in the end of tiny lung tubes in which pus collects). The only way a certain diagnosis can be made is by having a bronchogram performed by a specialist in lung diseases.

In the x-ray department of a hospital the doctor injects some lipiodol (oil containing iodine) into the windpipe with a catheter (tube). As this material settles in the lungs x-ray pictures are taken.

The iodine in the oil is radiopaque, meaning that it casts a shadow on the x-ray plate. If the child has bronchiectasis, pockets in the lung will be filled with lipiodol and show in the x-ray as little round shadows.

What the treatment will be is determined entirely by the degree of involvement of the lung. If the disease is not advanced, i.e., the pockets are small, antibiotics, medicine to liquefy the secretions and postural drainage (having the child cough while he is lying prone with his head and chest inclined far downward) will often clear up the trouble.

Surgical removal of the diseased portion of a lung is necessary when pus pockets are large and don't shrink following conservative management. Sometimes an entire lobe—one-half of a lung—has to be removed.

Nature is kind to us in furnishing more lung tissue than we need. It is safe to remove one or even two lobes of lung without handicapping the child or interfering with normal growth.

SINUSITIS

Whenever a child above four or five years has a severe cold some inflammation spreads from the nose through small openings into the sinuses in the bones on each side of and above the nose and in the frontal bones above the eyes. As the cold clears up, so do the sinuses.

A diagnosis of sinusitis in a child with prolonged nasal discharge following a cold frightens parents because they have a mental image of accumulation of pus, the need for sinus washings, painful probings, and possibly surgery—the treatment of chronic sinusitis in adults.

The truth of the matter is that children below twelve rarely have sinusitis that requires more than steam inhalations, instillation of nose drops to shrink the mucous membranes and time.

Sinusitis in children is rarely serious. Don't let such a diagnosis in a not too sick child frighten you.

CYSTIC FIBROSIS

"My baby was perfectly normal at birth and for two months thrived, gained weight, and acted as a baby should. Then he caught a cold and began to cough. The cough won't clear up. He has lost weight, is pale, eats poorly, and is very fussy. Recently I have noticed that his bowel movements are terribly offensive and that he is always full of gas."

This is a mother's description of the typical onset of cystic fibrosis. Sometimes in mild cases the unshakable cough and digestive disturbances don't appear until the baby is four to six months old.

Cystic fibrosis, affecting about one child in a thousand, is a serious, inherited ailment. When two people, otherwise perfectly normal, happen to have in their genes the inherited traits of cystic fibrosis, and they marry and have children, one in four of their children will have the disease. If the trait is dominant in one parent, cystic fibrosis will appear in more than one-fourth of the children. This illness does not occur in the Negro race.

Cystic fibrosis is not actually a disease but an inherited disorder in which the tiny glands in the bronchial tubes secrete thick, sticky mucus and the pancreas fails to secrete adequate intestinal juices. These abnormalities are responsible for persistent coughing and improper digestion.

To make a diagnosis, the baby is sent to a hospital where first of all a sweat test will be done. Salts in the sweat are high in cystic fibrosis. X-ray pictures will be taken of the lung to find telltale signs of infection. Tests will be made of intestinal juices. It is easily possible to make an accurate diagnosis.

Cystic fibrosis at this time is not curable but infection in the lungs can be partially controlled by continuous treatment with antibiotics, and digestion can be improved by administration of pancreatic extract.

Before the days of antibiotics, the average life expectancy of a child with cystic fibrosis was only eighteen months; since then it has risen to six years and today, in the hands of experts who give attention to every detail of treatment, it has risen to an average of fourteen years. From 10 to 15 percent of children, not too seriously affected, may grow up to adulthood but are never robust.

Shall the couple who have a child with cystic fibrosis have more children? Is it fair to bring another child into the world when his chances of dying an early death after prolonged illness are almost 25 percent? This is a cruel question which has to be met and answered. I suggest that parents in this dilemma write to the National Cystic Fibrosis Research Foundation, 521 Fifth Avenue, New York, New York 10017, for available material, carefully study it, and then with the guidance of doctor, pastor, priest, or rabbi come to a decision. My advice—just that of one person who has seen these children slowly fade away—is against further pregnancies.

PNEUMONIA

The sting has been taken out of pneumonia by the magic of penicillin and other antibiotic drugs. There are many kinds of pneumonia; some of the most severe types caused by pneumococci and streptococci are actually the least dangerous because these germs are extremely sensitive to antibiotic drugs. After a few doses the desperately sick child is sitting up in bed asking for food. Relatively mild pneumonia caused by staphylococci and influenza bacilli may persist for weeks because of their resistance to drugs.

You should suspect that your child has pneumonia if he has a severe chill followed in a few hours by a fever of 103 to 106 degrees and has a sharp, dry cough causing pain in the chest or upper abdomen. Needless to say, you call your doctor at once day or night. In most cases hospitalization is necessary for repeated hypodermic administration of drugs. The baby or young child can usually be taken to the hospital in the family car. Get the car warmed up if the weather is cold—it probably will be because pneumonia is a wintertime disease—wrap the child in a couple of blankets and cover his face lightly so a blast of cold air doesn't set off a spasm of difficult breathing or violent coughing. In those rare cases in which the child is unusually sick and cyanotic (has blue lips), your doctor will call an ambulance equipped to administer oxygen while en route to the hospital.

To see the desperately ill child improve in hours and recover in a few days is especially gratifying to those of us who, before sulfa drugs and penicillin were available, stood helplessly by while fate determined whether the child would live or die.

Less spectacular is the mild case of pneumonia as a sequel to a severe cold. The child instead of recovering from the cold in expected time continues to run a low grade fever. It is often difficult for the doctor to make a positive diagnosis without an x-ray picture. Symptoms and extent of pneumonia, usually a small patch or two of inflammation seen in the x-ray picture, will determine whether hospital or home care is in order. A child with minimal pneumonia can safely be treated at home. Antibiotic drugs can be given by mouth when treatment is not urgent.

General care is similar to that of the child with a bad cold and cough; aspirin for fever, aches and pains; diet as desired; sweetened juices and carbonated drinks for quick energy; closed bedroom windows—night air brings on coughing; humidification of air in his room by water vaporizer or steam kettle—the former is safer if there are other children in the family; simple cough remedies or a prescription for cough medicine containing codeine for persistent coughing. Nature and time are great healers. During recovery take his temperature four times a day and write down the readings. A normal temperature for a few days means that recovery has occurred.

Pneumonia caused by the staphylococcus, a common germ found everywhere, occurs almost exclusively in infants, the majority below one year.

The remarkable resistance staphylococci have slowly built up to antibiotics makes staphylococcal pneumonia in infants a serious infection. In fact, nothing is more feared in hospitals than an epidemic of staph. pneumonia and other staph. infections in a nursery. That's why nurses and other attending personnel wear face masks and why those serving these infants in any capacity are not allowed on duty if they have a boil or any other staph. infection anywhere on their bodies.

It is equally important that an expectant mother tell her doctor about any skin infection she or any member of the family may have or have had recently. The staphylococcus is a hardy germ which can live on skin, in clothing, and on furniture for a long time. Through hygienic measures, bathing with germicidal soaps, meticulous attention to the tiniest skin infection in herself or any member of the family, the mother should eliminate all harmful staphylococci before going to the hospital.

The baby who has staph. pneumonia must be in the hospital where cultures can be made to determine what type of staphylococcus is responsible. Sensitivity tests (mixing the responsible germ with different kinds of antibiotics) are performed to find out which antibiotic will be effective in checking the infection.

Staph. infections are like deep smoldering fires which slowly burn themselves out.

INFLUENZA

Influenza, or the "flu" is a loose term largely used to label epidemics of upper-respiratory diseases which don't fit into the category of ordinary colds or pneumonia. Nobody knows much about influenza except that it is caused by viruses.

Few epidemics, as that of 1918, the worst in history, are deadly; most are mild. Half the population in a community may suddenly be acutely ill but with few exceptions all recover.

The symptoms of influenza are much the same from year to year differing only in severity. During an epidemic a doctor can make a diagnosis by phone; every child has largely similar symptoms such as: a mild chill, headache, backache, lots of muscle pains, little or much fever depending upon the potency of the season's virus, a dry cough, a child who looks sick and says, "I feel just awful."

Since antibiotics are useless against the flu, treatment consists of routine home nursing care with liberal doses of aspirin.

In epidemics during which gastrointestinal (vomiting and diarrhea) symptoms predominate, especially troublesome in infants and little children, the disease is referred to as "intestinal flu." The baby sick with severe vomiting and diarrhea should be given no food for a time, maybe all day, only water or lightly sweetened weak tea. Medicines are often ineffective; those given by mouth are immediately vomited and those given in suppositories are promptly expelled. If he can retain no fluid or medication and diarrhea (frequent, watery, green stools), persists for twenty-four to thirty-six hours, hospitalization will be necessary for administration of intravenous liquids. Usually, however, the baby with intestinal flu will keep down some fluid, enough to carry him through the two or three days of acute illness. Put a little warm water in a hot water bottle, expel all the air and lay the baby on his face with the hot water bottle against his tummy. He'll like that.

Recovery from the acute symptoms of all types of flu usually occurs within a few days, but lassitude, lack of appetite, and a general run down feeling so typical as an aftermath of the flu may last for weeks. Influenza in mild epidemics is not a serious disease; in severe epidemics it is not influenza itself which is dangerous, but its complications. By lowering resistance to infection, the virus allows invasion of other germs such as staphylococci and streptococci. Complications of all kinds are most apt to strike the weak, below par, malnourished infant or any person chronically ill. The best home guide to the beginning of most complications is a careful record of the temperature taken four times a day.

Ask a dozen doctors, "Do you advise immunizing shots against the flu?" Six will say, yes, and six will say, no.

The vaccine is made from a number of viruses which in past years have been isolated from people who had the disease. Nobody knows whether these viruses will cause the flu next winter or whether a new group will take over. Therefore, I do not recommend flu shots for the average healthy child. Children hate shots; they've already been subjected to many for protection against specific childhood diseases. I'm on their side and vote against more injections. Now do as you and your doctor see fit. It is generally agreed, however, that children and adults who have heart disease, nephritis, chronic lung infections, or any long-standing ailment, should be given the vaccine with the slight chance but the hope that influenza may be avoided.

STREP THROAT AND RHEUMATIC FEVER

"I have been told that whenever a child has a severe sore throat a throat culture should be taken. The object of the culture, I believe, is to find out whether the sore throat is due to the streptococcus responsible for rheumatic fever. Do you think a doctor should be called to take a culture every time one of the children has a bad sore throat?"

Yes.

Many different kinds of streptococci cause sore throats but only one particular strain, the beta hemolytic streptococcus, is responsible for rheumatic fever. The only way this germ can be identified is by a throat culture studied in a laboratory. Whenever a sore throat is due to this particular strep, immediate treatment with penicillin is started by your doctor and continued for about ten days or until it has been shown by another throat culture that the infection has cleared up. Even though only about one sore throat in a hundred in which strep is the offender is followed by rheumatic fever, you can understand why routine throat cultures are so important.

Here is the way the streptococcus responsible for rheumatic fever does its dirty work. After an untreated strep throat infection has gotten well—sometimes as long as two weeks later—the child develops inflamed and painful joints. At the same time inflammation strikes the heart valves and heart muscle. The inflamed joints slowly get completely well and so do the heart valves but in the healing process the valves become puckered and thereafter are incapable of properly opening and closing. Inflammation of the heart muscle (myocarditis) leads to destruction of some muscle cells and their replacement by scar tissue. A heart so affected is, of course, a weakened heart.

After rheumatic fever has begun there is little to do but keep the patient in bed until the inflammatory process has burned itself out. All sorts of fancy drugs appear to be of little more value than large doses of aspirin taken for weeks.

Rheumatic fever differs from other infectious diseases in that no immunity follows an attack. In fact, a child who has had rheumatic fever is more susceptible to future attacks, each of which may cause more damage to the heart and its valves. For this reason, recurring strep throats must be avoided and this is accomplished by taking a daily dose of penicillin or one of the sulfa drugs, or by having an injection in the buttocks once a month of a long-acting antibiotic drug. This prophylactic treatment has to be kept up for at least five years; many doctors advise its continuation until age thirty.

For the pamphlet *Rheumatic Fever and Your Child,* write the American Heart Association, 44 East 23rd Street, New York, New York 10010.

CHOREA

Chorea, or St. Vitus dance, is a baffling ailment of children between ages five and fifteen years. The disease got its name centuries ago when afflicted persons sought help from Saint Vitus who was supposed to have curative powers. The same type of heart defects follow chorea as rheumatic fever. Girls are far more subject to this disease than boys.

Jeannie, a rather emotional but healthy girl age twelve, for no apparent reason became nervous, irritable, and cried easily. Her face twitched, she made purposeless movements with her hands and was awkward in such simple actions as eating and writing. These symptoms came on slowly over a period of weeks and were interpreted by parents and teachers as freakish nervousness and deliberate inattention. The poor girl couldn't help acting as she did; she had mild St. Vitus dance.

Sometimes symptoms come on suddenly and are so severe that the child can't stand, sit up, or even hold a spoon. Twitching and spasms are so violent that the child has to be put in a bed with padded sideboards to keep her from injuring herself or being thrown to the floor.

Whether the disease is mild or severe, the treatment consists of bed rest, sedatives, and lots of tender, loving care. These unhappy children simply cannot control themselves. Although weeks and months of treatment are necessary, they eventually recover from all nervous symptoms.

Since chorea is apt to be followed by heart defects similar to those of rheumatic fever, it is imperative that the patient be placed on prophylactic treatment with penicillin or sulfa drugs to prevent recurrent throat infections.

Be on your guard for this odd disease. The child who for no reason acts strangely, awkwardly drops dishes, develops peculiar jerky mannerisms, may not be willfully naughty but an unhappy victim of St. Vitus dance.

GROWING PAINS

When your child comes in from play and says, "I've got leg ache," you probably will be correct in brushing off his complaint with, "You are having growing pains. Rest awhile and they'll go away." If your child complains periodically of pain in one leg, then the other, is generally healthy, eats well, and plays hard your diagnosis is likely correct.

Nobody knows what growing pains are or what causes them. Children between eight and twelve years experience from time to time dull aching pain in the leg or legs mostly after strenuous exercise. Some children have the pains at night. Attacks last for a few minutes to an hour.

Growing pains are harmless. The only danger lies in that actual disease or malalignment of bones, joints and ligaments, flat feet, and rheumatic fever (without fever) may be overlooked and mistaken for growing pains.

Some doctors, notably professors of medicine, go so far as to say, "There is no such thing as 'growing pains.'" Such a dogmatic statement is made to stimulate doctors to make a diagnosis of growing pains only after careful physical and x-ray examination have ruled out possible specific causes. The fact remains that lots of children do have unexplained growing pains and eventually "outgrow" them. I did.

CROUP

Croup is a serious disease of little children; the younger the child, the more treacherous it is. The harsh, dry, crowing cough so typical of croup is due to inflammation of the larynx (voice box) and the trachea (windpipe) and, in medical parlance, is called *acute laryngotracheitis*. It may be part of a cold, or it may come on suddenly without any sign of an upper-respiratory infection. The reason croup is considered a serious disease is that the inflammation, if not checked, may obstruct breathing.

Croupy coughs usually come on during the night. You are loathe to call your doctor, so what do you do? Nothing is more soothing to a croupy cough than moist air. Get busy at once. Put your child in the smallest room in the house and humidify the air with a cold air humidifier if you have one, or with a teakettle on an electric plate.

For the child who sleeps in a crib, make a croup tent. Place a humidifier or steam kettle on the floor or chair near the crib and drape a large sheet over crib and kettle. Never put a steam kettle above the level of the baby—it might tip over and burn him.

For quicker results for the baby who is coughing continuously, take him into the bathroom and turn on the hot shower—not on the baby. Or take the child in the kitchen where you can quickly humidify the air by boiling water on all four burners. Saturation of the air with moisture to the point that water drips from the window panes will usually relieve the cough within an hour. Hold the child on your lap or, if he is too heavy, rig up some sort of makeshift cot of blankets for him to lie on. He probably will fall asleep; if so, don't put him back in his bed for a half-hour or more until the cough has completely stopped and then only in a humidified room. Keep one ear open for recurrence of the cough.

If you can't control the cough with these simple measures or if at any time the child shows the slightest difficulty in getting his breath, call a doctor at once and I mean, at once. If a doctor is not immediately available, wrap your baby in a blanket and rush him to the hospital. For a child gasping for air only a tracheotomy (an opening in the windpipe in the neck) performed as an emergency, can save his life.

I do not wish to frighten you about croup; the majority of cases can be cared for at home but those babies having difficulty in getting their breath need emergency treatment.

EARACHE

Earache, infection of the middle ear, is a complication of a cold. The virus spreads from the nose into the lining of the Eustachian tube (the canal that runs from the back of the nose to the middle ear), where it causes the same kind of inflammation that occurs in the nose. Whenever the tube becomes completely obstructed, other bacteria, staphylococci or streptococci, always present in the nose and throat, get a chance to grow. These bacteria fill up the obstructed space in the middle ear and form pus. The pressure of this accumulated pus is the cause of well-known earache.

Earache is most common in children between three and six years but may affect infants and children at any age. Some children have it with almost every cold; others probably because of larger

Eustachian tubes, never have it. Earache usually starts about two days after the onset of a cold. The baby who doesn't just cry but screams and rubs his ear undoubtedly has earache. The child old enough to point or talk leaves no question about the diagnosis. All infections vary in severity and so do earaches; some disappear spontaneously in a few hours or are relieved by hot applications, ear drops (phenol and glycerin) and a tablet or two of aspirin; others are severe and demand immediate medical attention.

Anyone who had earache before introduction of antibiotic drugs will remember how painful it was and will vividly recall the momentary excruciating pain experienced when the eardrum had to be punctured.

In those days, mastoiditis (inflammation of the bone behind the ear) was a common and dreaded complication, often requiring major surgery. Those days are happily past. Now antibiotics cure middle ear infections as if by magic in twelve to twenty-four hours. Therefore, when your child has earache call your doctor. While waiting for the penicillin to take effect, warmed ear drops and aspirin will relieve some of the pain.

Occasionally, during a mild attack of earache, the ear drum will rupture spontaneously and discharge pus. You may find it on the pillow in the morning. Don't be alarmed. Put a light plug of absorbent cotton in the ear and change it when necessary. In a few days drainage will stop and the hole in the ear drum will heal.

After middle ear infections deafness is not uncommon for a few weeks. Don't be worried unless it persists, in which case, an ear specialist should be consulted.

TONSILS AND ADENOIDS

Tonsils are lymph glands situated on each side of the throat where they serve as guardians against infection and, with very few exceptions, there they should remain.

In a typical case of tonsillitis both tonsils are acutely inflamed, fiery red, swollen, and covered with white spots. The throat is very sore, the temperature is almost always above 102 degrees, and the patient is acutely ill, often vomits and complains of headache.

Treatment consists of bed rest, aspirin to relieve pain and reduce fever, and a liquid diet because swallowing solid foods is painful. Your doctor will prescribe penicillin or other antibiotics. Gargles may be used but do little good because what medication they contain cannot penetrate the tonsils where the infection lies. The virtue of most commercial gargles is that they counteract foul tastes in the mouth. Salt and soda gargles are as unpleasant as they are valueless.

Medication with antibiotic drugs is the same as for strep throat. A throat culture is important because of the possible complications of tonsillitis. Medication with antibiotic drugs should be continued for ten days even though all symptoms have disappeared in four or five days.

Adenoids like tonsils are protective masses of lymphoid tissue high up in the back of the throat; they become inflamed as do tonsils. Adenoids are blamed for mouth breathing, snoring, underweight, lack of appetite, fatigue, retarded growth, earache, in fact, for almost anything that may ail a child. The only crimes adenoids can justly be accused of are causing earaches and occasionally mouth breathing.

Swollen Glands.   Many complications may follow tonsillitis but by far the most common is swelling of the lymph glands in the neck. The function of lymph glands or nodes in the neck as elsewhere is to filter out bacteria draining through lymph channels from an inflamed area. Glands in the groin enlarge from an infected leg or foot; in the armpit from an infected arm or hand. Almost every child has some enlargement of the glands or nodes in the neck after a sore throat. The enlargement often lasts for two to four weeks after the throat infection has cleared up.

So long as the glands are not painful and the child has no fever, leave them alone. Don't rub them with all sorts of advertised salves and ointments and don't put on hot packs; they have enlarged, as they should, to combat infection. However, occasionally a gland may have been so overwhelmed by infection that it breaks down, that is, forms an abscess. In that case, hot packs are useful in bringing the infection "to a head." After the abscess has softened, lancing may be necessary to let out the pus.

Persistent swelling of a gland in one side of the neck is a source of worry to parents. In a child who has had an unquestionable sore throat or an infected tooth, the chances are high that such a gland is chronically inflamed and that nothing needs to be done about it. However, see your doctor, he will decide.

TONSILLECTOMY AND ADENOIDECTOMY

Surgical removal of tonsils and adenoids, routinely referred to as T and A, is the most frequently performed operation on children.

Two generations of parents have inherited and cling to the mistaken notion that tonsils and adenoids are responsible for the frequent colds to which their children are susceptible. Numerous investigators have shown again and again that a T and A does not remove susceptibility to colds. Parents concerned about their poor eating, skinny, tired, uncooperative child seek a simple solution to the problem by requesting removal of the tonsils and adenoids. What such a child needs is not a T and A but considerate analysis of his real and imaginary problems.

Is tonsillectomy ever necessary? Yes, but rarely. The physician cannot tell from looking at tonsils whether they should or should not be removed, and I am quoting eminent nose and throat specialists. Enlargement of the tonsils is not an indication for removal. The child who for a number of years has had repeated attacks of tonsillitis, real tonsillitis with high fever and swelling of the glands in the neck, or has had tonsillitis complicated by quinsy (an abscess of the tonsil), probably should have his tonsils removed. Don't, however, expect the operation to eliminate sore throats; they are almost as common after as before tonsillectomy.

What about adenoidectomy? Every child has some enlargement

of the adenoids. Beginning at about age six they commence to shrink and in the course of years completely disappear. The child who has repeated earache and unexplained impairment of hearing likely needs to have his adenoids removed.

T and A is not the simple operation it is thought to be; it's a psychic jolt to children; hemorrhage, severe enough to require transfusion, is common; a few throats are permanently damaged. Reliable statistics are hard to obtain, but it is conservatively estimated that between 250 and 300 children die each year in the United States as a result of T and A. Unfortunately, there is no way of getting an answer to the question of how many children die each year because they did not have their tonsils removed. The fact that insurance will pay for T and A does not make the operation a bargain. You trust and admire your doctor; that's fine, you should. Now look him straight in the eye and ask: "Is this operation absolutely necessary?"

MENINGITIS

A rare but greatly feared complication of any kind of upper-respiratory infection is inflammation of the meninges or coverings of the brain, meningitis.

Of course, it is impossible for you to make a diagnosis of this treacherous disease. However, should your child, during any infection of nose, throat, or lungs however mild, rather suddenly complain of severe headache, vomit, become unusually irritable, or seem somewhat dopey and unresponsive, call your doctor. An infant, incapable of indicating symptoms, who suddenly develops high fever, cries whimperingly, looks knocked out and, when picked up, instead of naturally curving in your arms, holds his neck and back straight or has a convulsion, requires immediate medical attention.

These rather frightening symptoms are described only to emphasize that the earlier meningitis is recognized and vigorously treated the greater are the chances of recovery without permanent brain damage.

INFECTIOUS MONONUCLEOSIS

An odd disease of teen-agers is infectious mononucleosis, a mildly contagious disease caused by an unidentified virus. It starts like a simple cold with sore throat, a little fever, and headache. The victim feels depressed, knocked out, and best describes symptoms by, "I just feel lousy." Within a week lymph glands in the neck enlarge and are a bit painful. It is difficult for the doctor to do more than suspect infectious mononucleosis until specific laboratory tests have been made.

Fortunately, the disease is not a serious one because there is no specific treatment; antibiotics do no good. Aspirin relieves the headache, fever, and general misery. It often takes a long time; weeks or months to get completely well. During the long period of recovery, exhaustion and depression are persistent and annoying.

The infection is spread from person to person by viruses in the nose and mouth; it has been labeled "The Kissing Disease," probably because it occurs at an age when this activity is most popular. When this possible source of infection was mentioned to a girl rather miserable with infectious mononucleosis, she sighed, then brightened up and said, "It was worth it."

chapter Nine

CANCER

CANCER in children is altogether different from cancer in adults. Cancer of the stomach, bowel, lung, uterus, and breast is an extreme rarity in children. In the files of the Children's Memorial Hospital in Chicago for over a period of eighty-five years, there is no case record of cancer of these organs in children below sixteen years of age. Keep that fact in mind should your daughter have a lump in her breast or should any of your children vomit blood or pass blood in the stools. And yet, even though cancer is not common in children, it stands next to accidents as the number two cause of death.

Growths or tumors of all kinds appear anywhere in the body in children; most are painless lumps. They may be benign—growths which remain local and are harmless; or they may be malignant—growths which spread out and eventually invade the entire body.

Fear of cancer is universal for our children as well as for ourselves. When a lump or swelling is discovered, do not delay while you hope it will go away; get medical advice.

Tiny nodules in or immediately under the skin are most likely harmless. Nevertheless, get your doctor's opinion. Lumps of any size not easily identified and those showing any signs of growth during a reasonable period of observation should be removed. Parents are entitled to a diagnosis.

We would be remiss if after all our preaching about early treatment of tumors, we did not take out suspicious nodules. Unquestionably some harmless little lumps are going to be removed from time to time. A surgeon should not be called "knife happy" because he advises excision of a worrisome lump. In these days of scientific medical care all specimens are sent to a laboratory for microscopic examination by a competent pathologist. His report in most cases will be, "The tumor is benign, harmless," and parents breathe a deep sigh of relief. If the report is cancer, the fact of its early complete removal offers hope that it will not return. The surgeon will advise immediate, more extensive surgery if there is any doubt that the tumor was not completely removed at the first operation.

Lump in the Breast.   While it is important to remove questionable tumors to avoid spread of cancer, it is more important that certain lumps be left alone.

"My little girl has a tumor in her breast." The anxious tone in this statement revealed the mother's fear of cancer. A quick examination of the ten-year-old girl's breast was sufficient to make an unquestionable diagnosis. Directly beneath the nipple was a hard, fixed, painless swelling about the size of a lima bean.

The load of anxiety slipped from the mother's shoulders when the doctor said, "This lump in your daughter's breast is a premature bud of womanhood."

Development of such a swelling or bud in the breast of a little girl long before menstruation has begun is relatively infrequent and practically always confined to one breast. For no known reason it appears in a perfectly healthy child between the ages of nine and ten years, sometimes as early as seven or eight. The bud does not indicate that adolescence is about to begin and ordinarily it remains unchanged until the age of puberty when a similar bud appears in the other breast and both develop in normal fashion.

No treatment of any kind is necessary. The condition is common enough to be a source of deep concern to parents and uncommon enough to be mistaken at times for something serious. Surgical removal of the entire lump would be a tragedy; there would be no later breast development. A biopsy (removal of a small segment for microscopic examination) would result in later deformity of the breast. In spite of the fact that a premature bud in a child's breast feels exactly like a cancer in an adult woman, it must be left alone; it is not cancer. As I said before, cancer of the breast in girls before adolescence simply does not occur.

Mothers, don't get panicky if you find a lump in your little girl's breast. See your doctor; he will reassure you of its harmlessness. In time a similar swelling will appear in the opposite breast and your little girl will be a young lady.

Boys, too, develop little lumps in one or both breasts but not until well along in adolescence at about ages fifteen to seventeen.

An adolescent boy, otherwise perfectly normal, and with all the features and characteristics of manhood, discovers a slightly tender nodule directly beneath the nipple. The nodule may be as small as a BB shot or as large as a navy bean; it persists for a few months or as long as for two years and then completely disappears. It is estimated that almost 50 percent of boys have this minor problem sometime during adolescence. Being shy about mentioning the problem to mother, the boy asks his father who says, "Pay no attention to it. In time it will go away. I had the same thing when I was your age." His advice is excellent.

There are, however, rare exceptions to this rule of spontaneous disappearance. Occasionally, the nodules continue to develop until the boy has breasts quite similar in size and appearance to those of an eighteen-year-old girl. In all other respects he is a normally developed man. A psychological problem now presents itself. The boy refuses to undress except in absolute privacy; he will not go to a gymnasium, or swim, and will not be seen in a T-shirt. For such isolated cases surgical removal of both breasts is advised. The miniature nipples are left intact so that he will look like other boys.

Most Common Cancers in Children.   Although cancer in children is rather infrequent, the three most prevalent cancers are those of the brain, kidney (commonly called Wilm's tumor), and of nerves in the back of the abdomen (neuroblastomas, meaning tumors arising from nerves). Of all tumors in children those of the brain head the list. I hesitate to mention any symptoms of brain tumor for fear of rousing unnecessary worry, and yet parents should be suspicious of something seriously wrong in the brain if their child daily for a period of weeks complains of headache for no apparent reason, vomits without being sick to his stomach, loses coordination of movements, stumbles or staggers when he walks. Consult a neurologist.

The sad feature about kidney and nerve tumors in the upper abdomen is that they produce no early symptoms. Many are discovered accidentally by the mother who notices that her baby's abdomen appears large or by a doctor during routine physical examination. Blessed is the painstaking, unhurried doctor who, when he sees a child for any reason, even a cold, also feels the abdomen. That quick, passing feel may detect an unsuspected tumor which can be removed before it has spread.

The best treatment of cancer is surgical removal; often this can be accomplished, sometimes it cannot. Nothing is more heartbreaking than to have to tell parents that the tumor has spread and is not removable. "What is to be done now?" is the invariable question. The answer usually is x-ray therapy. Most tumors in children shrink rapidly under x-ray treatment but, unfortunately, cannot be completely eliminated. The fact that once in a long while growth of a cancer is permanently checked stimulates constant search for more effective x-ray treatment. X-rays are powerfully penetrating; however, only a limited amount can be given without destroying healthy cells, too.

Drug therapy of cancer has become popular in recent years and in certain cases is of some value. It is less effective than x-ray therapy but is definitely worth trying. An objection to its prolonged use is that drugs, if given in large enough quantities to do any good, are inclined to make the child sick and miserable for a day or two. One never gives up in the treatment of cancer in the hope that by some miracle the cancer may be arrested. However, after every means of treatment has been exhausted, I have often wondered whether, in a near terminal case, it is quite fair to the child to continue unpleasant treatments to prolong life possibly for a few weeks. I shall never forget a five-year-old girl whose frail little body was riddled with cancer. She was comfortable so long as she lay quietly in bed. She loved to hold a woolly bear into which a music box was fitted and played Brahm's "Lullaby." Whenever anyone came by her bed she would say, "Wind up my bear." As the music played a contented smile would creep over her face. It seemed to me that memory of the haunting melody and the smile it brought were worth more than a few extra weeks of life which might have been gained from further vigorous treatment.

Parents grasp at any straw that offers or is reputed to offer the slightest hope of saving their child. Vulturous quacks prey on this fact and sell all sorts of phony "cures." Whenever a "doctor" claims that he has a cancer cure and demands payment—usually exorbitant—in advance, shun him as you would the plague; he is not interested in your child, only in your money. Rest assured that, in these days of scientific investigation and rapid communication, report of a proven cure for any type of cancer will promptly spread all over the world.

Reports that cancer may be caused by a virus prompts parents to ask whether cancer is contagious. No evidence exists that cancer has ever been spread from one child to another by even the closest contact. Let your child visit and play with a friend who has cancer. It will be a kind thing to do.

LEUKEMIA

Acute leukemia or cancer of the blood is primarily a disease of children below eight years. Untreated, the average life span after the diagnosis has been made is only four months; with treatment, life expectancy can be lengthened to an average of nine months and occasionally to years. Chronic leukemia in older children and adults is less rapidly fatal. The younger the child the more rapidly fatal the disease.

Knowing that leukemia is a fatal disease parents are naturally inclined to be fearful whenever their child looks pale. Although pallor is one of the symptoms of leukemia, more indicative are rapid loss of weight, extreme fatigue, appearance of black and blue spots especially on the legs and arms with no history of injury, bleeding from the gums, and unexplained fever.

In acute leukemia the blood in most cases is loaded with leucocytes (white blood cells). The function of leucocytes is to fight infection but these abnormal cells have lost that power. Eventually, they invade every organ in the body.

Treatment is aimed at destroying these leucocytes with drugs and, for a time, from a few weeks to three or four months, is spectacularly successful; the blood count drops to normal and the child picks up lost weight and feels fine. These periods of improvement are called remissions. Rather suddenly all symptoms return. Each remission is shorter as the drugs lose their effectiveness. However, one never gives up treatment because once in a long while and for reasons unknown a remission may last for years.

There remains the question of how to handle a leukemic child. He will be happiest at home in familiar surroundings, treated insofar as possible as he was before the tragic diagnosis was made. Sudden, excessive pampering will confuse a little child and make him unhappy and difficult to handle. The less the child is hospitalized the better.

I am flatly opposed to the idea that a child with leukemia or any other hopeless cancer be told that he is going to die. It is claimed by advocates of this policy that the child will learn his fate in one way or another and that he therefore should be told the truth by a parent or sympathetic doctor. In general, the rule of telling children the truth is correct but not in these circumstances. Supposing your youngster learns of his condition from a playmate and comes to you and says, "Mommy, am I going to die?" I think the answer should be an evasion. Summon all your strength of self-control while with your face averted you focus your attention upon whatever you are doing and then quietly say, "Honey, we all are going to die sometime. Remember, grandpa died. He was very old. Grandma, Daddy, I, everybody will die some time. Nobody knows when. We all hope to live a long time. Now let's go have some fun." A favorite game, a shopping trip for some little treat will take his mind from the subject.

If hospitalization becomes necessary, the leukemic child should be put in a ward with children who have illnesses from which it is anticipated they will recover. In hospitals specializing in blood diseases, the placement of leukemic children in "leukemia wards" to me seems wrong. Children are smart. From comments of other children and members of the staff they are bound to learn about the seriousness of their ailment.

It takes courage to carry on as usual in the face of impending disaster. Andy was eleven years old when he was operated on for cancer. It couldn't all be removed, but after a series of x-ray treatments, he felt fine for about eighteen months. Then he began to feel not quite up to par. Evidence of tumor growth in the abdomen and in both lungs was found. More x-ray treatment and anticancer drugs were advised. The father considered the advice and said, "Maybe it isn't necessary to start these treatments at once. You see, I promised Andy a fishing trip in Minnesota week after next." He knew as well as we that the suggested treatment could only delay the inevitable.

They went fishing.

Upon their return, Andy's eyes shone as he told about the fish he caught. Beaming, he glanced at his father and said, "You know what? I caught the biggest fish, didn't I, Dad?"

As Andy was telling his story, his father, dry eyed, smiling, said without showing the slightest evidence of the anguish he felt, "We had a wonderful time."

chapter Ten

OTHER ILLNESSES
MAJOR & MINOR

APPENDICITIS

Acute appendicitis means inflammation of that useless appendage, the appendix, from two to six inches long, attached to the bowel and situated in the lower right side of the abdomen. Why it suddenly becomes inflamed no one knows, but we all know that when inflamed it should be removed without delay.

All children from time to time have stomachache and for many reasons. It is estimated that about one stomachache in fifty is due to appendicitis. To pick out here and there that case which needs emergency surgery is no easy task for the doctor. Where does that leave the parents in deciding whether their child's stomachache warrants calling the doctor?

Here are a few guideposts toward diagnosis; they aren't too clearly lighted for the simple reason that the symptoms of appendicitis is rare in an infant below one year of age, is uncommon before age two, and occasional between two and three. After four years, age is no factor.

In the standard or typical case of acute appendicitis, The sequence of events is as follows: the child complains of a nagging pain in the middle of the abdomen. Parents are under the impression that the pain of appendicitis is severe; it may be, but more often it is not; it is, however, persistent. Shortly after the pain comes on the child is nauseated and vomits. Children vomit easily for many reasons. If a child with pain in the abdomen does *not* vomit, he very likely does not have appendicitis. Within an hour or a few hours the pain moves down to the lower right side. By this time, the temperature will likely have gone up to 100 or 101 degrees.

A burden of worry would be lifted if appendicitis always followed the same pattern. The appendix may be inflamed only at the tip and cause mild symptons with no fever or the entire appendix may be acutely inflamed (red hot) causing violent symptoms and a fever of 105 degrees.

So what do you do about your child's stomachache? Call your doctor is good advice, but your doctor is not always readily available and actually it isn't necessary to call him for every little pain that crosses a child's abdomen. Unless the pain is severe, wait a bit to see what is going to happen. Take your child's temperature; do nothing else. Don't put hot or cold packs on the abdomen and don't give any medicine of any kind; it's important not to mask symptoms.

Calmly review in your mind all the possible reasons why your child may have stomachache. Does he have any kind of respiratory infection such as a cold, sore throat, earache? Any of them may cause pain in the abdomen, vomiting, and fever. The well-known cramping pain associated with diarrhea differs from the pain of appendicitis in that it comes and goes. Likewise constipation may cause abdominal cramps. Has your youngster had anything unusual to eat or drink—excessive fruit, notably green apples, contaminated picnic food, too much ice water when he was overheated, too many carbonated drinks? Was he excessively fatigued before eating? Has he had such attacks of pain before? Do they come on at certain times of the day, for example, just before school time or when it is time to dry the dishes? Has he just been in a fight or a highly competitive game?

You run through the gamut of causes of stomachache and find that none apply. Maybe he does have appendicitis. The best thing to do still is nothing. And *don't*—no matter what anybody says— give the child a cathartic or physic of any kind. The peristalsis (contraction) stirred up by the cathartic may rupture the appendix. If he has not had a bowel movement for two or three days, an enema of one pint of soapy water will do no harm. Doctor books advise against enemas as dangerous; they are dangerous only if big ones are given. A one pint enema will do no harm and will eliminate constipation as a cause of pain. If no worsening of symptoms occurs, take the child's temperature again in two hours. Elevation of temperature of even one degree is significant. Stomachache without vomiting and without fever is practically never appendicitis. If the nagging stomachache steadily gets worse or persists unchanged for about two hours, call your doctor. You have gone as far as you may safely go. If he makes a diagnosis of appendicitis, the treatment is immediate operation. Go to the hospital, but don't rush. That appendix is not going to rupture within a few hours. Take time to explain to your child with the aid of your doctor exactly what's going to happen. A cool, unhurried attitude will give you and your child confidence. A few days after surgery he will leave the hospital feeling fine. Within two weeks he'll be back in school bragging about his operation.

In spite of most attentive medical care, an inflamed appendix, producing minimal symptoms or masked by some other disease, will occasionally rupture. Consequently, there is some spillage of intestinal content into the abdominal cavity. This unsterile material plus infection from the inflamed appendix cause peritonitis (inflammation of the lining of the abdomen and the covering of the intestine). Spread of infection throughout the abdominal cavity causes generalized peritonitis; nature, however, is kind and usually seals off the rupture in the appendix thus limiting infection to a small area called local peritonitis.

Before the days of antibiotics, the words ruptured appendix struck terror in everybody's heart. After the operation there was little to do but stand by and hope that the patient would successfully combat the infection. Today, the magic drugs have changed the outlook; deaths following rupture of an appendix are uncommon but still do occur with sufficient frequency to warrant careful consideration of acute appendicitis as the possible cause of stomachache.

HERNIA

While bathing the baby or changing his diaper, you suddenly notice a bulge in the groin on the right or left side. The bulge gets a bit larger as the baby cries. Later you look again and see nothing. Again when the baby cries the bulge reappears. The diagnosis is unquestionable; your baby has an inguinal hernia or rupture in the groin.

Of all inguinal hernias in children, 80 percent appear in boys, 20 percent in girls. A hernia or rupture in boys rarely causes any signs of discomfort, but in girls—especially infants below six months of age—colic, constipation, fussiness, and excessive crying occasionally occur because an ovary has slipped through the defect or rupture in the abdominal wall where it is caught; it's the slight pull on the ovary which causes the symptoms.

You take your baby to the doctor who confirms the diagnosis and sends you to a surgeon. Hernia is very common in infants; in fact, surgical repair of hernias is the most common operation performed by children's surgeons. Every mother has a series of questions she wants answered.

Q. What is a hernia?
A. A hernia is a protrusion of the intestine through a weakness in the abdominal wall; this weakness is called a rupture. A hernia and a rupture are one and the same.

Q. Is it my fault that the baby has a rupture? Did I let him cry too much?

A. No. In every baby before birth there is a sac or finger-like protrusion of peritoneum (the lining of the abdominal cavity) into the groin. This sac should have closed before the baby was born. It failed to close; therefore, when the baby cried or strained, he pushed the intestine into this sac. One cry is enough to produce a hernia. If the sac hadn't been there no amount of crying would have forced the intestine through the abdominal wall into the tissue right under the skin.

Q. My baby has a hernia on only one side. Will he get one on the other side?
A. He may. The chances are one in ten that a baby who has a hernia on one side has a weakness on the other side which may pop open at any time.

Q. I have heard that surgeons advise operation on both sides even though a rupture has appeared on only one side. What do you advise?
A. Your baby is only three months old. I think I can feel a sac or potential hernia on the side where no bulge has appeared. I therefore would advise the double operation. If your boy were two years old, I'd advise a single operation for this reason: Since no hernia has appeared in two years, the chances are that it never will.

Q. Is the operation serious?
A. To us it is not; to you, any operation on your baby is serious. We consider it a minor procedure. Of course, your baby will have to have a general anesthetic. There is no operation that is not attended with some danger. However, the danger of an operation is far less than that of not having an operation.

Q. What do you mean by that?
A. Sometimes the intestine gets stuck in the sac and can't be pushed back into the abdomen. We call this an incarcerated or strangulated hernia. When this happens, the blood supply to the segment of incarcerated intestine is pinched; it's like tying

a string tightly around your finger. If the hernia can't be reduced, i.e., if the bowel can't be pushed back into the abdomen,
an emergency operation will be necessary to prevent gangrene
of intestine.

Q. How long will my baby be in the hospital?
A. Twenty-four to thirty-six hours. He'll be admitted, for example, on Sunday afternoon, will be operated on Monday
morning, and go home that evening or Tuesday morning, depending upon how he feels.

*Q. I still hate the idea of an operation. What about putting on
a truss?*
A. A truss will not cure the hernia; it will serve only as a support to hold back the intestine. He'll have to wear a truss for
the next seventy years. And another thing—people who tell
you that hernias get well by themselves or with the aid of a
truss are wrong. An unquestionable hernia can be cured only
by operation.

Q. What are the chances of its coming back?
A. One in two hundred.

Hydrocele. A collection of water in a sac in the groin, a hydrocele
looks and feels very much like a hernia except that it remains constant in size. They are perfectly harmless. In children below six
months of age most of them go away spontaneously. Only in older
children are they operated upon if they become very large.

UNDESCENDED TESTICLE

When you notice or your doctor calls attention to the fact that one
or both of your son's testicles are not in the scrotum, you are naturally much concerned about future male development and fertility.
Present opinion of the medical profession concerning this problem
should relieve some of your worries.

During fetal life the testes (male glands) develop in the flanks beneath the kidneys, slowly move downward, and at the time of birth have reached their normal position in the scrotum. For some unknown reason, one or both occasionally stop their descent somewhere along the way, usually in the groin.

Non-descent of one gland presents an altogether different problem than non-descent of both. A boy with one gland in the scrotum will grow up to normal manhood and be fertile. A testicle in the scrotum produces normal spermatozoa; one in the groin does not for the simple reason that the temperature in the scrotum is a few degrees lower than in the groin. It seems strange that variation of a few degrees in temperature can have such a profound effect, but so it is.

If your boy has only one gland in its normal location, take him to your doctor who by careful examination will determine whether there is true non-descent or whether descent may spontaneously occur later; it sometimes does. Surgical placement of the gland in the scrotum in cases of unilateral descent is usually not advised until the boy is about ten years old.

"Why operate at all if one gland is sufficient?" For the simple reason that two glands function better than one and for psychological reasons—disturbing comments in locker rooms and the deep-down feeling of being not quite a man.

If both glands are undescended, most surgeons believe that one at a time should be operated upon at about age four. Because there still is some question about growth and development of glands in the groins, earlier operation is advised than when only one is undescended. The boy with neither of the glands in the scrotum will grow up to normal manhood, but will not be fertile. Following successful operation, the chances of normal fertility are good.

For a short time about thirty years ago, injections of male hormones were widely advocated to bring down one or both testicles. The hormones were successful in a small number of cases, but they also brought on precocious puberty in some children. Little boys six and eight years old developed the appearance and impulses of eighteen-year-old men. The only time hormones should be used is in the case of a boy about twelve years old who has bilateral non-descent of the testicles and then only during the weeks immediately preceding operation.

DIABETES

David was five years old and had always been healthy. His mother noticed that for five days he was unusually thirsty and made frequent trips to the toilet. She took a specimen of urine to the doctor. Diagnosis: diabetes.

Harold, after being dry at night for two years, started wetting the bed. His urine was loaded with sugar.

Susan, always a poor eater and skinny all of her eight years, developed a tremendous appetite but still lost weight and was pale and tired. Examination of the urine solved the mystery.

Jerry was three years old. Instead of recovering as usual from a bad cold, he became dopey and slipped into unconsciousness. Diagnosis: diabetic coma.

Diabetes in adults comes on slowly in contrast to children, in whom symptoms usually appear in a matter of days or weeks.

Treatment of the diabetic child should always be initiated in a hospital. Since diabetes is controllable but not curable, it is important for the mother to learn as much as she can about diet, calories, insulin, and urine-testing for sugar while her child is in the hospital. Find a doctor who has taken special interest in treating diabetes in children and stay with him.

Diabetes is a lifetime disease and the wisest policy is to begin and stay with scientific treatment. Until you have learned to estimate caloric values of a slice of bread, a pat of butter, or a dish of carrots, etc., it will be necessary to weigh every bit of food your child eats. Your doctor will write out a diet sufficiently generous to satisfy needs and promote growth, and will prescribe proper amounts of insulin. By frequent examination of the urine for sugar, the insulin dosage will be balanced with the diet.

After a week or two in the hospital you will have the task, and it is a big one, of weighing food, injecting insulin, and examining many specimens of urine. On top of these daily burdens is that of slowly, patiently instilling into the child's mind that there may be no exception to the routine. It's going to be tough to watch your youngster munch on a stalk of celery while the other kids are eating cookies. Children are wonderfully adaptable; they respond to love and your sympathetic interest in their misfortune and soon accept the new way of living.

A mother of a six-year-old diabetic boy stressed a number of "dos and don'ts."

"Don't tell your diabetic child he is normal. He isn't and he knows it. Stress all the positive things he can do, such as playing ball, swimming, and going to parties.

"Be sympathetic when he cries about an insulin shot. Tell him it's absolutely necessary; firmly, but gently and quickly give it and then give him a hug.

"Don't baby your child or allow special privileges not given other children; this will only increase his feeling of being different.

"Never vary from the diet 'just this once'; you are only hurting him. When other children have cookies or candy, give him diabetic gum or calorie-free soft drinks.

"Let him go to parties. Explain to the hostess what he may eat or send food along.

"Diabetic control demands a great deal of discipline from the entire family. Don't try to make a 'little man' of him; he is just a little boy."

For instructional material, write to: The American Diabetes Association, 18 East 48th Street, New York, New York 10017.

EPILEPSY

It is not a disgrace for a child to have epilepsy—a misfortune, yes, but not a disgrace. Parents and their solicitous friends should quit talking in hushed whispers about epileptic "fits." A child has seizures and they should openly be referred to as such. Epilepsy is a disorder of children rarely appearing before age three or after adolescence.

Seizures are petit mal (pronounced petty mahl), meaning momentary loss of consciousness, or grand mal, the well-recognized spell with loss of consciousness, falling, and convulsive jerking of the entire body. Little is known about epilepsy except that something acting like an electric shock, suddenly strikes the brain and brings on an involuntary seizure. Needless to say, any kind of a spell suggestive of epilepsy should send parents to their doctor for evaluation, because the earlier a diagnosis is made and treatment begun, the better the chances of cure.

Seizures are controlled solely with drugs. Finding the right kind and the proper dosage requires time, patience, and good judgment. Be frank with your doctor; if he is not interested in carrying out the prolonged and exacting treatment, ask him to refer you to someone who makes a specialty of treating epilepsy. Drugs will have to be taken for years. Approximately 60 percent of epileptics can be permanently cured, that is, kept free from seizures, and 25 percent can be largely controlled, having only a rare seizure. Unfortunately, that leaves about 15 percent who continue to have uncontrollable seizures. Nothing is more important than continuing medication for about five years even though during that time no seizure has occurred. Many parents forget medication after a year or two without a seizure.

A child who falls on the floor with a seizure should be left alone. Keep calm, don't throw water on his face or slap him or bring him back to consciousness. In a few minutes the jerky movements will stop, he'll get up, and except for being a bit dazed, will soon be all right. Minimize the embarrassment of his having possibly soiled his clothing during the seizure.

Dr. Samuel Livingston, outstanding authority on epilepsy at Johns Hopkins University, has these answers to questions about epileptic children:

They are as smart as average children.

They should go to regular schools.

Treat them as normal children; don't pamper. When the child is old enough to understand, explain what epilepsy is and what limitations of activity, if any, are necessary.

Teachers should be told of the possibility of a seizure. Should one occur in the classroom, she should explain to classmates what has happened and urge them to treat the child as normal.

There is no reason why the grown epileptics, free or practically free from seizures, should not marry and have children. The chances of their children having seizures is about one in forty.

For further information write to: The Epilepsy United Association, Inc., 111 West 57th Street, New York, New York 10019.

HEADACHE

"Mom, I've got a headache." How many times have you heard your children make this mournful complaint!

Ordinary headache associated with colds, fever from any cause, fatigue, emotion, excessive exposure to the sun, and many other conditions are easily relieved by a tablet or two of aspirin. Severe, persistent headache, however, in a child who has any kind of respiratory infection or contagious disease and fever is quite another matter. A child who has such a headache not relieved by aspirin, who looks sick, vomits, and says, "My head hurts just awful," should be seen by a doctor. Danger of spread of infection to the brain is not great (see meningitis, page 163), but is a possibility. Early treatment affords the best chances of complete recovery without consequent brain damage. Parents hesitate to call a doctor about a headache. Children have many headaches; those which don't respond to aspirin call for medical appraisal.

Migraine headache never killed anybody, but has tortured innumerable people to near the limit of human endurance. Children below six or seven years rarely have migraine headaches but older children and teen-agers may have attacks similar to those of adults. The healthy youngster who rather suddenly gets a pounding headache, often confined to one side of his head and is "sick to his stomach," probably is having an attack of migraine. If there is a history of migraine in the family, there is little doubt about the diagnosis. Don't, however, conclude that your child has migraine because he has an occasional unexplained headache. If the attacks recur, consult your doctor. Migraine follows excessive fatigue, nervous strain, unusual excitement, and emotional upsets. Girls are apt to have migraine just before or during a menstrual period. Adults can tell when a migraine headache is coming on by the appearance of zigzag flashing lights in their eyes. Children rarely have this warning signal. Eye strain may cause migraine; any child with unexplained headache should have a careful eye examination by an eye doctor (ophthalmologist).

Just a suggestion: Observe whether your youngster gets one of his typical headaches after eating chocolate. Not a few children sensitive to chocolate are relieved of their troubles by eliminating it from their diet. The youngster, usually a teen-ager, with suspected migraine should, of course, have a complete physical examination, urine and blood tests, and a patient, sympathetic analysis of his or her way of living. For the attack of migraine headache various drugs including aspirin are helpful. More important is correction of the manner of every day living: regular, sensible meals, proper sleeping habits, elimination, if possible, of emotional strain in the home, and a reasonable work and play schedule. High-strung, tense children may get rid of their migraine headaches by cutting out some of the extracurricular activities in high school.

Adults are not averse to developing a sudden headache as an escape from some unpleasant situation. Children learn fast. The causes of headache are still much of a mystery.

URINARY INFECTIONS

The sneakiest infections are those of the bladder and kidneys in infants below two years of age. The only outstanding symptom is repeated attacks of high fever lasting for a few days and coming on after a cold or for no apparent reason. These attacks are apt to be ascribed to "the flu." Unfortunately, the baby can't describe his symptoms of burning on urination and the discomfort of an over-filled bladder. All he can do is cry.

Examination of a baby's urine may be neglected because the specimen is thought difficult to collect; actually it is not. The doctor will give you a soft plastic container easily attachable to boys or girls to catch a small amount of urine; a teaspoonful is enough for a routine examination.

The diagnosis of urinary infection is made when pus and bacteria are discovered in the urine. Now the child is sent to the hospital for further studies by a specialist to find out what is back of these infections. The answer is almost always the same—partial obstruction to urinary flow somewhere in the kidney, ureter, or at the bladder opening, and due to a defect the baby was born with. Any defect obstructing the normal flow of urine slowly causes hydronephrosis (ballooning out of the kidney) and distention of the ureter and bladder. In these distended structures urine stagnates, becomes infected, and brings on attacks of fever.

After the obstruction is removed these irritable, poor-eating, unhappy babies suddenly change to normal robust life.

Older children also have urinary infections, girls far more frequently than boys because the bacteria find their way upward from the vagina into the bladder. Most of these infections clear up with drug therapy; if they don't, again suspicion arises that there may be blockage somewhere. Children through their teens rarely have kidney stones.

PIN WORMS

A chic mother brought her five-year-old child to her pediatrician and said, "I think my daughter has pin worms because she is always scratching herself. I'm so embarrassed. I thought only dirty people get pin worms."

The doctor took a piece of scotch tape, pressed the sticky side against the folds of skin about the rectum and made a microscopic examination of adherent particles.

"Your suspicion is correct," he said. "I have found the eggs; your child has pin worms. For your comfort may I say that at least 40 percent of children in the United States, including suburbs, at some time have pin worms. It's not a disgrace."

Pin worms are tiny creatures about one-eighth to one-half inch long. They live in the intestine where they developed from eggs which were swallowed. The female worm crawls out of the bowel at night and deposits a few thousand eggs in the folds of skin about the rectum. (At night is the only time one is apt to see the worms.) The child scratches at night, gets the tiny eggs under his fingernails and on his night clothing, and in the morning gets some in his mouth. These eggs hatch and the cycle is repeated. It's easy to understand how other members of the family get infected. Some children heavily infected are nervous and irritable. In hot climates pin worms sometimes grow so extensively in the bowel that they produce symptoms resembling those of appendicitis.

It's easy to clear up pin worms with medicine. The entire family will have to take it. To prevent reinfection, to kill all the eggs, these few suggestions should be followed for about ten days.

At night put on each child a tight panty under the night clothes.

Boil or soak in ammonia water (1 cupful to five gallons of water) for one hour all sheets, night clothes, bath towels.

Scrub the hands before each meal and, of course, after going to the toilet.

Keep fingernails cut short.

Wash floors with soap and water and vacuum rugs, carpets, and upholstered furniture.

That's right, if the pin worms come back you'll have to go through the entire regime again. Watch for indications of pin worms in your children's playmates; if you see suspicious signs, diplomatically talk about pin worms with their mothers. Sometimes, all the children in a schoolroom become infested.

ALLERGIES

Allergy is a strange ailment. For reasons unknown, about 19 million people in the United States are sensitive to things which are harmless to others. There is some comfort in the fact that misery has lots of company. Allergies usually show up during childhood, but a person free from allergies for thirty or forty years may suddenly develop hay fever or skin sensitivity. Allergy is inherited; a child's chances of having allergy of some kind are about 20 percent if one parent is allergic and 50 to 75 percent if both are allergic.

During the first year allergy is most commonly caused by milk, wheat, eggs, or orange juice. The baby who continues to have colic beyond the time it normally disappears, has red, scaly patches of eczema and cries a lot, may be suffering from allergy. Rather than jumping into a series of skin tests, you and your doctor try to find the guilty substance by eliminating one food at a time. Substitution of soy bean formula for milk will frequently solve the problem.

Allergy in older children who are not sensitive to foods, is most commonly due to feathers, house dust, germs (especially molds), cat and dog fur, horse dander, or wool. The symptoms at this age are stuffy nose, frequent unexplained "colds," excessive sneezing, coughing, itchy eyes and nose. Again, with the aid of your physician, eliminate the most likely causes; farm out all pets for a few weeks; get rid of feather pillows; tightly cover the mattress with plastic; ease away all woolly bears and bunnies. Getting rid of house dust is a tough problem; you'll have to figure that one out yourself.

After all simple measures fail, consult an allergist. He will know of dozens of less common causes of allergy. Finally, a series of skin tests may be necessary in the hope of finding the criminal. Frequently, it is found that the child is sensitive to a number of things. Desensitizing injections against all the offenders may do some good, but don't expect miracles. A few patients will be greatly benefitted. The majority will be improved.

Don't take this allergy business too seriously. The more you worry and fuss about it, the more nervous you and your child become and the worse will be the allergy. There is no doubt that stress and strain in the home is a large factor in allergy. Reduce to a minimum exposure to whatever your child is sensitive to and be patient, the chances are good that the allergy will remain mild.

Hay fever is most often due to ragweed pollen appearing about the middle of August and to tree, rose, and grass pollens appearing in spring and early summer. After the offending pollen has been identified by means of skin tests, desensitizing injections offer the best chance of partial relief. Popular drugs, all containing antihistamines, help relieve symptoms. Air filtered through an airconditioner into a tightly closed bedroom makes the nights more comfortable.

ASTHMA

Asthma belongs to the same congregation as allergy—just sits in a different pew. Allergy affects skin and noses; asthma affects bronchial tubes. Any of the irritants mentioned under allergy may also cause asthma.

Wheezing is the outstanding symptom of asthma. As an irritant strikes the lining of the bronchial tubes, it swells and secretes thick, sticky mucus. In the walls of the bronchial tubes are tiny muscles which, in the allergic child, contract, go into an asthmatic spasm when an irritant strikes them, and thereby narrow the air passages. Forceful breathing through these constricted tubes with strings of mucus strung across them produces wheezing, the "musical rales" heard with a stethoscope.

Asthmatic attacks vary greatly in severity. One need not be too concerned about a little wheezing in a baby below six to twelve months when it occurs only during a cold. However, attacks of asthma coming on repeatedly at any time require a search for the substance to which the child is sensitive. As with allergy, elimination of one possibly causative factor at a time is more successful in catching the culprit than innumerable skin tests. Allergists don't advise skin tests for babies. Even in older children skin tests are resorted to only after long study because attacks of asthma are precipitated by so many things. Anger, fear, temper tantrums may bring on asthma and there's no skin test for them. It is well recognized that emotional outbursts are a common cause of asthmatic attacks in children as in adults.

So what does the harassed mother of an asthmatic child do? She tries to keep her child from catching cold (difficult), keeps him out of dust, denies the poor little fellow his live pets as well as stuffed woolly animals, eliminates from his diet suspicious foods (often the ones he likes), and tries to provide a relaxed atmosphere in a home free from violent emotions. All these things are done with the hope that if the attacks of asthma can be limited and lightened, the child will outgrow them. A fair number do.

Allergists are divided in their opinions about the effectiveness of "shots," desensitizing injections, for asthma; some feel they are effective, others resort to them only in severe asthmatics. If, after elimination of the usual causes of asthma, the child continues to have relatively mild and infrequent attacks, the doctor tends to prescribe medication (nasal sprays), for wheezing, and to let it go at that. Parents willingly accept this conservative attitude hoping that the attacks will get no worse and may disappear at adolescence.

For mild attacks of wheezing, humidified air, aspirin, a sedative, nasal spray prescribed by your doctor, and time are all that are necessary.

Severe asthmatic attacks are an altogether different matter. Nothing is more distressing than to see a child, pale and covered with sweat, gasping and fighting for air. To relieve the suffering of a severely asthmatic child, hypodermic injections of adrenaline or ephedrine are necessary. It is wise for the mother to learn how to give an injection; it is not always possible to get a doctor to make an emergency call. The injection will be more effective if it is given early in the attack.

Whether it is wise to move to another climate for the sake of a severely asthmatic child is a question that you, your doctor, and your financial status will have to decide. Moving is often disappointing; the youngster takes his asthma with him.

SKIPPED HEART BEATS

The very fact that Mr. M. took off an afternoon to bring his son, Paul, to the doctor, at once suggested more than ordinary interest in his twelve-year-old boy's ailment.

For a year Paul had been complaining of "funny feelings" around his heart which he described this way: "Every once in a while it feels as though my heart skips a beat. After the skip there is a real hard beat. Whenever one of these hard beats comes, it feels as though my heart was doing a flip-flop in my chest."

The boy looked healthy and said he felt fine. Physical examination, and electrocardiogram (heart tracing), and x-ray pictures of his heart proved that Paul's heart was normal. The diagnosis was extrasystole (extra-syst'-o-le). This word, describing a common and usually harmless irregularity of the heart, needs some explanation.

Normally, a tiny electrical impulse stimulates the auricles to beat, hesitates a moment, then spreads downward to make the ventricles beat. And so our hearts beat in a regular lub-dub, lub-dub fashion. If, however, an impulse to beat arises anywhere outside of the regular circuit, a feeble heart beat results and is called an extrasystole. Following this beat, a delayed, excessively strong heart beat follows, and it is this heavy beat which gives the sensation of the heart doing a flip-flop.

Extrasystoles are very common in older children and young adults. Some people have them all their lives. The cause of extrasystoles in children is unknown; in young adults they are made worse by excessive fatigue, overwork, loss of sleep, excessive smoking, too much coffee—all conditions which increase irritability of heart muscle. The only treatment for extrasystole in persons whose hearts are otherwise normal is reassurance that the condition is harmless. Exercise may be unrestricted. In fact, during violent exercise extrasystoles disappear.

The reason for the father's visit with his son now came out. He said, "When I was a boy my son's age, I had exactly the same symptoms. My mother took me to the doctor who explained nothing. I don't think he knew what the trouble was. He simply advised that I take it easy. That was enough for my mother. Father had died of a heart attack at age forty-seven. Mother interpreted the doctor's advice, 'take it easy,' to mean no competitive athletics. Not until I was a junior in college did I go to a heart doctor who told me that I had no heart disease, nothing but skipped beats, extrasystoles, and could do anything I liked in the way of physical exercise.

"Thank you for your advice to my son. I feel more kindly to the medical profession now than I did twenty-five years ago."

HARMLESS HEART MURMURS

Just because your child has a heart murmur is no reason to fear that the end is in sight.

Some heart murmurs are due to disease or defects in the heart, but the majority of murmurs in children heard by doctors in day to day practice are harmless, or as they are called in medical circles, functional. Pediatric cardiologists, those who specialize in heart disease of children, claim that functional murmurs may be heard at some time before adolescence in as many as 40 percent of children.

Little is known about functional murmurs or what causes them. One day the murmur, a sort of a purr instead of a clear, sharp sound, is distinctly heard; the next day it is scarcely audible. Sometimes the murmur, distinctly heard when the child is standing, disappears when he lies down. Exercise may make the murmur disappear. It is most often heard during high fever.

It is, therefore, easy to understand why parents are confused and criticize their doctors. One says the child has a murmur; the next says he hasn't. Both the doctors are right; they simply listened to the heart at different times.

Actually it requires years of experience to interpret correctly the many causes of heart murmurs in children. If a child's heart is normal size for his age as shown in an x-ray picture, if his electrocardiogram is normal, and he feels and acts well, there is little to worry about; the murmur is most likely harmless, even though the murmur may be due to a small defect or to a previous mild disease. Many people have gone through life with a slight heart murmur and attained a ripe old age.

And another thing we might as well clear up right now. At times your youngster says his heart pounds hard, so hard that he can feel it slamming against his ribs. That's *palpitation* and it doesn't mean a thing. Fear, anger, excitement, violent exercise will make a heart palpitate. That's normal. After mind and body rest, the heart returns to normal beating. Forget it.

FUNNEL CHEST

A funnel chest is due to depression of the sternum or breast bone. Children are born with this deformity; it is usually inherited.

Parents are disturbed by the appearance of a deep funnel chest and are inclined to think that a deformity so apparent must certainly require surgical correction. Funnel chests are harmless except in those instances in which the breast bone lies so far back that it interferes with heart action; such cases are rare.

To correct a funnel chest surgically for appearance sake alone is not justified. Tell a boy that he was born with this harmless defect which will never cause any trouble or interfere with athletic activities and he will be content. There need be no concern about a girl with a funnel chest. When she matures to full womanhood, the deformity won't show; in fact, it will accentuate femininity.

ATHLETE'S FOOT

Ringworm of the feet, ordinarily called athlete's foot, is a fungus infection almost universal in high-school children.

Little blisters on the soles and the sides of the feet, fissures, and raw areas between the toes, cause itching and burning. There is no known way of preventing ringworm nor is there a permanent cure. Foot baths in locker rooms have been abandoned because the germicidal solutions can't safely be made strong enough to kill the fungi. The first time your youngster gets ringworm of the feet, you'll probably seek medical advice; thereafter, recurrences will be home cured.

Small blisters on the feet should be aseptically opened. Sponge the blisters with alcohol, then with a needle tip, sterilized in the flame of a burning match, open the blisters and apply a disinfectant. Opening the blister won't hurt. For infections between the toes, soak the feet in hot soapy water each evening, rub vigorously with a rough towel to remove the soggy skin, and apply denatured alcohol. The alcohol will sting. Many prefer advertised preparations available at any drug store. Walking barefoot in sand at the beach in the summertime rapidly clears up extensive ringworm; the sand wears away dead, soggy skin, and the hot, dry air kills the fungi.

The child whose feet perspire freely is most susceptible to ringworm. He should change socks every day, wash his feet every evening, and put a drying powder between the toes. From time to time shoes should be set out in the sun or on a radiator until completely dry. Fungi can live only in moist surfaces. Severe and resistant types of ringworm respond to a new antibiotic, Griseofulvin, prescribed by your doctor.

WARTS

Everybody recognizes warts for the simple reason that practically every youngster has or has had them. Warts may appear anywhere on the body, but most commonly occur on the backs of hands and fingers and on the soles of feet (plantar warts). All are supposedly caused by a virus. The virus spreads and produces a number of warts on one's hand, but they are not easily transferred from person to person.

The most important treatment for warts on the hands is patient waiting for spontaneous disappearance. The fact that all of a sudden and for no reason warts vanish, accounts for the many silly methods of charming them away. Whatever treatment or hocuspocus was used just before the warts disappeared gets the credit. The wart that persists or is in an inconvenient spot may be taken off with the touch of an electric needle, dried up with some chemical, or frozen with carbon dioxide snow.

Plantar warts on the soles of feet occur in older children and adults, and rarely disappear spontaneously. The warts look like calluses, but are very painful.

I doubt if there is any minor problem which a doctor hates more to encounter than a miserable plantar wart. Treatment is painful, cure is difficult, and recurrence common. After simple methods of local application of drugs fail, x-ray treatments are tried. If they fail, the wart has to be destroyed with an electric needle or cut out. Either process is painful. It's actually less trouble to get rid of a gallbladder full of stones than a stubborn plantar wart.

INGROWN TOENAILS

Ingrown toenails are an unnecessary evil brought on by ill-fitting shoes and improper cutting of toenails.

All ingrown toenails occur on one or both sides of the big toe. Pressure from a too narrow and too short shoe makes the skin roll over the edge of the nail. After a time when the side of the toe gets sore where the nail is digging into the skin, the nail is trimmed far up on the side to relieve the pain. Now a vicious cycle begins: The more the nail is trimmed away, the more the skin pushes up. Constant irritation eventually causes infection and the well-known, painful, ingrown toenail.

Prevention of this difficulty is so simple: Buy shoes large enough and wide enough across the toes to prevent crowding and teach your children to cut their big toenails straight across. The edges of the nail on both sides should project just beyond the end of the toe. By cutting the big toenail a bit shorter in the middle than at the edges, excessive wear on the end of the sock will be avoided.

It's not easy to cure an established infected ingrown nail. Cut out the toe of an old shoe to relieve painful pressure. Each evening soak the foot in warm water, dry it, and then with a toothpick tuck a small piece of cotton soaked in alcohol between the swollen tissues and the nail. Patiently stick to this procedure until the nail has grown out beyond the end of the toe. You may need medical help to clear up this pesky trouble. Sometimes the nail has grown so far to the side that surgical removal of a strip of toenail will be necessary.

When your corns are hurting from too narrow shoes, be reminded to tell your children how to avoid ingrown toenails.

BOILS

A boil is a staphylococcal infection in the skin. Many boils are man-made. Teen-agers may turn a pimple into a boil by trying to squeeze out the tiny white spot of pus. The pressure forces germs into the skin and, presto, there is a boil. The hated, white topped pimple should be left alone until a bit of pus can be wiped away with a piece of gauze. Kids, don't squeeze pimples.

The large, painful, hard boil with redness and swelling about it should be treated with hot packs to relieve pain and bring the infection "to a head." Heat a quart of water in a pan and put in it a tablespoonful of epsom salts. Soak a small bath towel in this solution, comfortably warm, wring it out just so it is not dripping, fold and lay it over the infected area. Place a dry towel over the wet one and cover with any kind of plastic—the cover over a suit from the cleaners serves well.

To keep the compress warm, lay a hot water bottle against the pack, not on top as the weight of it will cause pain. Wet compresses carefully covered with waterproof plastic may be kept warm with an electric pad. Be careful with an electric pad, don't turn it up to full heat. Never cover an electric pad with a towel.

Hot dressings are usually changed every four hours and kept on from morning until bedtime. The patient sleeps better without being hampered by cumbersome dressings. In a few days the boil will point. Leave it alone. Nothing is accomplished by having it incised. When the boil begins to discharge, wipe away the pus with an antiseptic solution to prevent spreading germs to the surrounding skin and lay on a piece of sterile gauze each time you change the dressing. After the "core" discharges itself, stop the hot dressings and cover with a bandage. Carefully dispose of infected gauze and boil towels contaminated with pus to prevent development of another boil.

This simple home method of applying hot compresses may be used to draw out infection from all sorts of minor, superficially infected cuts and scratches. Any time the infection is severe enough to produce fever and/or red streaks in the skin, call your doctor.

A Stye is a little boil occuring in the base or follicle of an eyelash; it usually gets well without treatment. Hot packs hurry its cure, but are difficult to use on a baby. A child old enough to stand up at the sink may hasten recovery by applying to his eye a wash cloth repeatedly rewarmed with water from the hot water faucet.

chapter Eleven

YOUR CHILD GOES TO THE HOSPITAL

THE IMPACT OF HOSPITALIZATION

Going to a hospital is an ordeal for any child. He cannot understand why he must be torn from home and parents and go to a place associated in his mind with insecurity and pain. Adults when ill do their best to avoid hospitalization and go only because they know they must do so to get well. Imagine how a child feels. It is the duty of all of us, parents, doctors, nurses, when dealing with children who face hospitalization, to soothe the fears of their uncomprehending minds.

When hospitalization becomes necessary, explain to your child as simply as possible what he can expect. If you tell him that some things are going to be unpleasant, that there will be some little hurts, he will not later harbor resentment or feel that he has been tricked. Of course, he'll cry but at the same time will understand and appreciate your sympathy and interest in his welfare. Explain that the doctors and nurses are there to help him and will take good care of him. Emphasize that he will be with other children, will have lots of toys to play with, and books to color.

The most likely response to your honeyed speech will be a vociferous, "I don't want to go," or "I won't go unless you stay with me." And that brings up the question of ward or private room care. Private rooms are fine but most young parents can't afford the extra cost.

Infants are best cared for in the usual four-bed ward. They are indifferent to surroundings and content so long as someone attends to their simple needs. More important is the fact that they get four times as much supervision in a ward. Each time a nurse comes in to attend one patient she routinely glances at the other three to see if they are all right.

Older children often prefer the congeniality of a ward. The two year old presents the biggest problem in hospitalization. He is too young to understand why, when placed in a ward, his mother can't stay with him all night. The highly sensitive, the overprotected, and the only child should, if economics allow, be placed in a private room where a parent can constantly be with him. There is no way of gauging damage to the emotional pattern of a terror-stricken child, but I am sure it may be considerable.

Let your child take along to the hospital the toy, woolly animal, or blanket to which he is so firmly attached. No matter how worn and dilapidated it may be, let him take it along and don't allow any germ-proof observer of rules take it away from him. If there is any time he needs his little idol, it is while in the hospital.

After he has gone through the rigmarole of admission, go along on the elevator with him to his bed; it most likely will be in a ward. Stay with him while he is getting into his hospital gown, having his temperature taken, is being weighed, and is going through the usual routine. Stimulate friendly relations between him and other children in the ward. Eventually you will have to leave. Give him a hug, tell him what a good boy he is, and assure him that you will be back tomorrow and then—go. If a loud wail brings you back to him, it will only make final parting more difficult.

Visit your sick child in the hospital as often as you can. Visiting hours in children's hospitals and children's sections of general hospitals have slowly changed from the barbarous restriction of an hour or two a day, to hours from midmorning to seven at night. The evening hours have been added to give fathers a chance to see their children. The idea that a child will adjust to hospitalization better if not seen by the parents is a sadistic misconception. Were you ever lost, couldn't find your way home, separated from parents in a crowd? If so, you will remember the terror and indescribable relief when you again saw a familiar face. That's how some children feel in a hospital—forgotten and deserted. Visit often, stay as long as you can, bring along little presents to remind him of you and tell him again and again that you'll be back. At the earliest possible date take your child home.

The sensitive three- to four-year-old children requiring hospitalization are the ones for whom I am sorry. While seriously ill they haven't enough energy to scream for their parents, but the moment they feel better they begin hollering for mommy. Many times I have seen such little children standing in their high-sided cribs, their faces stained with tears, sobbing interminably, "I want my mommy." One can pick them up, offer them toys, tell them over and over that mommy is coming. Their only response is more wailing and, "I want my mommy now." A three-year-old child has no sense of time; "pretty soon" means nothing. What he wants he wants right now and nothing will satisfy but the sight of mother walking through the door.

Five to ten year olds and even children in their teens feel lonely, get homesick, and look forward to the touch of a familiar hand. I repeat, regardless of age, visit your sick child in the hospital as often as possible. Don't be concerned about indulgences and over-attention; any spoiling done while in the hospital can later be neutralized at home.

Preparation for Operation.   Never, but never, let your child, old enough to understand, be taken to an operating room before someone, preferably the doctor who is going to operate, has explained in simple words what is going to happen. He will not like the idea of an operation but will not harbor resentment if told what he may expect. The explanation needn't be elaborate, but honest and suited to the child's age.

The evening before operation the three- to five-year-old child is told: In the morning you will ride in an elevator and be taken to a special room where you will see nurses and doctors with funny things over their faces called masks. You will be put on an extra fancy table. Then a doctor will put a thing something like a space helmet over your nose and mouth and you will blow up a balloon. (The age of the child determines how much explaining is necessary about connections between face mask and balloon [anesthetic bag] and about the fact that gas will be inhaled as the balloon is being inflated.) As you blow up the balloon you will get sleepy. While you are fast asleep the doctor will "fix that sore place," "get rid of those bad tonsils," "make your heart better." When you wake up you will be back in your room and mommy and daddy will be there. (Be sure you are at his bedside when he wakes up from the anesthetic. Occasionally you may have to break some rules to be there. Go ahead, bust 'em. You promised your child you'd be there when he woke up. Promises are sacred to children.) The older child, six to eight years, is likewise told in words that he can understand exactly what will happen. After his fears of bad-smelling anesthetic gas and of waking-up during the operation have been dispelled, he is content and goes to sleep. Mother is given the sleeping pill.

A nine-year-old child after explanation of anesthesia and operation said, "You don't have to tell me all that stuff. I know all about it. I saw it on TV."

"And where are you going?" I said to a pert little five-year-old girl I happened to see on the elevator.

Her snappy answer was, "I'm going to the operating room to have my tonsils out." Her tone of voice suggested that she was on her way to a party instead of the operating room.

Then she added, "Do you know what? My daddy took the whole day off just to be with me." She would expect mother to go along to the hospital but to think that daddy cared enough to take a whole day off from work just to be with her—well, that was something special.

Contrast this story with that of a seven-year-old boy who was admitted to the hospital for repair of a rupture. When I went to see him he lay in bed sobbing and inarticulate. Finally, his story was pieced together. His playmates had told him that he would be tied to a table and put to sleep with some awful-smelling stuff. Then the doctors would cut him all to pieces. The poor little guy. I said to him, "I'll tell you what we'll do; we'll go visit some children who have had an operation and you can see for yourself that your friends were just trying to scare you for fun." I'll never forget that cold, little moist hand in mine as we walked through the hospital. As he watched children sitting in bed coloring pictures and reading story books, the cloud of fear lifted from his face. He went through the operation without a whimper.

Children are such trusting little creatures. Tell them in simple words why they have to go to a doctor, or to a hospital, or why they have to have an operation and, in most instances, they will cooperate in a fashion that adults might well emulate. Faith and trust are unbroken when a child is dealt with honestly. The child sunned by love and security will be able to withstand the storms of illness and pain.

chapter Twelve

WHAT TO DO ABOUT:

DISCIPLINE

If you are puzzled about how to discipline your child, you belong to the majority. I can't give any pat answers, but from the mistakes I made with my own children and from observation of all sorts of children from smiling, cooperative little angels, to ornery, impossible nonconformists, I have learned that love, understanding, and friendly relationships are the basic guiding principles to obedience. Children are not bad. Often they are not even naughty; they are just little folks eager to learn the right and wrong way of living.

The dominant tone of discipline is too often punishment, and that's mostly wrong. A child can't be forced into obedience with harsh words and whippings; he must gently but firmly be led into the spirit of cooperation. The word discipline comes from the word disciple, and disciple means follower.

Love a child with your whole being, not just with honeyed words, and that child will love you, and with few exceptions, will want to conform to the pattern of life you set for him.

The two- or three-year-old child doesn't know the difference between what you recognize as good or bad. He does all sorts of exasperating things. He is imitating you when he tries to pour milk in a glass but because of inexperience, clumsily spills some of it on the floor; he wants to be helpful when he dusts the table and knocks over a pot of flowers; he is trying to please you when he brings in a handful of unopened peony buds. If a child is punished for these innocent mistakes he becomes confused. Repeat punishment and harsh words often enough and he rebels. His feeling of security is replaced by fear. Soon he becomes a belligerent nonconformist. "So you mean to tell me I should let my child do anything he likes?" I can hear you say with some heat. The answer is definitely, no! Simple explanations about why certain things may or may not be done usually suffices. Accentuate the positive, minimize the negative, be liberal with praise, and the problem of discipline will be well on the way to solution.

Children enjoy orderly living. They are happier in an atmosphere of wise and patient discipline than in an atmosphere of indulgence. Expect children to obey but don't ask the impossible. When you make a mistake, as you will, admit your error and say you are sorry. His respect for you will go up; his feeling of being an important member of the family will be assured by the realization that you are trying to be fair.

There are times when the spirit of cooperation flies out of the window and the question: to spank or not to spank, arises. "Spare the rod and spoil the child" is an adaptation of Solomon's advice in the Bible (Proverbs 13:24), "He that spareth his rod hateth his son, but he that loveth him chasteneth betimes." (Spanketh once in awhile.) Except for short periods of time when misguided psychiatrists advocated complete permissiveness, this advice has remained unchanged for thousands of years.

Spanking a child, i.e., giving him a few resounding smacks on his bottom with the flat of your hand, must be distinguished from beating a child. Let this be crystal clear, not all children require corporal punishment in any form, not even a slap, in the process of learning discipline. Some hypersensitive children quail at a cross look; others take a spanking without much more than a shrug of the shoulders.

Willie was playing train in the back yard while his mother was hanging out the wash. Willie was chugging up and down raising clouds of dust with his bare feet. Mother said, "Willie, don't play train there, the dust is getting on the clean clothes." Willie hesitated, diminished the shuffling, but didn't quit. Mother repeated her request a bit more emphatically, whereupon Willie "piled on the coal" in his imaginary train. The dust billowed up. Did Willie need a spanking? I'll say he did and he got it. (I was called Willie when a boy.)

There are times when arguing and sweet requests avail nothing. Sometimes, and it better be during childhood, everybody has to learn to conform to a few rules. If such lessons can be learned without spanking, fine; if not, spank. Spanking a child sounds cruel but isn't if done with cool judgment, in great moderation, and only immediately following deliberate and willful disobedience. To threaten a child with a spanking by father when he comes home is silly. How can a father punish a child for something done hours ago?

There is a tremendous difference between teaching a child to obey and making him obey. You can't *make* a child obey without "breaking" him as a colt or dog is broken to respond to commands. Children are intelligent little people who absorb the principles of obedience and good behavior through example and teaching.

Eddy comes in from play and his hands are filthy. His mother says, "Eddy, please wash your hands." Compliance or refusal depends upon your previous attitude toward similar situations.

If Eddy *does* wash his hands and as a reward receives a pat on the head and "That's a good boy," he will have learned in a small way that cooperation makes him happier than obstruction.

Supposing Eddy makes no move to wash his hands, then what? Stoop down to the child's level, take his hands in yours and say, "Look at those dirty paddies. Come along, let's wash them." He is distracted from the command by looking at his hands. He is pleased by your interest in him and goes to the sink.

"But you don't know my boy! If he makes up his mind not to do something he won't do it without a fight."

That's the time to be a little better than human. Don't lose your temper. (How easy it is to give advice.) Without slapping or jerking by the arm, with no harsh words, gently steer, if necessary pick up and carry, the little fighter to the sink and wash his hands.

After the storm is over say, "Look at those nice clean hands. Now let's play a game." Spend a few minutes on the floor with him.

Into Eddy's subconscious mind will have filtered the knowledge that you, not he, is boss in the home and that you love him. The basic principle of discipline will have been learned.

TEMPER TANTRUMS

Soon after birth a baby learns to get what he needs by crying. As he grows older he steps up crying to screaming and adds kicking, jumping up and down, throwing himself on the floor, beating with hands and feet to attain this objective. I doubt if there ever was a normal child who hasn't displayed temper tantrums. Sad but true, temper tantrums, differently expressed, continue far beyond childhood.

Your eighteen-month-old baby in his playpen screams. You run to see if he is all right. He promptly stops crying, even favors you with a smile. It worked; he'll try it again. If you are unresponsive, he'll increase the tempo. Not until he discovers that his antics are useless will he quit. Give him some toys or a pan to bang on and leave him alone. Go to him once in awhile and play with him when he's quiet. He'll learn. Disregard temper tantrums about food, about getting dressed or undressed; he's too little to understand that his actions are anything but normal.

The four- to six-year-old child who puts on a first-class temper tantrum while screaming, "I hate you, hate you," arouses in all but the saintly a desire to respond in kind. That's a mistake. Talking, scoldings, or spanking during a tantrum won't do any good; in fact, will only stir up rebellion. A child must never get what he wants by use of a tantrum, no matter how furious or persistent he is. The best treatment is indifference. Walk away. A tantrum loses its effectiveness without an audience.

At times when you can't stand the shrieking and kicking another minute, send him to his room, close the door, and leave him there. If he won't go under his own steam, try to control your temper as you put him in his room without jerking, dragging, and literally throwing him in. Take a deep breath—more likely ten will be necessary—then tell him gently that when he can behave he may come back to the living room. Even when dealing with a child, "a soft answer turneth away wrath."

After the storm has passed turn on the sunshine of your love. The chances are he'll say he's sorry. You may then be able to get across to him that such outbursts make him unpopular with family and playmates.

When children are tired or, because of weather have been cooped up in the house too long, outbursts of temper are bound to occur. Try to avoid situations which you know will lead to a tantrum. Attention can sometimes be turned away from the trigger mechanism by suggesting a different kind of play, a TV show, telling an interesting news item, or appealing to his feeling of importance by asking him to help you do something.

Don't be too disturbed by occasional temper tantrums; they are unavoidable, not serious, just annoying. When your son is a grown man the only remnant of his early outbursts will be an uncontrollable desire to throw a golf club after a poor shot.

STUTTERING

At about age three or four most children stutter; words tumble over each other and are chopped up in repeated syllables. The child's mind is faster than his speaking apparatus. At an airport I overheard a little boy trying to tell his father about a plane he had seen take off. "Daddy, you, you know what I saw? I saw a p-plane an, an, an the plane it st-start-started and then then it went 'woosh.' " As he said "woosh" he threw up his arms in excitement. The father listened attentively to the story without interruption.

The secret of prevention of stuttering or stammering lies in a nonchalant attitude toward repetitious babbling of children. The stumbling speech of children is normal; attempts to correct it lead to frustration and, if continued, set up a block in the child's mind. Because stuttering is a recognized handicap, parents become frightened when their child repeats syllables; they stop him during his telling about some event, exciting to him but inconsequential to them, and instead of quietly listening, say, "Now stop a minute. Take a deep breath. Don't talk too fast." What they are saying in their minds is, "Don't stutter." Their anxiety is transferred to the child and, instead of helping him, they are adding to his frustration.

Students of speech of primitive tribes not only found no stutterer but no word in their languages to describe it. Stuttering is a man-made problem of civilization.

When your three- or four-year-old child, just learning to master the difficult art of speaking, garbles his words, pay no attention to his errors. What he is trying to say is important to him; let it be the same to you. Relax and listen. He doesn't know what stammering is; don't teach him. And another thing, if you take him to a doctor don't discuss the problem before the child. Focusing upon the condition will help create a problem that doesn't exist. Overly domineering parents who expect their children to be perfect may mold a sensitive one into a pattern of a stammerer. Such parents should themselves consult a psychiatrist the moment their child begins to stammer.

TICS

A tic means spasm or twitching of a group of muscles, mostly of the face. Tics vary from scarcely noticeable wrinkling of the forehead or blinking of the eyes to violent facial distortions, neck stretching, shoulder jerking, or combinations of all. A tic is a first cousin to stammering.

Practically all tics begin between ages seven and ten years and are due to nervous tension in home, school, or environment. Dr. Else Tarup, a pediatrician in Copenhagen, found the incidence of tics greatly increased during the German occupation of Denmark in World War II.

When your boy—boys are three times more apt to develop tics than girls—screws up his face in odd ways when excited, the most important thing to do at the moment is nothing. Scolding or punishing for "making silly faces" will fix the habit. Look for the cause; it likely will be tension: sibling rivalry, conflict between parent and child, difficulties in school, too much pressure to excel, or just the reaction of a highly tense and sensitive child to a competitive world.

As in early stammering, the most effective way of stopping tics is to disregard them while at the same time you search for the cause. Time, patience, and a little extra love are the most effective treatment.

Most of us have some little tic which has become part of our personality. Notice how many people under tension scratch their noses, pull their ears, clear their throats, touch their hair, make all sort of purposeless gestures. A woman explained how she transferred a tic from her face to her toe. Whenever she became excited she concentrated on wiggling her big toe. Her face remained calm. Not a bad idea, worth trying.

NAIL BITING

"Stop biting your nails," a mother repeats time after time. She emphasizes this command by stamping her foot or slapping offending hands, but all to no avail. The nail-biting habit once established is hard to break. Not all nail biting is due to nervous tension; although it is the primary cause, many children develop the habit through imitation.

When a child only a few years old begins to gnaw on his nails or pick at them don't call attention to his acts; he doesn't know he is in the first stage of becoming a confirmed nail biter. Cut his finger nails short, file down rough edges and corners, and let it go at that.

The nail-biting habit firmly fixed in an eight- to fifteen-year-old child is difficult to uproot. Boys are apt to continue the habit; pride makes most girls eventually quit. Instead of telling a girl how horrible her fingers look, tell her how pretty she is and how nice hands look with full fingernails. Nothing is more effective than appeals to pride and vanity.

A snappy little ten-year-old girl came to my office for a routine matter. I noticed her nails were bitten far back and in an offhand manner said, "Such a cute little girl and such pretty hands. Too bad you spoil them by biting your nails." Three weeks later I got a letter from her stating, "I thought you would like to know that I have quit biting my nails."

An eager twelve-year-old Boy Scout came in for examination for a merit badge in "Personal Health." I noticed his deeply bitten fingernails and said, "You've passed but I'll sign this form two weeks from today if your nails have grown out." It was a sort of mean thing to do. To my surprise, he came back in two weeks with full fingernails. I would have then signed anything for that earnest little fellow.

MASTURBATION

Inherited from past generations is the false notion that there is something vile about masturbation, that it leads to insanity, is an indication of sexual impotence, and that during puberty it causes acne.

Between the ages of two and five, normal children are all explorers; they find their genitals and in handling them experience a pleasurable sensation. It is normal, in no sense whatsoever abnormal, for children to play with their genitals or masturbate. It is accomplished in many ways: by fingering, riding on toys or pillows, rubbing the thighs together, rocking on hands and knees, etc.

Parents err in making an issue of masturbation by jerking their hands away, slapping them, and by look and word indicating that they are doing something dirty and disgusting.

Masturbation in children is in a sense like thumb sucking, a pleasurable escape from boredom and unhappiness. It is far more important to find out why the child engages in this practice than forcibly trying to stop it.

The cause of masturbation is not depravity of character but a product of excessive frustration. The more a parent furnishes substitute pleasures and diversions the sooner the habit will disappear. In any case, as the child grows older and develops interest in other activities at home and in school, he will spontaneously quit the habit.

During puberty, especially in boys, masturbation reappears. Again, the only harm arising therefrom is a feeling of guilt; some parents consider it a sin.

Stop worrying about this problem. Almost without exception little children and adolescent boys experiment with handling their genitals. The practice is physiological, not evil; no harm will come from it. Remember that.

BED WETTING

The seeds of later bed wetting may be planted by too persistent attempts at early toilet training. A child will practically train himself at age two and within a year will learn to remain dry most nights. When you put the child in training pants praise success and never, but never, scold or punish for errors. In the same spirit of friendly cooperation, discontinue diapers at night when you think the proper time has arrived. Again, give praise for a dry night and show no resentment about an occasional wet one. A child is less apt to become a chronic bed wetter who grows up in a family where happiness is dominant, criticism minimal, and a spirit of nonchalance prevails.

The three- to five-year-old child who not only wets the bed at night but has little control during the day should be thoroughly examined by a specialist. You may safely take it for granted, however, that the child who remains dry all day, and wets only at night has a normal urinary system.

For reasons unknown, four out of five bed wetters are boys. Up to age four or five the less said or done about occasional or even nightly bed wetting the better. It takes some children a long time to develop continence. Psychological disturbances brought on by stress, insecurity, insufficient attention, and a too critical attitude are the causes of most bed wetting. Take every opportunity to establish a relaxed atmosphere in the home. Avoid too much excitement, too scary TV programs, be liberal with praise to establish self-confidence. Some children are pleased with gold stars for the nights they remain dry. Time and patience eventually pay off.

What to do for the confirmed bed wetter six years old or older is a question not easily answered. Cutting down liquids after five o'clock in the afternoon doesn't do much good.

Getting the child up just before you go to bed may be helpful. The mistake usually made is that the child is not thoroughly wakened before going to the bathroom. He should walk, not be carried. The light should be turned on. He should be so wide-awake that he knows what he is doing. If still half-asleep, he doesn't distinguish between going to the toilet or going in bed.

The child who is anxious to correct his trouble may be helped by giving him an alarm clock which is set to ring before the time he usually wets. He gets up, turns off the alarm, and then goes to the toilet. The fact that he is considered mature enough to use an alarm clock, instead of being taken to the toilet by a parent, in itself is beneficial.

There are on the market a number of electrical devices which are placed on the bed or attached to the child: The moment urination begins a bell sounds or the child receives a slight electrical shock. He then gets up and completes urination in the toilet. Some doctors are very partial to these devices.

Shaming, punishing, making the boy wash his bed linen is all wrong. Promise of a new bicycle may be a good idea. Probably the bike had better be given before the bed has remained dry for a week, as a matter of faith. If the boy doesn't remain dry and doesn't get the bike, the bed wetting will be worse than ever.

Drugs to relax the bladder and tighten the sphincter (the shut-off muscle at the opening of the bladder) may do some good. I'm inclined to think that the faith transmitted from doctor to parent and child is more effective than the medicine.

The most comforting fact is that eventually very nearly all bed wetting stops. Oh, glorious day.

TEETH GRINDING

The habit of teeth grinding during sleep appears in mentally re-tarded children and those who live in the atmosphere of unhappy and broken homes.

To find and eliminate the cause is time consuming. In the meantime, a set of teeth have to be saved and, if I interpret rightly the tone of letters I receive, the sanity of parents who say they can't stand the noise of teeth grinding another night.

Go to your dentist and have him make a plastic tooth guard somewhat similar to those made for football players. The guard, worn at night, will not stop the teeth-grinding habit but it will stop the noise and save the teeth.

FRUSTRATIONS

Frustrations begin in early infancy and continue throughout life; they are unavoidable. So much has been written about the harmful effects of frustrations in children that fear of them leads parents to permissiveness, overprotection, and indulgence. A little frustration during childhood is a good thing. If controlled it immunizes the child against bigger frustrations during adult life. No one now or in the foreseeable future will be able to go through life without the crushing jolts of disappointments. So why not let a child struggle with and overcome a few frustrations instead of trying to shield him against them?

The three year old tries to build a house with blocks; they continue to fall over and in a fit of anger he scatters them about the room. Sitting down on the floor and building a house for the child does no good; it only makes him feel more inadequate. At this point the art of teaching comes in—the ability to guide without taking over, encouragement with a light attitude of "Whoops, they fell over, try again," then a word of praise for even a minor success.

Children are eager to progress beyond their abilities, a noteworthy characteristic to be fostered, yet at the same time held in check. Children have to learn that failures are a part of life. Frustrations can't be avoided. All we can do is to try to teach a child to accept with equanimity a broken dolly, a stuck toy, a lost roller skate key, so that later in life he will be strong enough to meet the impact of not making the team, of disappointment in love, of failure to get a coveted promotion.

A good motto to hold before child or adult is: If you can't get what you want, get something better.

BAD LANGUAGE

Spirited children almost without exception go through a phase of bad language. They pick up words from neighbor children as well as at home. Father may be in the garage fixing his car. Something goes wrong and he lets loose with a forceful expletive not realizing that his son is standing by. Children hear spicy words, are impressed by their forcefulness, and innocently use them.

Expressions such as "lousy," "you stinker," "you dirty rat," "drop dead," are inelegant but less meaningful to children than adults. "Kill you," simply means removal of an interference, nothing more. A seven-year-old boy disliked his teacher and wrote a poem, the last two lines of which read, "I'll grind you to a bloody pulp and then I'll eat you gulp, gulp, gulp." His teacher was smart; instead of punishing, she laughingly said, "That sounds like rather rough treatment but I like the rhyme and rhythm of your poem." Shortly thereafter the boy said to his parents, "You know, I'm beginning to like my teacher."

It is maddening to have to listen to your child's objectionable words repeated again and again, but be patient, he is only letting off steam and trying to act older than his age. Instead of showing annoyance dress up one of his expressions. He says "fool"; you say, "Oh, fool, schmool." Beat him at his own game.

Even though children have no knowledge of the meaning of profane or obscene words, they should be told that such language is not permissible and may not be used. Telling a child that he is a nasty, dirty boy is wrong because he is not; he is only repeating what he has heard. Punishing or washing his mouth with soap will only make him angry and stimulate him to use the words away from home. A child old enough to use taboo words is old enough to understand that good manners do not allow their use. Needless to say, a good example at home is quite essential. I'll admit it is a bit difficult to stop a boy's use of simple profanity when he hears on television a past President of the United States say, "Give 'em Hell" and "I don't give a damn."

LYING

"Lying is an abomination unto the Lord and an ever present help in time of trouble." This was the youngster's answer to the Sunday School teacher's request for a definition of lying.

Every adult has, upon frequent occasions, utilized this jointed quotation as an escape from a difficult situation.

Children four or five years old don't know what lying is. Living in an age of fantasy they make up all kinds of stories. The smarter and more imaginative they are, the taller the tales. The child who feels neglected and belittled increases his own feeling of importance —so necessary for every child's happiness—by concocting stories about his prowess and possessions. Enjoy rather than criticize his outlandish tales. The very fact that you listen attentively to his fabulous yarns—even add a few touches of your own—is a means of giving the child the attention he craves.

The age of discretion—the ability to distinguish between right and wrong—doesn't develop until about age seven or eight. Then is the time to point out by word and deed, mostly deed, what honesty is. In spite of your best intentions your child will sometime catch you in a lie. A neighbor drops in and says, "How do you like my new hat?" You kindly say, "I think it's lovely." That evening you jokingly describe the hat to your husband and say how awful it looked. Your child pipes up with, "Mommy, you told a lie." Right then and there you will have to battle with the problem of differentiating between bad lies and white lies. Explain the difference to your child by examples. "Supposing you threw a ball through a neighbor's window. If, to escape punishment or paying for the window, you said you didn't do it, that would be a bad lie.

"You heard me tell our good neighbor that her hat was pretty. She would have been hurt if I had told her that I thought it looked terrible. We are good friends and want to stay that way. No one was harmed by my little lie. You see the difference?" A bad lie is one you tell to protect yourself or to avoid trouble of your own making; a white lie is one that is told to avoid hurting somebody's feelings.

Children rapidly learn to tell the truth by example rather than by precept. The father who openly boasts about a shady business deal or bribes a policeman will not accomplish much at home in preaching honesty to his children.

STEALING

The three-year-old child who tries to take a toy from a four year old gets a quick, sharp lesson in the meaning of possession. A child, even at age two, should begin to learn the meaning of having certain things which belong to him and him alone. At the same time, he should be taught that other members of the family have similar rights of ownership. Parents will have to act as arbiters when a fight is on for possession and explain the meaning of "mine and thine."

Children often take some toy or object from a neighbor's house. Don't make a scene about this natural instinct. The child saw something he liked and took it; he didn't steal it. Simply explain that the item will have to be returned. If he is old enough to recognize that there was a touch of thievery in his act, don't humiliate him when you insist that he take it back. Emphasize, without heat, that we don't take things that don't belong to us.

I doubt if there is a school child who has not at some time done a bit of pilfering. It's so easy to take a nickel or dime from mother's purse for that irresistible candy bar. When the evidence is unquestionable, you will have to point out that taking money from mother's purse—even though it's in the family—is stealing and that stealing is wrong. Give the youngster a weekly allowance and make him live with it. You won't be doing your child a disservice or be planting seeds of mistrust if you keep your purse out of temptation's way for a time.

Seven-year-old Helen came home from school one day, sad and noncommunicative. She went directly to her room where her mother found her weeping and asked what had happened. Between sobs Helen said, "I—stole—a—candy—bar." Her mother relieved that nothing worse had happened said, "You know what? I once stole a weenie from a butcher shop when I was a little girl. Your grandmother made me go to the meat market the next day and pay for it. Tomorrow you go to the school store, pay for the candy bar, and tell the storekeeper you are sorry. He will understand. I know you will never do it again."

A child who steals is not a criminal. He will learn honesty from honest parents.

Stealing by junior high or high school students is quite another and serious matter requiring reevaluation of home and school influences and investigation of motives; if persistent, it would be wise to consult a counselor, religious leader, or psychiatrist before a police record is established.

GUNS

"Michael runs around the home with his toy pistol and shouts, 'Bang, bang you're dead.' Every time I hear him say this I cringe and wonder whether I should take the gun away from him."

Let Michael have his gun. Every boy loves to have a toy pistol; it gives him a feeling of being independent and grown up. I don't believe a toy pistol does any child in a respectable family the slightest harm. When a child says, "Bang, you're dead," he is only playing; the idea of actual killing doesn't enter his head.

"Cops and robbers" played with toy machineguns is a harmless popular game. Arguing about who is "dead" seems to be half the fun. Boys from seven to ten years old like to support the image of being the tough little savages they actually are.

Toy guns are no more a bad influence than cowboy suits. Both represent freedom from restraints. That's why adults like "Westerns."

A child is no more apt to become an outlaw from playing with guns than he is to become a saint from playing with toy churches.

Real pistols or revolvers have no place in the home. The danger of someone being killed or wounded by accidental discharge of weapons in the home far outweighs their value as protection against marauders. Hunting rifles and shotguns should be kept in securely locked cabinets. A dismantled gun or one from which the ammunition has been removed is unsafe. Nothing is more fascinating to a boy than assembling a real gun. He might find ammunition. Then "Bang, you're dead" might become a reality.

chapter Thirteen

CALORIES & GROWTH

CALORIC REQUIREMENTS OF INFANTS AND CHILDREN

While mothers are figuring out ways of reducing their own intake of calories, they are worrying that their skinny children are getting too few.

Babies and children need lots of calories to grow. After growth is complete this whole business of calories becomes extremely simple. Every calorie, regardless of the form in which it is consumed, alcohol or broccoli, furnishes a certain amount of energy which is spent in activity or stored up as fat. Eat more calories than are needed for the wear and tear of daily living and you get fat; eat fewer than are needed and you lose weight. That is all there is to weight control. However, I'm not writing about adults and far be it from me to so simplify the matter of weight control that all the fun is taken out of discussing the newest dietary fad over a luncheon of creamed chicken, hot buttered rolls, and date pudding with whipped cream.

So, let's get back to the calorie requirements of children. During the first year of life an infant requires daily about 50 calories per pound of body weight. These calculations are based on what the average baby should weigh from month to month.

For example, a baby weighing seven pounds will require about 7 times 50 or 350 calories per day. When the baby is six months old, he should have about 700 calories per day on the basis of an average weight of fourteen pounds. Remember that the number of calories a baby should have, and what he will take, often don't match. Some babies to the great pleasure of the mother "eat like little pigs" and are overweight; others with a different kind of metabolism are skimpy eaters and are underweight. So long as both are healthy and growing, why worry. We adults are not alike by far; neither are infants.

At about age eighteen months the child's appetite lessens and his caloric requirements begin to fall. (This is the time when mothers try to keep up the high caloric intake and when the less hungry infant rebels.) By age three years the caloric requirements have fallen to 40 calories per pound of body weight. An eighteen-year-old boy, weighing 140 pounds, will require 3500 calories or approximately 25 calories per pound.

	AGE	WEIGHT in Pounds	HEIGHT in Inches	CALORIES per Day
INFANTS	1– 6 mos.	6–13	21–24	330–750
	6–12 mos.	13–21	24–29	700–950
CHILDREN	1– 3	27	34	1300
	4– 6	40	43	1700
	7– 9	60	51	2100
	10–12	79	57	2500
BOYS	13–15	108	64	3200
	16–19	139	69	3700
GIRLS	13–15	108	63	2500
	16–19	120	64	2400

Above are the figures of average heights and weights of children from ages one month to nineteen years, and the average number of calories they require for normal activity and growth. Most children tend to be skinny, some are average weight, and a few are fat. Look at a picture of a group of children ages nine to twelve at a summer camp where clothing is minimal and you will see an odd assortment of shapes and sizes, all normal.

Just because your children weigh more or less than indicated in these tables or are a few inches shorter or taller, don't conclude that they are abnormal. I repeat, these are average figures.

CALORIES COUNT—SO COUNT 'EM

Every calorie we eat comes from carbohydrates (sugars and starches), protein, and fat. The amount of water taken with or between meals has absolutely nothing to do with calories. Each gram (450 grams in one pound) of carbohydrate or protein yields 4 calories; every gram of fat such as butter, digestible oils (there are no calories in mineral oil), and the fat of meat or fish yields 9 calories.

A calorie to the scientist is that amount of heat necessary to raise the temperature of 1 gram of water 1 degree centigrade. To us ordinary people a calorie is the amount of energy derived from the digestion and assimilation of a certain amount of food.

People often go astray in calculating the number of calories in a meal because they forget that a small amount of any kind of fat adds many calories.

For example, an ordinary serving of spinach, or any other leafy vegetable, contains only about 4 grams of starch and protein, the rest is indigestible roughage. These 4 grams multiplied by 4 calories per gram equals 16 calories in the spinach. The "good" cook makes the spinach tasty by adding a pat of butter which weighs 5 grams. This weight in fat multiplied by 9 calories per gram adds 45 calories or almost three times the number of calories in the spinach itself.

The obvious answer to food preparation for the youngster (yourself or your husband), who wishes to lose weight, is to cut down sharply on fats; addition of fats is in order for the underweight child or adult.

The accompanying table lists the common foods eaten by most children. The caloric values are listed for specific portions, but bear in mind that such figures, although taken from authentic sources, are variable. For example, lean meat contains fewer calories than meat richly grained with fat. Incidentally, cheap cuts of meat are just as nutritious as expensive cuts. A slice of standard commercial bread contains fewer calories than a slice of home-baked bread.

Look over these food values. It will be fun to figure out the calories in the average meals your children eat. It will be a good idea at the same time to calculate the calories you eat.

Food and amount		Calories
CEREALS and **BREAD**	Bread, 1 slice	75
	Cracker, saltine (1)	15
	Cracker, graham (1)	40
	Cream of Wheat, ½ cup cooked	70
	Dry cereal, 1 cup	80
	Griddle cake, 4″ diameter	75
	Oatmeal, ½ cup cooked	75
	Waffle, 1 average size	225
DAIRY PRODUCTS	Butter, 1 pat	50
	Butter, 1 teaspoon	35
	Cheese, American, 1 small serving	80
	Cream, 20%, 1 tablespoon	30
	Egg, boiled (1)	75
	Egg, fried (1)	100
	Ice cream, ¼ pint	150
	Milk, skim, 6 oz. (1 med. glass)	65
	Milk, whole, 6 oz. (1 med. glass)	125
	Milk, breast, 1 oz.	21
FRUITS	Apple, 1 large	100
	Applesauce, ⅓ cup sweetened	55
	Banana, 1 small	100

	Fruit cocktail, ⅓ cup	65
	Grapefruit, ½ small	45
	Orange juice, ½ cup	50
FRUITS	Orange, whole, 1 medium size	75
Continued	Peaches, canned, 2 halves in syrup	75
	Pears, canned, 2 halves in syrup	75
	Strawberries, frozen, ½ cup	55
	Tomato juice, ½ cup	25

	Baked beans, ⅓ cup	105
	Beets, diced, ⅓ cup	25
	Cabbage, cooked, ⅓ cup	8
	Carrots, ⅓ cup	20
	Corn, canned, ⅓ cup	60
	Corn, fresh, 1 medium ear	100
VEGETABLES	Lettuce, ¼ head	10
	Peas, canned, ⅓ cup	35
	Potato, baked, 1 small	85
	Potato, mashed, ⅓ cup	100
	Spinach, cooked, ⅓ cup	15
	String beans, ⅓ cup	12
	Tomatoes, cooked, ⅓ cup	12

	Bacon, 3 slices	100
	Chicken, stewed, ½ breast or 1 thigh	195
	Fish, broiled, 1 serving	150
	Frankfurter, 1 average	100
MEATS	Hamburger, 1 medium size	140
and	Lamb chop, 1 broiled	215
FISH	Pork chop, 1 medium size fried	235
	Pork roast, 1 serving	170
	Roast beef, 1 slice 3 x 2 x ¼"	100
	Sausage patty, 3 small	180
	Steak, 1 piece 4 x 1 x 1"	105

	Food	Calories
	Apple pie, ⅙	265
	Carbonated beverages, 6 oz. bottle	65
	Chocolate malted milk shake, regular	480
	Chocolate soda, fountain	400
	Chocolate sundae, ½ cup	375
	Fig bar (1)	55
	Ginger snap (1 small)	20
SWEETS	Hershey bar, large size	270
	Honey, 1 teaspoon	16
	Jams, commercial, 1 tablespoon	60
	Jelly beans, 10 beans	66
	Maple syrup, 1 tablespoon	50
	Orange ice, ⅓ cup	95
	Sugar, 1 teaspoon	16
	Maltose, 1 tablespoon	28

	Food	Calories
	Almonds, shelled, ⅓ cup	300
NUTS	Peanut butter, 1 tablespoon	100
	Peanuts, shelled, ⅓ cup	210
	Pecans, shelled, 12 halves	104

Fatty. Joe was nine years old and weighed 120 pounds. His father weighed 225 pounds and his mother a solid 175. And there is the answer to most cases of obesity in children.

Statistics show that when both parents are overweight about 75 percent of their children follow the same pattern; if one parent is overweight the percentage falls to 45, and if neither are overweight to 10 percent.

Heredity may play a small factor in obesity but the basic cause remains monotonously the same—just too much food. "Something wrong with the glands," is a popular but mistaken excuse for obesity. Not more than one child in a thousand is obese because of some disease of the glands. There is no escaping the truth; children and adults are fat because they eat too much.

The old cliche that a fat child is always happy and jolly is wrong. Obese boys and girls are frequently unhappy; often they are miserable. They may seem placid because they sit around the house during their spare time and watch television, but actually they would much rather be outside playing if it were not for the taunts—not meant to be cruel—that are hurled at them by the neighborhood children.

No child likes to be called Fatty. Joe was no exception. He didn't play with the other boys because he couldn't run fast and because the kids teased him.

Solution to Joe's overweight problem is absolutely hopeless unless the parents lead the way and make weight reductions a project for the family, and an interesting game for the child. All the doctor can do is to emphasize the importance of weight reduction for the entire family and explain quite frankly that overweight is a menace to health.

It's easy to outline a proper diet for weight reduction but difficult to furnish incentive to carry it out to the point of success. Treatment of overweight is very much like the treatment of alcoholism; until the victim makes up his or her mind to lose weight all the diets and preaching are totally wasted.

Joe's parents were not too interested in a family plan of weight reduction; they just wanted Joe to reduce. To expect young Joe to lose weight in an environment of rich gravies, tasty cookies, and evening snacks is unrealistic.

I'll lay a wager and give long odds that when Joe is twenty he will weigh 200 pounds.

Obesity, a Psychological Problem.   There is a vast difference between the active, well-adjusted, chubby child, and the lethargic, introverted, obese child.

Chubby boys or girls who live in well-adjusted family environments eventually solve their own weight problem. Your assistance in such simple measures as avoiding rich foods (bad for adults, too), supplying sugar-free soft drinks, skim milk instead of whole milk, offering for snacks fruit, carrot sticks, and unbuttered crackers, and gently, very gently, suggesting smaller servings of mashed potatoes will help to keep weight stationary.

Shortly after puberty when your chubby daughter begins to ogle the boy across the street and decides that he might be more apt to return the look if she were not so fat, weight reduction is about to begin. Appeals to vanity are justifiable: "You are a very pretty girl. You would look awfully cute in that little dress we saw in the window." Chiding about diet control won't work.

The chubby boy in his teens can, by very subtle suggestions, be stimulated to take interest in athletics, Boy Scout activities, camps, and outdoor play of all kinds which will keep him away from sitting in the house and nibbling. Pride in his slowly developing athletic prowess plus lots of praise for even the slightest progress in weight control eventually will win. Indulge in violent arguments about the amount of food he eats and all will be lost.

Most pitiable is the obese child who is so because of psychological stress brought on by a variety of causes. The possessive mother constantly feeds her child because she doesn't want him to leave her. He mustn't play rough for fear he'll be hurt. She plies him with food to keep him at her side.

In a broken home loss of security is compensated for by food. The hopelessly spoiled child who gets everything he wants may turn to food. The unwanted, unloved child discovers that there is comfort in eating.

Suddenly, and often with a feeling of guilt, the mother consults her doctor and asks for a strict diet that will get her obese child thin quickly. She wants drugs to stop the appetite and hormone injections that will whip up the metabolism. None of these will do any permanent good.

Reducing is not the cure for obesity in psychologically disturbed children. Only recognition of the basic cause of obesity will be successful, and only after a long struggle. Talk with your doctor, visit a psychiatrist, and with them study your problem. The going will be rough; it's hard to change habits and traits which are already ingrained. Stay with it. Your child will eventually be grateful to you.

Breakfast.   Children should eat some breakfast, more than just a swallow of orange juice, before dashing off to school. The youngster who eats no breakfast becomes irritable and inattentive by midmorning. During recess he eats a candy bar or two. Consequently, at lunchtime he is not hungry, and again at about three o'clock in the afternoon, he droops.

Irregular eating habits in the family, slack discipline about getting up in time, association with playmates who brag about staying in bed until the last minute, and lack of appetite are responsible for the no-breakfast attitude. The family which routinely on school days has a specific time for breakfast will not have the problem of children skipping this important meal. Children trained to get up at a specific time and accustomed to eating breakfast regularly during preschool years will continue to do so. It is in those families where it is a custom for each member to make his own toast or get his own cereal that skipping breakfast becomes routine.

An orderly household doesn't always solve the problem; some children with capricious appetites don't like the standard breakfast of fruit, cereal, toast, eggs, bacon, or any of these items. There's nothing wrong in catering to the child with a nonconformist appetite. A high school girl said, "I'd eat breakfast if you let me have a bowl of soup and crackers." She got it. Why not? It's no more work to open and heat a can of soup than to fry an egg. A skinny boy stopped rebelling at breakfast when his mother agreed to prepare a hamburger for him each morning. Some youngsters will gladly eat a peanut butter and jelly sandwich for breakfast.

I can hear the reverberations of mothers emphatically retorting, "I don't run a short order restaurant." True, you don't, but by catering to a few eccentricities you'll avoid unpleasant arguments, most of which you'll lose, and your child will be getting the food he needs. Don't worry about vitamins, he can get those at dinner time.

Improper Dieting.　Your teen-age high-school girl reads a glamour magazine, looks in her mirror, and decides she's too fat. Without medical consultation and contrary to your advice she goes on what she considers a reducing diet. Breakfast consists of a slice of toast. At 11 o'clock she is famished and eats a candy bar. For lunch all she will eat is a sandwich and a coke. After school is out the pangs of hunger are stilled by potato chips. For dinner she eats a piece of meat and a huge serving of lettuce (doesn't know that lettuce contains practically nothing but roughage and water), and perhaps some fruit for dessert. A few more potato chips, or popcorn and a soft drink or two close the day.

The calories consumed, approximately 1,300 if only 20 potato chips are eaten (8 calories per large chip), are mostly just units of energy deficient in essential vitamins and minerals.

Such a diet maintained for weeks results in weight reduction but does not furnish the anticipated glamour and sparkle. In fact, the result is just the opposite: a sallow, pimply face, and no pep. No wonder she's irritable and hard to live with.

Dr. Robert W. Hillman of New York says, "The teen-age girl is the worst fed member of the household. Up to three-quarters of the teen-aged girls may be deficient in such nutrients as vitamins, calcium, and iron. The serious implication of this," he adds, "is that many of these girls become teen-age mothers. One-third of first-born children are born to girls under twenty."

It is a rather sorry reflection upon our education in nutrition that in a country with bulging granaries so many people are improperly fed. We are not ill-fed because of economic status; many good foods are cheap.

Fads in dieting are silly. Eventually all fail and one comes right back to the necessity of eating proper foods from year to year. Loss or gain of weight is purely a matter of the number of calories that go into the stomach. Yes, calories do count.

Diet For Your Teen-Age Girl.   The average teen-age girl requires 20 calories per pound to maintain weight. The eighteen-year-old miss, five feet four inches tall, should weigh about 120 pounds, plus or minus ten pounds.

The girl 20 percent or more overweight at age eighteen should stop the trend toward obesity now. Her caloric intake for maintenance should be 20 calories per pound of what she *should* weigh not of what she *does* weigh. To reduce she should eat not more than 10 calories per pound.

On page 228 is a reducing diet, taken in part from *The Teenager's Guide to Diet and Health,* by Robert S. Goodhart, M.D., to bring "Fatty" back to her proper weight.

On this diet of approximately 1100 calories—no candy bar (200 cal.), ice-cream soda (400 cal.), or potato chips (8 cal. per large chip) between meals—loss of weight at the rate of about one pound a week is guaranteed.

To maintain this diet requires determination, will power, no cheating, and a lot of moral support from you. There is no easy road to weight reduction.

This diet contains the five building blocks of all foods: carbohydrates (starch and sugar), protein, fat, minerals, and vitamins.

The teen-ager should weigh herself in the morning twice a week but not expect to get rid of that blubber in a couple of weeks. Everyone's weight varies a pound or two from day to day so warn her not to get mad if some week she seems to have lost no weight.

If she will take some exercise daily, continue this well-balanced diet for a month, she will feel better, look better, and have more zest for life.

After she has gotten down to her desired weight, she may slowly add to her diet, but should continue to weigh herself every week.

REDUCING DIET FOR TEEN-AGERS

	Calories
½ glass orange or tomato juice or ½ grapefruit (no sugar)	50
1 slice bread	75
½ pat butter	25
1 egg boiled or poached	75
1 glass skimmed milk	85
Coffee	0

Dry cereal, ½ cup skim milk, and 1 level teaspoonful of sugar, may be substituted for the egg, toast and butter.

	Calories
1 thin slice of lean beef, lamb, chicken, or a small frankfurter	100
Average serving of cooked or raw vegetables, string beans, tomatoes, carrots or	
a large serving of lettuce, cucumber, spinach, cabbage, broccoli, cauliflower, or similar leafy vegetables	25
1 slice bread	75
½ pat butter	25
1 glass skim milk	85
Raw fruit: peach, small apple, pear, orange	50
Calorie free soft drink	0

A sandwich of two thin slices of bread with peanut butter or a small hamburger (no fat) on a bun, a glass of skim milk, and raw fruit may be substituted for the above.

	Calories
Small serving of lean meat or a modest portion of broiled fish	150
Vegetable similar to those under Lunch	25
Salad: Lettuce, tomatoes, cucumbers (calorie free dressing)	25
1 slice bread	75
½ pat butter	25
Fresh fruit or dietetic cooked fruit	50
1 glass skim milk	85
Coffee—tea	0

Height Is Inherited.   Parents want their sons to be tall and broad shouldered; their daughters to be slim and petite. What they want and what they get have no relation to each other; that was decided generations before they approached the marriage altar. "Short" genes and "tall" genes are passed in pure or mixed form from one generation to another. Children inherit growth potential just as they inherit blue eyes or black hair.

The fact that children today, in general, are slightly taller than their grandparents doesn't mean that a race of giants is about to be produced but that the childrens' total growth potential has been attained through better food and adequate vitamins. Excess vitamins will not increase growth.

Every normal child has in his cells an inborn factor that determines whether he shall grow to 6 feet 6 inches or shall stop growing at 5 feet and, as of now, nothing can be done to change it. Illness lasting for a year or more may slow growth but if followed by complete recovery will not stunt growth. As soon as health is restored a growth spurt follows and continues until the delay has been overcome. However, the child who has chronic incurable anemia, digestive disturbances, heart or kidney disease will almost certainly be stunted.

What parents want is a hormone to make their boys grow and an "anti-hormone" to slow the process in their daughters; no such substances are available.

"Now hear this!" Hormones will make only that child grow who is deficient in hormones. The thyroid gland in the neck and the bean-sized pituitary gland at the base of the brain furnish growth hormones. Deficiency in secretion of one or both of these glands causes certain types of dwarfism; extracts from these glands will stimulate growth but they will not increase one bit the stature of a child whose glands are normal.

Administration of pituitary extracts to a normal child may upset the hormonal balance and cause permanent damage to ovaries or testicles. Laboratory tests are available to determine whether the thyroid and pituitary glands are functioning normally. Avail yourselves of these tests before subjecting your undersized boy to "growth shots" in the faint hope that they may do some good.

At present research scientists at the National Pituitary Agency in Baltimore, Maryland, are seeking a pure growth hormone. In the future growth may be increased in the normal child; today it is impossible.

All you can do for your tall daughter is to advise her to accept her stature, to walk up straight, and learn to carry herself gracefully. A tall girl who looks the world in the eye surrounds herself with an aura of stateliness and charm. To the boy who is short and unhappy because he is ineligible for many sports, you can only emphasize that it is what's above the neck that counts.

chapter Fourteen

MENTAL & PHYSICAL RETARDATION

MENTAL RETARDATION

A baby is born; it is anticipated that he will be normal. When at any point steps of advancement, such as smiling, sitting up, walking, talking, are not being taken or are far behind schedule, the question of mental retardation creeps into your consciousness. As a normal mother you wait weeks or months while you hope and pray that your worries are unfounded. Finally, you consult a doctor.

Except in obvious cases, it is often difficult for a doctor accurately to diagnose mental retardation or to determine its degree, especially in infants below one year of age. Your doctor most likely will refer you to a psychiatrist or a child guidance clinic for evaluation where you learn the awful truth that your child is definitely retarded.

First of all you ask, "Why did this happen to me? What have I done wrong?" Neither you nor your husband have done anything wrong. Clear from your minds any feeling of guilt. It is not your fault. A kind and loving God never sent anybody a deformed child

231

as punishment. Only because something went wrong with your child's brain before birth, or as a result of infection or accident, do you have a mentally retarded child.

Wipe away feelings of guilt and bitterness to make room for planning with your husband and other children in the family a program of doing what you can for your unfortunate child.

His intelligence quotient is a rather fixed thing. Destroyed brain cells cannot be replaced but the good cells remaining can, by patient training, be stimulated to raise the child's status to a higher level.

Seek the aid of a social worker who specializes in handling retarded children. Instead of hiding your backward child from friends, bring him out with no apologies and make him part of the family. Open recognition of your problem at home and in the neighborhood will get helpful cooperation.

Write to the National Association for Retarded Children, Inc., 386 Park Avenue South, New York, New York, for pamphlets, leaflets, and a reading list. Go to your local library and get Pearl Buck's book, *The Child Who Never Grew,* about her own mentally retarded child.

Public attitude toward mental retardation has changed from hopeless indifference to intelligent interest since the Kennedy Foundation invested millions of dollars in its study. The fact that about 2 to 3 percent of children have some degree of mental retardation means that you will find others in the community with similar problems. Get together, form study groups, learn and get strength from each other. You will be surprised at what can be accomplished in the development of a mentally retarded child toward fitting him into some simple niche in society.

Leonard was mentally retarded. He went to public school a few years but could not advance beyond the first grade. His parents, in the low middle income bracket, could not afford private schools or tutoring. With the aid of volunteer teaching and home tutoring, Leonard learned to read simple words, write, and do simple arithmetic. Having noted that Leonard was happiest when puttering about in their small garden, the parents went to the local florist to see if they could get him a job. The florist, an understanding man with a character as fine as his flowers, gave Leonard, at age sixteen, a menial job. He has worked in this greenhouse fifteen years and is quite content. Except for a little spending money, all his earnings are set aside for the day when his parents will no longer be around to care for him.

To such parents I bow in profound admiration.

CEREBRAL PALSY

Injury to the brain before or during delivery is the primary cause of cerebral palsy. The extent of brain injury and its location differ in all cases and determine how seriously the baby is affected.

Parents hear the words, cerebral palsy, and get a mental picture of a totally helpless, spastic child. That's not right. A child who has suffered brain damage may be spastic in one or all extremities or may have nothing more than paralysis or spasticity of isolated muscles.

Mental levels depend entirely upon which portion of the brain has been damaged and how severely. Cerebral palsy varies in degree from total physical and mental helplessness to such a minor thing as drooping of one eyelid.

What shall be done for the spastic child is, of course, related to the degree of handicap. Home care for educable children, during early years when love and security of parents are of utmost importance, appears to be most successful. Need for special schools or training centers is determined later. Each state has a Crippled Children's Service to lend aid to children who require operations, braces, physical therapy, help in learning to write, walk, or talk.

For guidance and information write to: The National Society for Crippled Children and Adults, 2023 West Ogden Avenue, Chicago, Illinois 60612, or to the United Cerebral Palsy Association, 321 West 44th Street, New York, New York 10036.

A classmate in medical school was severely spastic but mentally alert, in fact, above average in mental ability. Writing, walking, talking were a tremendous effort. His determination was boundless. He asked no help. Today he is a famous radiologist (x-ray specialist). I'm sorry I never met his parents; they must have been outstanding.

MONGOLISM

Mongolism, one of the commonest causes of severe mental retardation, is due to an error in the development of the chromosomes (centers of life), in every cell in the baby's body. Each cell instead of having the normal number of forty-six chromosomes has forty-seven. Why the forty-seventh develops and how it causes such profound changes is unknown.

There is no treatment for the disease itself. All mongoloid children are mentally retarded, some more severely than others; none are educable in the sense that they will be able to take normal places in society and become self-supporting.

The slanting or Oriental eyes and other characteristics make it possible in most instances for the doctor to diagnose mongolism at birth. There is no escaping the fact that parents should be told the tragic news at the earliest appropriate time. After many questions have been answered and tears temporarily dried, this question arises: "Shall the baby be cared for at home or sent to an institution?" The answer almost invariably is and should be: "Take the baby home." Mongoloid babies do far better at home than in an institution; they are easy to care for, are affable and happy. The idea of avoiding attachment by institutionalizing the baby shortly after birth seems altogether wrong. A feeling of guilt often tortures parents who send their baby away before he is given a chance in the home.

When the baby is three to five years old, then, after consideration of the child's mental condition, other children in the family, economic circumstances, religion, and a lot of other factors, a reasoned decision can be made. The parents and they alone must make the final decision between home or institutional care.

HOME OR INSTITUTIONAL CARE

"Shall a hopelessly, mentally defective child be placed in an institution?" This question might be answered with a quick yes, by those who haven't faced the problem. The answer is not quite that simple.

In my syndicated newspaper column, a letter written by a woman who faced this decision was published. She wrote:

"We have three normal boys. Three years ago our daughter was born. Slowly we realized she wasn't developing normally. Two specialists told us our child had what they called cerebral agenesis (lack of development of the brain). They said nothing could be done and advised institutional care.

"My husband favored this move but I am still hoping for a miracle. I can't bring myself to part with my daughter. She's mine. I gave birth to her. I'm worried about how my boys will feel about having an idiot sister in the home. Supposing something should happen to me, who then will take care of her? Please tell me what to do."

Feeling inadequate to answer this mother's call for help, I sought the opinion of our readers. Answers were many and mostly from parents of severely retarded children; 56 percent advised institutional care, 44 percent advised keeping the child at home.

Excerpts from two letters from each group follow:

"I am a mother of two severely retarded boys, ages nine and eleven. The boys are deaf, dumb, and blind and completely helpless. They had to be spoon fed and diapered. The younger one had convulsions. They both cried out in the night.

"Five years ago my daughter was born. She is all our boys are not. We didn't know how wonderful life could be until she came into our lives.

"In desperation we made application for the boys to be admitted to the Lincoln State School, Lincoln, Illinois. After a long wait they were accepted. We visit them every three or four weeks.

They are always clean and well cared for. We have met many nice people who have their children there and we seem to feel close because we share the same grief.

"We are a family once again and can do things together. It's wonderful to be able to walk out of the house, just to the store after being in for almost ten years."

"We have three children: a daughter sixteen, a son eleven, and a three-year-old daughter we call our 'Special Baby.' When told that our baby was mentally hopeless we were brokenhearted. Our other children were the ones who saw us through the difficult months that followed. Their friends and ours come to our home just as they always have.

"The thought of institutionalizing her has never crossed our minds. We receive more from this baby than we can give her."

"I firmly believe the retarded baby you speak of should be institutionalized immediately. I would never burden my children with the care of such a child after I am gone. I lived with a retarded brother forty years."

"We have a mentally retarded boy who is twenty-four years old and a great consolation to us. The other four children are married and gone. We feel we have someone besides ourselves to care for."

Although I favor institutional care for noneducable, mentally retarded children, the following experience with a patient jolted me.

A couple from southern Illinois brought their seven-year-old boy, Marvin, to the Children's Memorial Hospital in Chicago. He was a "blue baby," but worse, he was severely mentally retarded. He could not be toilet trained. He was able to speak no word; his only response to attention of any kind was a guttural grunt. He was able to walk, but because of his deformed heart, had to sit down after walking a half-block.

When the parents requested operation it was explained that

his heart defect could be corrected but that the operation would not improve his mental condition.

Operation on his heart was successful. Upon their return for a checkup examination six months later, the mother, with tears of gratitude in her eyes, clasped my hand and proudly said, "Doctor, it's wonderful. Now Marvin can walk with me all the way to the post office without sitting down."

After considering all phases of what shall be done with severely mentally retarded childen, only this I know for sure—the depths of mother love have never been measured.

PHENYLKETONURIA (PKU)

All newborn infants before leaving the hospital should be tested for PKU, a metabolic disorder which causes mental retardation. About one baby in ten thousand lacks in his system an enzyme or substance needed to break up completely a protein called phenylalanine which, if it builds up in the blood, causes brain damage.

Laws have been passed in some states making tests for PKU obligatory on all newborn children. If a test is positive, all that is needed for normal mental development is to put the baby on a special diet which excludes the protein harmful to the brain. The diet, not prepared at home but purchased ready-made, is expensive. State health departments defray the cost to those who need financial help.

PHYSICAL HANDICAPS

What would you do if the misfortune of giving birth to a deformed child should befall you? We are not concerned with such minor defects as a hairy mole, an extra toe or finger, a missing lobe of an ear; these and other simple deformities are easily corrected or, in the course of years, are accepted as part of one's appearance.

We are concerned with approximately 2 percent of babies born with serious defects of lip, palate, spinal cord, heart, lungs, diaphragm, esophagus, intestine, rectum, urinary bladder, or extremities. Some of these deformities require surgical correction as soon after birth as possible, and in this sense are emergencies. However, with few exceptions, delay of surgery for twenty-four, even forty-eight hours, is not going to jeopardize the outcome.

Parents are helpless when suddenly faced with any of these unanticipated problems about which they, of course, know nothing; they have never even heard that such deformities occur. When emergency surgery is necessary a surgeon with experience in operating upon tiny newborn infants must be found. Babies with serious deformities are apt to weigh a pound or two less than average.

Your baby should be operated upon where skillful surgery and experienced aftercare are available; maybe in the hospital where he was born, maybe elsewhere. Parents are foolishly shy about asking their doctor questions, fearful of revealing their ignorance. Your baby's life and future may be at stake; that's no time to quake and hesitate.

Without apology, ask the doctor who delivered your child, the pediatrician in attendance, or both, if there is a man on the staff of the hospital where your baby was born who has had special training in this particular type of infant surgery. They will honestly guide you. If a man capable in children's surgery is not available, suggest that your baby be transferred to a hospital where expert service is available. Such action is not unethical, too demanding, or in any way inappropriate.

No man in the world knows all about all kinds of surgery; he's lucky if he has a fair amount of knowledge in one branch of surgery.

Capable surgeons and hospitals with skilled nurses experienced in the painstaking care of infants are within two hours travel time from any but the most remote parts of the United States. Don't let finances make your decision. If you can't afford private care get help from state or county, or from the Crippled Children's Service. Help through one agency or another is available, if needed. This is your baby. Insist that he gets the best care available.

ADJUSTING TO HANDICAPS

Given plenty of encouragement, the physically handicapped may rise above their disabilities.

Lynn was six months old when she lost her left leg above the knee. At age two she was hopping around the house like a bird, and one year later got her first artificial leg. During the next fifteen years Lynn was fitted with three proper-sized artificial legs, each of which was lengthened a number of times.

Lynn, now a sophomore in high school, walks without a limp, rides a bicycle and goes to dances. Schoolmates don't feel sorry for her; they don't have to. Lynn does almost everything other girls do and has just as much fun.

Twenty-two years ago a three-year-old girl fell from a mowing machine on which she was being given a ride. Her right arm and leg were severely mangled and had to be amputated.

Recently there appeared in the daily papers a picture of this girl as a radiant bride.

A twelve-year-old girl badly burned over her face, neck, and left hand at age two, is nonchalant about the scars on her face and proud of her skill in using the stumps of two fingers.

David was born blind and with a defective heart. (His mother had German measles when she was six weeks pregnant.)

When David entered the hospital at age eight for a heart operation, he methodically said to each nurse, "Just tell me your name when you come to my bed; I'll remember it." He did. "Explain what you are going to do and I won't make a fuss." He didn't. I doubt that any child ever got more kindly service from nurses. What a wonderful boy! In June, 1963, David was graduated from high school with honors and went on to a college for the blind. His mother has normal vision but has learned to read braille with her son.

Success stories don't just happen; they are painstakingly written out by loving parents who never lose faith. Assistance is obtained from doctors, nurses, trainers, and therapists, but the spirit of hopefulness, the will to try, and the determination to succeed are generated in the heart of a child by those who care.

chapter Fifteen

THE CHILD WITH
A DEFORMED HEART

A FEW children are born with deformed hearts—we don't know why. If a mother has had German measles during the first eight weeks of pregnancy, her baby is liable to have a deformed heart, defective eyes, and poor hearing. In the vast majority of children born with malformed hearts, no cause for this calamity has been discovered. Actually, the percentage of children born with serious congenital heart disease is small, probably about one in two hundred.

The process of embryological development of the heart during the third to eighth week of pregnancy is nothing short of phenomenal and so complicated that it is surprising, not that defects occur, but that they are so rare. Approximately three weeks after conception, when the fetus is less than a fourth of an inch long, the beginning of a heart appears as a bulge in a tiny blood vessel. The heart develops rapidly; twists, bends, miraculously remolds itself to form compartments and valves, and begins to beat. By the time the fetus is eight to ten weeks old, the minature heart is completely formed and has taken over its lifetime task.

The subject of congenital heart disease is of special interest to those parents whose child is born with a crippled heart. Because a murmur is heard, or a chance x-ray picture is taken and shows enlargement of the heart, or symptoms such as pallor, failure to gain weight, too frequent colds, or cyanosis (blueness of the lips and fingers) present themselves, the child is sent to a heart specialist.

A rather wide variety of congenital heart defects appear in children; some are easily and permanently corrected, some can be improved, and a few are today hopelessly irremediable. It is most pleasant to write about a heart defect that can be cured—the patent ductus arteriosus.

PATENT DUCTUS ARTERIOSUS

Before a baby is born there is always a connection, or ductus, between the pulmonary artery, which carries blood to the lungs, and the aorta, which distributes blood to the entire body. Because the lungs of the unborn child are collapsed, full of fluid and, therefore, resistant to blood flow, the tiny heart is unable to pump all the blood through them.

The ductus arteriosus acts as an escape valve, allowing the blood to be shunted into the aorta. At birth the lungs expand, and immediately it becomes important that all the blood now go through the lungs to supply the infant with oxygen.

The ductus arteriosus has filled its function as an escape valve and should promptly close. When it fails to do so, blood flow through this opening is now in the opposite direction—from the aorta to the pulmonary artery. If the ductus is wide, large amounts of blood escape from the aorta to the pulmonary artery and put a strain on the heart. Eventually the heart wears out because of excessive work.

The majority of children with an average-size patent ductus arteriosus—about one-fourth inch in diameter—appear perfectly healthy and can keep up with their playmates. If the ductus is large, heart failure may occur during the first year of life.

A diagnosis usually can be made by a doctor with the aid of nothing more than a stethoscope. A loud, rumbling, continuous murmur like the noise of a humming top is practically diagnostic of a patent ductus arteriosus.

In retrospect, it seems strange that before 1938 nothing could be done for these children. In that year Dr. Robert Gross first successfully tied a string around a patent ductus and cured a child. Since then the surgical treatment of this condition has been perfected and is routinely successful. After the ductus has been surgically closed, the child has normal life expectancy. The most suitable age for operation is between two and five years. The operation should be done before the heart begins to show signs of strain. If the ductus is large, heart failure may appear during the first few weeks of life and necessitate immediate operation; if the ductus is small—three millimeters in diameter—the heart may show no sign of strain before thirty or forty years of age.

COARCTATION OF THE AORTA

Some scientist with a love of big words introduced the word coarctation, which simply means constriction, or narrowing. Why coarctation of the main blood vessel in the body should occur is still a mystery, and why it should practically always appear in the same place in the aorta, about six inches from its origin from the heart, is equally mystifying.

Children with coarctation of the aorta grow up quite normally, and the condition is not suspected until somebody hears a mild heart murmur, takes the blood pressure, and feels for pulses in the legs. If the blood pressure in the arms is high, the pressure in the legs low, and the pulse in the groin weak or absent, the person has coarctation, or narrowness of the aorta.

The parents' question is then, "What must be done about it?" It is explained that the most suitable time for operation is between the ages of seven and twelve years. To the question, "What will happen if nothing is done?" the answer is rather clear-cut. The blood pressure in the arms, and more significantly in the head, will continue to rise and eventually, probably in ten to twenty years, a stroke will occur, the aorta may rupture, or the heart may go into failure. Operation is advised during late childhood before irreversible changes have occurred in the blood vessels. Parents are apt to ask: "If the aorta is constricted, how does blood get to the lower two-thirds of the body?" A reasonable question. Nature is very adaptable. Collateral vessels develop; i.e., branches from the aorta above the constriction, to the aorta below the constriction develop and carry enough blood to keep the lower two-thirds of the body properly supplied.

It is rare that a child with coarctation of the aorta has any complaints. In severe cases the child may complain of his legs being cold and of their going to sleep. Even though the blood supply to the major portion of the body is diminished, normal development is the rule.

The operation is a long and tedious one, but not particularly dangerous. The chest is opened and the constricted segment of the aorta is exposed. Special nonslipping clamps are applied, and the narrowed segment is cut out. With carefully placed stitches, the ends of the aorta are sewn together with fine silk. That's about all there is to the operation. A certain amount of skill is required to sew the ends of so large a vessel together in such a manner that no leaks occur. Resident surgeons in training get experience in this sort of tricky sewing on animals before they attempt a human case.

BLUE BABIES

Infants and children are cyanotic, or blue, because they don't get enough oxygen. The typical "blue baby" is blue because the flow of blood to the lungs is partially impeded by an obstruction to its flow through the pulmonary artery. Part of the blue blood returning from the body, unable to get to the lungs, escapes through a hole inside the heart and is pumped back through the body by way of the aorta. Obviously, the greater the obstruction to blood flow to the lungs, the more blue blood is shunted into the general circulation, and the more serious is the child's condition. In mild cases, the child's lips and fingertips are blue only after exertion; in severe cases, the child is constantly blue.

Many different kinds of congenital defects in the heart may cause blueness, or cyanosis, but the most common is the defect ordinarily spoken of as the tetralogy of Fallot. This is a combination of four defects in the heart and great vessels, which interferes with blood flow to the lungs.

Oxygen-starved infants with tetralogy of Fallot do not thrive; they gain weight slowly and because of constant discomfort are fussy and irritable. As they enter childhood they slowly learn to walk, but have to stop frequently to "catch their breath"—get enough oxygen to proceed. Their red blood cell counts, instead of being normal (between four and five million per cubic millimeter), are usually around seven million. This rise is nature's attempt to furnish more cells to carry oxygen to the tissues. These children are pitiable little creatures; because they get blue when they cry and sometimes faint due to insufficient oxygen, parents naturally indulge them until they become thoroughly spoiled.

Before 1945 nothing could be done to help these unhappy children and most died during infancy or early childhood. In 1945 and 1946 operations were devised to relieve these oxygen-starved children by shunting blood from the artery to an arm or directly from the aorta to the lungs. These procedures were called "shunt operations." By means of these two methods of increasing blood flow to the lungs, thousands of children were given a new lease on life. Parents all over the world besieged heart centers with the hope of having their oxygen-starved children relieved from the torture of gasping for air. Although these operations were eminently successful in changing blue babies to pink, an inherent fault in both was that the deformities inside the heart remained uncorrected.

In 1955 extracorporeal circulation was developed. This phrase means that the blood is purified outside the body in an oxygenator and is then returned to the body and circulated by means of a mechanical pump. Greatly simplified this is how extracorporeal circulation is accomplished: all the blood returning from the body is siphoned off just before it reaches the heart and is run through an oxygenator. The purified blood is then pumped back into the aorta—the main vessel of the body—just beyond the heart. In this way the heart is bypassed and, being free from blood, can be opened for correction of defects. Then the heart is stopped; it lies absolutely motionless. This is done to allow the surgeon to work more efficiently inside the heart. After the operation has been completed the heart is started and normal circulation is restored. It is hard to believe that a heart can be stopped for a half-hour or even an hour and then be stimulated to resume beating in normal fashion, but so it is. I agree, it does seem miraculous.

Today, the heart defects commonly referred to as the tetralogy of Fallot are corrected by what is popularly called "open-heart surgery," with the aid of extracorporeal circulation. Through an incision in the right ventricle, the obstruction to the pulmonary blood flow is removed and the hole between the two ventricles is closed with a patch of plastic material. The operation is not an easy one nor without danger, but does give the child a good chance to live a normal life. To perfect the technique—it is difficult and demanding —a surgical team that contemplates doing open-heart surgery on children first performs the operation on dogs again and again until all the details—and they are many—have been mastered. The operation is attended with more danger than the shunt operations, but it does have the advantage of giving the child a better chance for normal life. For this reason, parents are usually willing to accept the greater surgical risk.

HOLES IN THE HEART, OR SEPTAL DEFECTS

The heart is divided into four chambers. The right auricle is separated from the right ventricle by the tricuspid valve; the left auricle is separated from the left ventricle by the bicuspid, or mitral valve. Between the auricles and between the ventricles there are walls, or septa. A hole in the wall between the auricles is called an interauricular septal defect; a hole in the wall between the ventricles is an interventricular septal defect. A septal defect, unless very tiny, is serious.

The left side of the heart is stronger than the right. Consequently, with each heartbeat, some blood is pumped through the defect into the right auricle or ventricle. To pump to the lungs this "escaped" blood plus the blood returning from the body obviously put an extra strain on the right side of the heart. And the increased amount of blood returning from the lungs puts a strain on the left side of the heart. It is, therefore, obvious that over a period of years the heart slowly wears out because of excessive work.

Symptoms will depend entirely upon the size of the defect. The average child with an opening the size of a nickel in the auricular wall or the size of a dime in the ventricular wall is liable to develop symptoms between the ages of two to five years. The child will tire more readily than normal, and an x-ray picture of the chest will show that the heart is somewhat enlarged. If the hole in the heart is so small that the heart does not enlarge and the child is perfectly well except for a slight heart murmur, he does not need an operation and may be unrestricted in his activities. Cardiologists find out how large a hole in the heart is by catheterization (introducing a long, fine tube through a vein into the heart to take samples of blood), and through cardiograms, x-ray pictures of the inside of the heart.

Operative closure of septal defects with the aid of extracorporeal circulation has become so safe and so successful that most holes of any size are either sewed up or covered with a patch.

THE UNFINISHED STORY

The story of surgery for congenital heart disease is a happy one written during the past twenty years, but not finished. Refinements in diagnosis and technique of surgery constantly demand that each chapter be rewritten at least once a year. There are some sad chapters in this story; some defects cannot be corrected. One of the most distressing tasks confronting cardiac surgeons is to have to say that nothing can be done for a child. Parents, told by their doctor that the child has a congenital heart defect, travel long distances to heart centers and, with shining hope in their eyes, anticipate that some magic operation will be performed and that their child will be normal. It's a terrible blow to learn that some defects cannot be corrected.

Only a few of the common heart defects with which children are born have been reviewed. Actually, at present there are seventeen different and specific congenital heart defects that can be cured or improved by operation. All this progress has been made in twenty years.

So long as we do not know why children are born with deformed hearts, and are therefore unable to avoid the misfortunes, surgeons will continue to correct the defects as best they can while constantly seeking new operations and improvement of those already in use. Transplantation of a heart or installation of an artificial heart is far in the future, not just around the corner.

WHEN your boy rides his bike and proudly says, "Look, ma, no hands," are you going to curb his venturesome spirit or take pleasure in his achievement? Parents are constantly stirred by opposing impulses: one, to overprotect their child for fear of accident; the other, to allow uninhibited learning by experience. Different proportions of each impulse are needed in the long process of teaching children of widely different temperaments the rudiments of self-protection.

Accidents are bound to happen. After taking all reasonable precautions all one can do is hope that fatal accidents will be avoided. When your child gets hurt, bind up his little wounds, have the big ones attended to by your doctor, and at the earliest possible moment send him out again to play.

chapter Sixteen

ACCIDENTS

CUTS

When your child gets a cut anywhere between the crown of his head and the sole of his foot, do a little investigating before you dash to the telephone to call your doctor. The red splashes of blood on clothing are sure to frighten you into overestimating the amount of blood lost; a tablespoonful, even a teaspoonful, makes a great showing on a white shirt.

Take the youngster to a washbowl or sink. First wash your own hands thoroughly with soap and water, then with wet absorbent cotton or a freshly laundered towel, or with water from the faucet if it is an injury to an extremity, wash away the clotted and fresh blood so you can see the size of the wound and decide whether stitches will be necessary or whether a simple bandage or bandage strip will suffice. In either case, wash the wound well with plenty of soap and running water. There is no better way of avoiding later infection than by getting rid of tiny pieces of dirt and bacteria immediately after the wound has occurred. A thoroughly washed wound needs no antiseptic. If the wound is small, put on a sterile dressing and let nature do the healing. There is no such thing as a "healing salve."

A gaping wound requires the services of a doctor. Often he will be able to bring the edges of a small skin wound together with a strip or two of adhesive tape. Watch the procedure, and you'll be able to handle the next little cut yourself.

Really severe bleeding, so extensive as to endanger a child's life, practically never results from accidents about the home. You may see blood spurt from little arteries, but such bleeding soon stops spontaneously. The best and safest way to stop bleeding is to place a sterile piece of gauze or a freshly laundered handkerchief on the bleeding point, make pressure with your finger, and keep it there for five minutes. If, when you release your finger, blood still spurts, repeat the process. Don't use a tourniquet to stop bleeding in a child. Tourniquets are dangerous; they often do more harm than good.

Simple brush burns which bleed only a few drops require nothing more than washing to get rid of the dirt; they heal better if left exposed to the air.

Deep brush burns with particles of sand, soot, cinders, carbon of any kind embedded in the skin, require diligent cleansing. If soap and water won't remove the particles, bubble them out with hydrogen peroxide. The peroxide stings but is effective. Black or colored particles of dirt left in the skin remain as permanent tattoo marks. Black material of any kind ground into the skin of the face, if not removable by simple measures, may have to be scraped out at the hospital under anesthesia; it is easy to remove such stains immediately after injury, difficult after the skin has healed.

Cuts in the scalp bleed very freely for a few minutes. You see blood dripping down the child's face and over the front of his shirt, and if it's your first experience with such an accident, you will immediately call your doctor who sends you to the emergency room at the hospital. There the doctor washes the blood out of the youngster's hair while you anxiously stand by fearful about the extent of a wound which bled so freely. Usually the wound is far smaller than you anticipated. It may require a stitch or two; maybe nothing but a dressing. The next time such an accident occurs, wash away the blood as you would following any cut, and then decide whether the wound needs medical attention.

It will be a great day for children and a load of worry off parents' minds when glass bottles are replaced by acceptable shatterproof plastic. Seventy-five percent of severe lacerations of hands and feet in children are caused by broken glass.

In case of a cut in the inside of a finger, palm, or wrist, the size of the wound is of secondary importance. Of vital importance is: Can the patient move his fingers? At the age when children get serious cuts in their hands they are usually old enough to cooperate in answering that question. After thoroughly washing the injured hand, have your child move his fingers, slowly closing and opening them as far as they will go to find out whether a tendon has been cut. Such movement will hurt a little, but try to get him to cooperate. If there is the slightest question about normal use of all the fingers take him to the hospital at once. A severed tendon in the hand is a serious matter; it should be repaired as soon after injury as possible. A cut tendon in a foot is of little consequence.

In case of a badly crushed finger, the first question a parent asks is, "Will the finger be lost?" If the finger is not cut off, the answer is almost always no. Even though the nail is torn off, the bone broken, and the skin mangled, the finger heals and, except for some temporary stiffness and scarring, usually regains normal appearance and function.

A finger completely cut off never survives no matter how soon or how carefully it is sewed back on, as it is impossible to sew the tiny blood vessels together. A completely severed arm may be replaced, and will sometimes live because the arteries and veins are big enough to be reunited and to maintain circulation.

A thin slice cut from the tip of a finger, if promptly replaced, may live. If the tip of the finger is lost, a small skin graft from the leg may be placed over the raw finger tip. To maintain normal touch it is important to have the end of a finger covered with skin rather than scar tissue.

After minor cuts, scratches, and brush burns, a booster dose of tetanus toxoid is unnecessary; following severe injuries and puncture wounds, it is routinely given.

"Will there be a scar?" a mother invariably asks when her daughter sustains a wound of the face. The answer is yes. Any cut all the way through the skin will inevitably leave a scar no matter how expertly the wound has been closed.

BURNS

Severe and fatal burns are most common in children below four years of age, and in adults over sixty-five. Little children haven't developed judgment for self-protection; the elderly have forgotten.

Distraught parents are deeply remorseful when their children are severely burned because often the tragedies could have been prevented.

Hospital histories are sadly monotonous:

"Baby reached up and pulled down handle of saucepan full of hot water standing on front burner of stove. Burns over face, neck, and chest."

"Youngster stuck screwdriver in open electric socket. Severe burns of both hands."

"While mother went out of the bathroom to answer the telephone, the two year old turned on the hot water. Both legs burned."

"Child was playing with matches (lighter). Clothing caught fire. Extensive body burns."

A severe burn is one that involves 10 percent or more of the body surface. Burns of the face or of the genital region are more toxic than similar-sized burns elsewhere.

A first-degree burn means redness of the skin; a second degree, redness and blistering; a third degree, destruction of all the layers of the skin.

Don't put oil, lard, any kind of grease or ointment on an extensive burn. Do not remove clothing burned and charred by fire. Remove clothing, if possible, from child burned with hot liquids. In either case, wrap the child in a freshly laundered sheet, cover him with a blanket, and take him to the hospital without delay.

It will be impossible in most instances for your doctor to tell you immediately how deeply the skin has been burned, whether it is a first- or a second-degree burn which leaves no scars, or a third-degree burn which always results in scarring. He won't be able to predict the period of hospitalization nor tell you whether later skin grafting will be necessary. The object of treatment during the first few days is to combat the shock of a severe burn.

For a small, superficial burn of the hand, arm, or leg, have the child hold the burned area in cold water to relieve pain or, if you have it, put on a pain-relieving spray. Cover with a bandage. Be sympathetic but inwardly thankful that he has gotten a small burn which may support your lectures about being careful with fire.

Sunburn. This is the same as a first- or second-degree burn from any other cause. When the sun is hot and the air deceptively cool, don't let your winter-pale youngster be exposed to the sun for more than a half-hour the first day out. Allow increased times of exposure as tanning develops.

Blondes and redheads tan poorly and are always subject to sunburn. Suntan lotions furnish excellent protection but not against a whole afternoon of brilliant sunshine. Sunshine is deceptive; by the time one's skin feels delightfully warm and tingles, it's too late. Four to six hours later these pleasurable sensations will be replaced with burning and pain.

There's not much to do for a sunburn but learn to be more careful next time. The burning pain can be relieved somewhat by soothing sprays purchasable at the drug store.

Many vacations are spoiled by severe sunburns. It's tough to be a killjoy and order children to wear shirts and blue jeans when on the beach. The alternative is to spend the night comforting the sunburned child.

Frostbite.   Local blanching and numbness are the signs of frostbite. First aid treatment consists of placing frostbitten fingers or toes
in mildly warm water, and of applying warm wet towels to frostbitten nose or ears. Do not rub with snow. This time-honored practice is wrong; it tends to break the skin and cause infection. Do not
massage; let the warmth restore circulation.

During thawing the skin will get fiery red and the pain will be
just as severe as after a burn. Give suitable doses of aspirin. If
blisters form leave them alone. Cover fingers or toes with a bandage
to prevent blisters from breaking.

A totally white and numb finger, toe, or ear is badly frozen.
Call your doctor. It is well to remember that frostbitten parts will
be more sensitive to cold for the rest of the winter and will therefore
require extra protection.

Chilblains of the feet, the equivalent of trench foot in soldiers,
are due to prolonged and excessive chilling of wet or damp feet.
Most children's feet are sweaty.

Treatment is simple: Soak the feet each evening in hot soapy
water. Dry by rubbing briskly with a towel. Apply foot powder or
calamine lotion to relieve itching. Put on freshly laundered wool
socks each morning. Keep the feet dry.

BUMPS ON THE HEAD

Children frequently bump their heads. Fortunately, the brain is protected by a firm, resilient container and usually escapes injury.

Your baby falls from his high chair or crib and lands on his
head. He screams. A little later he vomits and shortly thereafter
falls asleep. The fact that he falls asleep is not a bad omen but
rather a sequel to a frightening and exhausting experience. So long
as he lies quietly and breathes normally you need not fear that he
may be unconscious. However, if there is any question in your mind
about the possibility of unconsciousness, rouse the baby; he'll go
back to sleep and wake up later feeling fine. The lump on the head
will disappear in a few days.

The child who has received a severe blow on the head but can run crying into the house is not seriously hurt. Swelling and discoloration will appear where the scalp has been bruised. Holding an ice cap or some cracked ice in a towel against the sore place will lessen the pain somewhat and prevent more swelling.

Total loss of consciousness even for a few minutes *immediately* after a head injury means some damage to the brain. Hospitalization for close observation for a few days and x-ray pictures of the skull are advisable. Minor injuries to the brain in children usually heal without leaving any aftereffects.

The boy who is hit on the head, falls over stunned, immediately gets up and in a spirit of bravado continues in a game but later complains of headache or dizziness, or is to any degree mentally confused, should be seen by a doctor without delay. He may have a seeping hemorrhage pressing on the brain.

BROKEN BONES

After a child has fallen some distance or has been in a serious accident, parents wonder if any bones have been broken. Any visible deformity, of course, leaves no doubt. A leg is probably not broken if the child can walk without too much pain, nor is an arm apt to be broken if it can be moved without wincing. Before rushing to your doctor wait a few hours to see what happens. In the absence of deformity and swelling nothing is lost by waiting. Slowly increasing swelling, persistent pain, and tenderness upon touching the sore place, strongly suggest that a bone has been broken; only an x-ray picture can give the final answer.

Parents are disturbed when told that their child has a fracture, and often say, "I hoped it was just a break." A broken bone and a fracture are one and the same thing. Confusion arises from the fact that there are different kinds of fractures.

A greenstick fracture is an incomplete break of a bone. Children's bones are soft, and like green twigs, bend and crack on one side.

A complete fracture is, as the words imply, a break all the way across a bone. Complete fractures occur with or without displacement. A fracture without displacement is one in which the broken ends are in alignment; it needs only a cast to hold the bones while they heal. A fracture with displacement has to be set; that is, the bones have to be realigned before a cast is put on.

A compound fracture is one in which a fragment of bone sticks through the skin. Such a fracture is serious because the protruding piece of bone has been contaminated by clothing or dirt and may become infected.

First aid treatment of fractures is largely a matter of using common sense. The child with a broken arm can be taken in the family car to the emergency room of the hospital. Put the arm in a sling to support it and avoid further damage while en route.

If a child's leg is obviously broken, don't pick him up and carry him into the house. Movement of the sharp, broken ends may injure important blood vessels or nerves. Leave the child lie, reassure him that he will be all right, cover him with a blanket, put in an emergency call for help. Let those who have been trained put on a temporary splint if necessary before placing him in an ambulance. If you must move him a short distance be sure someone holds the broken leg as rigidly as possible.

In case of a compound fracture don't move the injured extremity. Swab the protruding piece of bone with a disinfectant, put on a sterile bandage, or cover with a freshly laundered towel, and call for help.

Sprains and Strains. A sprain means actual tearing of the capsule or supporting structure around a joint; a strain means just what the word implies, excessive pull on joint ligament or muscle. An ankle is sprained or strained by a misstep which suddenly turns the foot inward.

Whether an ankle is strained or sprained can be determined only by the symptoms which follow. A strained ankle hurts for a matter of a few hours or less and swells little if any, whereas a sprained ankle continues to be painful and in a short time gets puffy on the outside. Bluish-black discoloration is a sign that some bleeding has occurred under the skin.

Whether an injured ankle needs medical attention is a matter of judgment. If the pain is severe, elevate the leg and put ice packs on the ankle to lessen swelling and relieve pain. The doctor will decide whether an x-ray picture is necessary. If the ankle is not broken, just sprained, he will strap it with adhesive tape to protect the joint while it heals. An ankle sprained or strained gets well faster if used in moderation.

EYE INJURIES

A "black eye" results from an injury not of the eye but of the tissues about the eye. Our eyes are well protected by protruding bones. A bruising blow causes bleeding under the loose skin of the eyelids. The escaped blood slowly darkens, later turns yellowish-green, and eventually is completely absorbed.

Injuries to the eyeball itself may or may not be serious. Always consult your doctor immediately.

Shooting sharp, pointed arrows and air rifles provides lots of fun for children playing Indian or hunting "big game," but the sport is dangerous. How restrictive parents should be in the use of these playthings which are actually weapons, I don't know. Having had a bow and arrows and a "Daisy" air rifle when a boy, I should be lenient; but the danger of shooting someone in the eye—I have seen three such tragedies resulting in loss of sight in injured eyes—forces me to be a mean old killjoy.

chapter Seventeen

FIRST AID

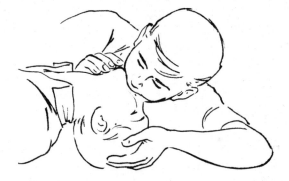

ARTIFICIAL RESPIRATION

Everybody should know how to give artificial respiration to a person who has just been pulled out of the water, overcome by gas, knocked unconscious by electric shock, or who for any reason is unable to breathe. All complicated methods have been discarded in favor of simple mouth-to-mouth breathing. The procedure is the same for children and adults with these small variations: The nose is pinched shut when mouth-to-mouth breathing is being given to an adult; both nose and mouth are covered by operator's mouth when resuscitating a small child. Blow vigorously into an adult's mouth at twelve times a minute; blow gently into a child's at twenty times a minute.

The procedure:

With the sweep of a finger clear the mouth of fluid, gum, vomitus, or foreign body.

Place the victim on his back.

Tilt the head far back by lifting the lower jaw with both hands; this will keep the tongue from falling back in the throat and obstructing the air passage.

259

Place your mouth over the victim's mouth, and blow. The chest should rise as you blow, and fall as you raise your mouth and turn your face to one side to take a breath.

If there is no air exchange, that is, if the chest doesn't rise and fall with each breath, turn the victim—if an adult, on his side; if a child, lift him up by his ankles—give a couple of sharp blows on the back between the shoulder blades to dislodge anything obstructing the air passages, and again clear the mouth.

Replace the victim on his back and resume breathing.

Don't give up. Continue artificial respiration until the victim begins to breathe for himself, or until professional aid arrives.

CONVULSIONS

High fever is by far the most common cause of convulsions in children between ages one and four years. Why fever causes convulsions and why only children are subject to them is unknown. Suddenly, and without warning, the child's eyes roll back, he stiffens, becomes unconscious, his face twitches and is distorted, his arms and legs jerk. If it's the first convulsion you have seen you will be terrified and will telephone your doctor.

While awaiting his call, try to reduce the fever. You will be too nervous to take the baby's temperature; simply feeling his forehead will tell you that his temperature is elevated. Take off all his clothing and sponge him with cool water or alcohol. Some doctors advise holding the convulsing baby in lukewarm (coolish) water in a bathtub. Within five to ten minutes the convulsions will stop. Rarely does a convulsion last as long as fifteen minutes. Then give him, if he is about two years old, two baby aspirin tablets to further reduce the temperature. After a convulsion the child is exhausted and will likely fall asleep; that's good, cover him lightly and let him sleep.

Don't cancel the call for your doctor. He will want to examine the child to determine the cause of the fever and be sure that it brought on the convulsion.

Yes, the next time your baby has high fever he is apt again

to have a convulsion. Therefore, any time your child is coming down with any kind of upper-respiratory infection take his temperature every two hours. If it goes above 102 degrees give him a cooling sponge bath and aspirin. Febrile convulsions are not a sign of brain damage nor do they cause brain damage. After age four or five, febrile convulsions rarely occur.

FAINTING

A simple fainting spell is in no way related to a convulsion. Some children as well as adults faint easily at the sight of blood, in fear of being hurt, or when overcome by violent emotion. Fainting occurs when the blood pressure falls to the point that the brain gets insufficient blood to maintain consciousness; it is purely a psychic phenomenon, not an indication of weakness or abnormal traits, but of a sensitive and responsive nature. Little children don't faint. They can watch gruesome spectacles without effect, presumably because they do not relate the incident to themselves.

A feeling of faintness is usually preceded by such symptoms as yawning, nausea, dizziness, and a feeling that the room is hot and stuffy. When such symptoms appear have the youngster or adult lie down. In a few minutes blood will flow back to the brain and the feeling of faintness will pass. The pallor and sweating occurring during and after fainting are of no significance.

DROWNING

Insist that your children learn to swim. Some children at age four or five are hysterically afraid of the water. Give them time, respect their fears, and let them play in shallow water until of their own accord they become more venturesome. By age seven or eight most children should be able to swim.

Precautions:

Never leave little children unattended at pool or beach.

Be sure floating toys or inner tubes are leak free. Don't let children float out of reach.

A child who cannot swim should never go into a small boat without a life preserver on—not just in the boat—but on.

Impress upon your older children:

To have respect for the water. Disdain for its temperature, depth, currents, and undertow will lead to disaster.

Never to go swimming alone.

Not to swim after a big meal.

Never to dive into water unless sure of its depth.

To swim only where lifeguards are on duty unless someone in the group is trained in lifesaving.

If you can't swim a stroke, think before you leap into deep water to save a drowning child; it may seem heroic and who wouldn't be inclined to do it? The result will almost certainly be two casualties instead of one.

SMOTHERING

Stories about normally healthy infants found smothered to death in their cribs are unfounded. Sudden deaths do occur but are almost always caused by an overwhelming infection, not suffocation. A healthy infant sleeping in any position in his crib, even when encumbered with loose clothing, has strength enough to turn his head so that he can breathe. It is recognized that a premature infant too sick or weak to move must be protected against smothering. Pillows have no place in any infant's crib.

For an exhausted mother to take her fussy baby into bed with her is unwise. Accidental smothering under such circumstances is highly improbable, but should it occur the mother will never forgive herself.

In case of suffocation by carbon monoxide, smoke, or escaped gas from a stove, remove the child to fresh air and give artificial respiration by mouth breathing as previously described.

Don't let children play with plastic bags big enough to put over their heads.

CHILDREN WILL SWALLOW ANYTHING

Anything small enough for a baby to put into his mouth, he will swallow. Small objects such as coins, buttons, beads, marbles, easily go down the esophagus and through the bowel. Pins, phonograph needles, tacks, screws, small open safety pins, and other objects even with pointed or sharp edges are usually passed without trouble.

Standard-size safety pins when swallowed are apt to get caught in the throat, esophagus, or duodenum (the portion of the intestine just beyond the stomach), and usually have to be removed surgically. The answer to the open safety pin problem is prevention. Keep open safety pins out of the baby's reach. While changing a diaper close each pin as it is removed. Sticking pins in the bedding is hazardous. The telephone rings. When you come back a pin is missing. Had you closed each pin you wouldn't have to worry whether the baby had swallowed one because a closed safety pin is passed without difficulty.

Older children, too, put into their mouths and accidentally swallow keys, lockets, brooches, toy watches, miniature figures, and a host of other things. If an x-ray picture shows the object in the stomach, yet the child is symptomless and can eat without distress, it is safe to wait a week or ten days for it to move on. Objects which can go through the stomach and duodenum will move on and be passed.

Give no cathartic. Give the youngster some leafy spinach; the object may become enmeshed in the leaves and be carried on. My confreres slyly scorn the spinach treatment, but I have found it effective. Anyway, the treatment is harmless and the spinach might even be good for the child.

Choking.   Objects which children can put into their mouths can be inhaled into their windpipes or lungs.

Inhalation of a bead, pin, or peanut far into the lung causes violent coughing for only a short time. Thereafter, the only indication that something may have lodged in the lung is a mild cough which lasts for weeks or months. Unfortunately, such things as peanuts or pieces of any kind of vegetable matter do not show on an x-ray film. When consulting the doctor about the chronic cough, the mother forgets to tell him about the violent coughing episode. Consequently, the possibility of a foreign body is overlooked and slow damage of the lung continues until a foreign body is eventually suspected and removed. Do you know what object children most frequently inhale into their lungs? It's the peanut. So common is this misfortune, it is advised that children below four years of age not be allowed to eat whole peanuts. Satisfy them with peanut butter.

Large objects such as safety pins and pieces of jewelry are apt to get stuck in the windpipe. You won't be able to see the foreign body in the throat. If the child, although coughing violently, is definitely not blue, take him to the hospital and call your doctor. If he is literally choking—can't get his breath—don't waste precious minutes calling your doctor. Turn the child over your knees with his head far down and give a sharp blow or two on his back between the shoulder blades to force the object out of the windpipe. Try mouth-to-mouth breathing for a few minutes and repeat the maneuver of turning him over your knees and striking his back. Then call for help.

NOSEBLEEDS

Injury to the nose by fall or fist, too vigorous blowing, and picking are the most common causes of nosebleeds. Practically all bleeding from the nose originates from the lower part of the septum between the two nostrils.

In case of nosebleed have the patient sit in a semireclining position, put cold cloths on the face, and wait. Within ten to twenty minutes the bleeding will usually stop. Children don't die of nosebleeds.

If bleeding doesn't stop in a reasonable length of time call your doctor. Watch him pack the nose as outlined below, and you will be able the next time to handle the problem yourself in case medical help is not immediately available. Have your youngster blow his nose vigorously to remove all clots. Wipe his face and nose with a wet cloth so you can see from which nostril the blood is coming. Blowing the nose will increase bleeding, but the nostril must be cleared before packing. Then take a piece of absorbent cotton, a small strip of gauze, or piece of soft cloth, and with the eraser end of a pencil gently shove it into the bleeding nostril. Now with your finger, press against the packed side of the nose and maintain pressure for about ten minutes. The bleeding will slowly stop. Leave the plug in for about twelve hours, then very gently remove it.

Recurrent nosebleeds are due to engorgement of little blood vessels in the nasal septum. It may be necessary to have your doctor shrink them by applying some mild caustic.

ANIMAL AND INSECT BITES

Superficial dog bites incurred at home by one's own pet or by a neighbor's friendly dog require only prompt thorough washing with soap and water and application of an antiseptic. A deep puncture wound made by a tooth requires medical attention. "Clean as a hound's tooth" should be changed to "Dirty as a hound's tooth." No injury is more apt to be followed by a nasty infection than a severe dog bite.

When to give antirabic serum is a difficult question to answer.

For superficial tooth scrapes of the skin, antirabic serum need not be given.

In case of a severe dog bite, the offending animal should not be killed but impounded, or sent to a competent veterinarian for observation for ten days. If the animal has had antirabic shots and shows no signs of illness during the period of observation, antirabic serum need not be given.

Any person bitten by a stray dog, not apprehended, should be given the full course of antirabic serum.

Each summer a half-million children are bitten by dogs. Children have been told often yet must be *warned again and again:*

Don't tease dogs. They, too, have limits of endurance.

Don't pet strange dogs.

Don't ever try to take away a dog's food.

**Don't interfere with a dog fight. Turn the hose on them or
call an adult.**

Don't touch a sick or injured dog.

If you own a dog, be sure he has attached to his collar a license, your name, and a tag showing that he has been immunized against rabies.

Cat scratch fever is caused by a specific virus on the cat's claws. Thorough washing of a scratch with soap and water immediately after its occurrence will prevent this nonfatal but annoying disease.

Wasps, hornets, yellow jackets, and bumblebees can sting you again and again; the honeybee stings only once and leaves his stinger in the skin.

When stung by a bee look closely for the tiny stinger protruding from the skin and remove it with a tweezers or scrape it out with the blade of a knife. By squeezing on the skin about the puncture wound or by sucking, some of the poison may be removed. Put on some baking soda or calamine lotion.

A few children sensitive to bee venom may have severe reactions calling for medical attention. There are available extracts of the venom to desensitize these children.

Tell your boys to leave those beautifully constructed papier-mache homes of wasps, hornets, and yellow jackets alone or take the consequences of having stingers stuck into their hides.

SOMETHING IN THE EYE

There is probably something in an eye when it suddenly feels scratchy and waters.

Take hold of the lashes of the upper lid and draw it over the lashes of the lower lid. This maneuver may scrape out a foreign body. If not effective, draw down the lower lid and look for a cinder or speck of dirt on the white part of the eyeball or on the red surface of the lower lid. With the corner of a wet handkerchief or a swab made of cotton twisted over the end of a toothpick and wetted, flip out the speck. If you find nothing, then comes the trick of looking at the undersurface of the upper lid.

In a good light, take hold of the lashes of the upper lid while the patient looks downward, then with a pencil or any other slender round object press on the upper surface of the lid as you gently pull on the lashes. The upper lid will turn inside out. This maneuver requires some practice. You might try it first on some other member of the family whose eye is not watering and whose lids are not in spasm.

In case you have found nothing, and the eye still feels scratchy, try irrigation with ordinary tap water. With an eye dropper or syringe of any kind, direct a stream of water into the eye while the patient is lying down, his head tilted back. You may be lucky enough to wash out the offending speck. If all measures fail, cover the eye to keep the lid closed and find a doctor.

chapter Eighteen

POISONING

THE Number One killer of children between one and five years is not childhood diseases or pneumonia—it is poisoning. Of the half-million children poisoned in the United States each year, fifteen hundred die.

If some disease affecting this many children suddenly appeared, the drive to stop the epidemic would be tremendous. Frightened parents would rise up and demand that no effort or money be spared to control the killer. Yet, today, we go merrily on our way of leaving drugs and all sorts of poisonous substances within the reach of curious little hands.

Since no magic wand can be waved to make parents keep the aspirin bottle and all harmful substances under lock and key, here is a brief outline of what to do in case of poisoning.

With few exceptions, the first thing to do for most cases of poisoning is to get rid of the poison by making the child vomit.

Call your doctor.

He may not be available. If he is not, rush your child to the emergency room of a hospital, if one is nearby.

HOW TO INDUCE VOMITING

If you are on your own, and your child has taken an overdose of aspirin, sleeping tablets, or any drug from your medicine cabinet, the first thing to do is to induce vomiting. By far the majority of poisonings are due to drugs. Aspirin alone accounts for one-third of all poisonings in children.

Stick your finger or the handle of a spoon in the child's throat to make him gag and vomit. If he has recently eaten, it is easier to induce vomiting. If the stomach is empty, give him a glass of milk and repeat the stimulus to vomit.

One teaspoonful of dry mustard, or two teaspoonfuls of prepared mustard in a glass of warm water, or a tablespoonful of salt in a glass of warm water are equally effective in inducing vomiting.

Turn the child over your knees; support his head with your hand against his forehead as he vomits. This position is important to prevent aspiration. If he doesn't vomit promptly put your finger in his throat again. This is no time for coaxing or wheedling but for firm quick action.

Syrup of ipecac will induce vomiting. Many doctors advise that a bottle be kept in the medicine cabinet. One-half ounce in a half-glass of water is the standard dose; although effective, the only objection to its use is that it does not cause vomiting as promptly as the previously mentioned methods.

Be sure to save some of the vomitus for analysis. It is important in the immediate as well as later care of your child for the doctor to know without question what the swallowed material was and its concentration.

In most large hospitals in the United States and Canada there are Poison Control Centers where people are always on duty to answer your questions and tell you what to do. With the exception of volatile hydrocarbons, such as kerosene and strong acids and alkalies, the safest general treatment is to induce vomiting and give a glass of milk.

FOR OVERDOSES OF:

Aspirin
Bufferin
Excedrine
Oil of wintergreen
Remedies for colds,
    headache, and pain
Alcoholic liquors
    (rubbing alcohol)
Unknown liquid or
    tablet medicines

Induce vomiting. Give a glass of milk.

Sleeping Tablets
    Phenobarbital
    Allonal
    Amytal
    Seconal
    Nembutal
    All Barbiturates
    Tranquillizers

Induce vomiting. Give a cathartic. Epsom salts is preferred. If signs of sleepiness appear give a cup of strong coffee.

Opiates
    Morphine
    Codeine
    Opium
    Paregoric
Atropine
Belladonna

Give glass of milk, induce vomiting. Keep child awake. Artificial respiration may be necessary.

FOR POISONS SUCH AS:

Ant poison
Rat poison
DDT
Weed killer
Arsenic
Chlordane
Dieldrin
Other insecticides

Give a glass of milk. Induce vomiting. Consult your doctor about further treatment.

Petroleum Products:
(Hydrocarbons)
   Kerosene
   Gasoline
   Benzine
   Naphtha
   Furniture polish
   Lighter fluid
   Turpentine
   Cleaning fluids

*Do **not** induce vomiting. Give water or milk and two tablespoonfuls of mineral or vegetable oil. Hydrocarbons are toxic poisons—one to two teaspoonfuls are dangerous. Call your doctor. He will decide whether stomach washing should or should not be done.*

Strong Alkalies:
   Lye
   Drano
   Bleaches
   Washing Soda
   Ammonia

*Do **not** induce vomiting. Wash mouth and face. Give two tablespoonfuls of vinegar in two glasses of water. Rush to hospital. The doctor will wash the stomach if you get there soon after the accident.*

Strong Acids:
   Nitric acid
   Sulphuric acid
   Soldering flux
   Muriatic acid
   Carbolic acid
   Phenol

*Do **not** induce vomiting. Wash mouth and face. Give two ounces of milk of magnesia or one teaspoonful of bicarbonate of soda. in two glasses of water. Rush to hospital. The doctor will decide about advisability of washing stomach.*

FOR THE CHILD WHO HAS SWALLOWED:

Ink
Dyes
Mothballs
Diaparene
Liniments
Toadstools
Mercurochrome
Boric acid
and innumerable
   other substances

Induce vomiting. Give a glass of milk.

The general belief that antidotes are available for most poisons is wrong. In the first place, antidotes are rarely kept in the home and, in the second place, there are no specific antidotes for many poisons.

External poisons: *For external contact with strong acids or alkalies, carbolic acid, or other corrosive substances, hastily remove clothing and as quickly as possible wash thoroughly with lots of water. Spatters of these substances in the eye should be washed with a stream poured from any container into the open eye. Never mind the rug, chair, or clothing, concentrate on washing away the chemical.*

For poisons in the air:

Carbon monoxide from automobile exhaust
Gas from leaking stove
Smoke
Noxious fumes of any kind

Remove patient to fresh air. Give mouth-to-mouth artificial respiration, if necessary. Have someone else call doctor.

To Prevent Poisoning.   Ask yourself these questions:

When you give your child aspirin do you put the bottle way immediately?

Do you call medicine candy? You are inviting children to take any medication they find.

Do you read the label before giving your child medicine?

Do you keep household products out of children's reach or in a locked closet, or do you merely store them under the sink?

Do you keep household products in their original containers? Children will drink anything poured in a cup or soft drink bottle.

How long since you've cleaned your medicine cabinet of partially-used prescriptions?

And, of primary importance, does your medicine cabinet have a child-proof locking device? There is now on the market such a device approved by the Poison Control Branch, Public Health Service of the federal government. For further information, write to General Bathroom Products Corporation, 2201 Touhy Avenue, Elk Grove Village, Illinois.

To climb up on the washbowl and open the medicine cabinet is alluring to children. Bottles and boxes are fascinating to look at and a challenge to open. Such beautifully colored capsules and pills must be as good to eat as candy. Why children refuse even to taste certain foods yet eat a handful of aspirin tablets, or chew up moth-balls, is beyond me. Such is the way of little investigators.

Lead Poisoning. Lead poisoning is common in children, especially in large cities.

Children get lead poisoning usually in one of two ways: They eat flakes of paint that peel off from old walls which have been decorated with paint containing lead (don't ask me why they develop perverted appetites for such unattractive morsels, but they do), or children use crib bars as teething rings and chew on furniture, window sills, toys decorated with paint containing lead.

After months of eating small amounts of lead each day, the bizarre symptoms of lead poisoning appear: irritability, poor appetite, stomachache, diarrhea, anemia, changes in personality, twitching of the face or hands, and in severe cases, convulsions. Lead is a potent poison.

If you happen to live in a rented apartment where paint is peeling from the walls, scrape off the loose paint—never mind how the walls look. You might talk the landlord into papering the walls.

Paint manufacturers do not put lead in paints, varnishes, or enamels designed for indoor decoration. Purchased toys are not coated with paint containing lead. On every can of paint that contains lead is this underlined caution: "Contains lead and lead compounds harmful if eaten. Do not apply on toys, furniture, or interior surfaces which might be chewed by children."

Whenever the impulse overcomes you to decorate your apartment or brighten your children's toys or furniture, be sure first to read the label on the paint can.

If your child swallows a sizeable amount of lead paint, have his stomach washed and give him a brisk cathartic. He will recover because the intestine does not absorb much lead at any one time. It's the small bits of lead swallowed day after day that eventually cause poisoning.

Food Poisoning.   Staphylococci are the cause of most cases of food poisoning. Staphylococci may grow and produce a poison called enterotoxin in foods such as soft pastries, custards, potato and meat salads, if not refrigerated. In the preparation of foods there is bound to be some contamination by the staphylococci found on people's hands. The germs themselves are harmless; it's only the toxin produced by their excessive growth which is harmful. In foods which are to be served cold but are not kept refrigerated, the germs may rapidly multiply and produce enough toxin to cause the typical symptoms of food poisoning—abdominal cramps, vomiting, and diarrhea. Recovery occurs in a few hours. It requires from six to eighteen hours at room temperature in the summer for enough toxin to form to cause symptoms. Most cases of food poisoning occur in the summertime when large groups of people are served cold foods prepared the previous day and not kept refrigerated.

A boiling temperature destroys the toxin. Therefore, cooked foods left standing at room temperature during a day or overnight are made perfectly safe by thorough reheating. Danger of food poisoning in one's own kitchen is rare. A piece of mother's superior lemon pie left from dinner is safe to eat the next day even though it was not put in the refrigerator overnight.

"Keep it hot or keep it cold" is the safe way of preventing food poisoning.

Acute salmonella infections in the bowel are often mistaken for food poisoning. The germs causing these infections are carried to foods by the contaminated hands of food handlers careless about sanitary habits. These germs also multiply rapidly in unrefrigerated foods and produce the same symptoms as those caused by the toxin of staphylococci. In most instances the acute infection promptly subsides but in some children it persists and requires diligent medical care and scrupulous attention to sanitary toilet habits.

Poison Ivy. Of all the useless and objectionable things in this world, poison ivy rates high on the list. Over a million children and as many adults have their vacations spoiled each year by this pest of the woodlands.

Almost all children and young persons—this includes those below forty years of age—are to some degree sensitive to poison ivy. Let those who proudly claim to be insensitive to poison ivy beware. Minor exposures may sensitize the skin without producing symptoms. Later exposures may result in a serious rash.

Poison ivy is a three-leaved plant growing as a climbing vine, small bush, or shrub. The top of the green leaf is shiny, the under-surface is fuzzy, and in the springtime slightly reddish. The best advice for the uninitiated in recognition of poison ivy is to leave undisturbed any plant in the woods that has three leaves.

One must come in contact with the toxic fluid released when the leaf, stem, or root is broken to get poison ivy rash or dermatitis. The poison is so potent that merely touching a shoe that has crushed a poison ivy plant a few days earlier may produce a rash. This fact explains the myth that highly sensitive persons may be poisoned by merely being in the vicinity of the ivy. You may safely look at poison ivy, but don't touch it.

Symptoms of ivy poisoning, burning, itching, redness of the skin, and blistering, usually come on twenty-four to forty-eight hours after exposure; they may appear within twelve hours and may be delayed for as long as twelve days.

After the first symptoms have appeared, the poison has fixed itself chemically to the skin, and the time honored bath with rough laundry soap or application of alcohol or kerosene, is useless. The child's clothing should be washed with soap and water and the shoes likewise scrubbed with soap to remove the tiny bits of poison which later, on contact, may reactivate symptoms.

Unfortunately, there is no known drug which applied locally will neutralize the poison and relieve the symptoms. The red, raw, blistered skin is best soothed by cool soaks, starch baths—a cupful or two of starch in a half-tub of water—and frequent applications of calamine lotion. Liberal doses of aspirin, taken by mouth, of course, will lessen the burning and itching.

Ivy poisoning may be prevented or lessened by vigorous washing with soap and water *immediately* after contact.

PART **4.**

<u>Parent-Child Relationships</u>

AND he who gives a child a treat
Makes joy-bells ring in Heaven's street,
And he who gives a child a home
Builds palaces in Kingdom come . . .

from
"The Everlasting Mercy"
by John Masefield

chapter Nineteen

A HAPPY FAMILY

A SIX-YEAR-OLD boy revealed in one quick sentence the secret of a happy family.

Father, mother, and their three children ages eleven, eight, and six, from a farm in central Illinois, came to my office for a checkup examination of the eight year old. After this routine matter was disposed of, I asked about life on the farm. It was fun to listen as the children enthusiastically told about what they did on the farm and at home.

Being impressed by the friendly harmonious atmosphere—the children did most of the talking, the parents just smiled and listened approvingly—I said to the father, "I would like to ask you a personal question. What is the secret of this happy family?" As quick as a wink the six-year-old boy said, "I know; it's 'cause we have so much fun."

In that one sentence there is more common sense about how to rear children than one can find in a hundred pamphlets about child-rearing.

The wisdom packed in that spontaneous remark prompted me

to tell the story in my newspaper column and ask readers to send in their secrets of a happy family.

Here are a few of the responses:

"We set aside every Tuesday evening as family night. Everybody gets specially slicked-up for dinner. After dinner we go to the playroom where we all take turns at being leader of the evening's activities. Whoever is in charge may do anything he wishes, read or tell a story, recite a piece learned in school, play some music on the piano or phonograph, and pick out the games he wants to play. We have lots of fun."

"On Friday night we all have picnic suppers on trays while we watch the children's favorite TV programs. After that we play games together. The kids look forward all week to Friday night. We have eight children. Some milk gets spilled on the floor but we don't care."

"In our family religion is the center of the home. Every evening after dinner we read a chapter from the Bible. We believe religion keeps the children out of trouble and holds the family together."

"Our home is a big, old, rambling house that is a sort of hangout for the neighborhood children. We welcome them and I see to it that there are always cookies and soft drinks on hand. On rainy days the smaller children play hide-and-eek in the house. It gets pretty noisy and is rough on the furniture but I say, 'Kids before furniture.' The teen-agers have dances in the basement on Friday or Saturday night. We make it a point to be at home that evening."

"I make it a practice to be home in the afternoon when the children come in from school. Often one will shout, 'Oh, Mom.' When I say, 'Yes, what is it?' the answer is, 'Nothing, I just wanted to know if you are there.' I think being home gives the children a feeling of security."

To make a happy home is not easy but tremendously rewarding.

The art is unconsciously passed on from one generation to another. To divide your time between attention to routine duties and attention to your children usually requires some neglect of housework. Let a few specks of dust lie quietly next to each other while you make a house a home where, as the six-year-old boy said, "We have so much fun."

GAMES, PLAY, AND FRIENDS

Children love to play. In fact, play is absolutely essential for normal physical and emotional growth from early infancy on. Beginning at age two or three expose your children to playmates.

Playing with toys and dolls fills many hours but soon children learn to love competitive games, such as parchesi, monopoly, innumerable card games and, as they grow older, scrabble, checkers, chess, and bridge.

Competitive games are ideal for teaching little children to play by the rules, to take their turns, play fair, to be good sports when they lose, and gracious when they win. Children keenly enjoy being teamed with father on one side, mother on the other. Actually, parchesi can even be fun for adults who sit on the floor and join their children in the spirit of enthusiastic competition. A little judgment has to be exercised in competitive games; sometimes it's wise to let a child win, but not always.

Help your preschool child find friends by inviting neighborhood children to a party. Serve the things they love to eat. A little supervision will be necessary but the less the better; leave the children alone to get acquainted in their own way. If there are no playmates of your children's age in the neighborhood, enroll them in a pre-school kindergarten. The fewer children in a family, the greater the need for association with other children. Adults cannot take the place of childhood companionship.

Nothing is better for growing children than uninhibited, unregimented outdoor play. In active play they learn to coordinate awkward muscles, work off boundless energy and, at the same time, absorb the rudiments of give and take. Competition is an essential part of all games but I seriously question the wisdom of overemphasized competition in highly-organized league play. Children between ten and fourteen are not sufficiently mature to take the physical and emotional strain of giving the last ounce of energy to win. Games should be fun for all children—the awkward and shy as well as the adept. Day in, day out, through long winter months and summer vacations, children get the most fun out of simple games played with neighborhood companions.

"Be a pal to your boy" is more a cliché than good advice. A father skilled in some sport may teach his son the rudiments of a game but that's about all. Of course, older boys love a ballgame or a weekend fishing trip with dad but, in general, children prefer play, parties, camping, and Boy Scout trips with others their own age.

As children grow up and go to school they will find their own friends. How to handle the problems of the bully, the undesirable companion, and how to settle inevitable fights which are bound to arise, requires the judgment of a Solomon. When you don't know what to do, the best solution is usually—do nothing. Children are brutally frank but not malicious; in their own way they dissolve misunderstandings and settle differences.

You won't have trouble finding friends for your children if yours is a fun house—a place where children can whoop and holler, laugh and giggle, where apples, cookies, or popcorn are freely dispensed, where parents accept children as they are, join in their fun and supervise activities without appearing to do so.

Read Me A Story.   One of the finest things you can do for your children is to read them stories. Whether you choose the old standards, such as Mother Goose rhymes, "The Three Bears," "The Three Little Pigs," or more modern stories makes little difference so long as colored illustrations appear on every page.

Beginning at about two years a child looks forward with keen anticipation to the bedtime story. You will soon find that certain stories are particularly popular and are requested again and again.

Soon they learn the story by heart as they look at the pictures.

Father has a wonderful opportunity after dinner, when he is in a relaxed mood, to establish friendly relations by taking his son or daughter on his lap and reading a story or two. Put lots of expression into reading "The Three Bears." Say in a deep gruff voice, "Who has been sleeping in my bed," and the children will shout with glee. Add a few words or expressions to a well-known story and the child will interrupt with, "Daddy, you're just making up stuff." Secretly, they are pleased that you are embellishing the story and taking an interest in its reading.

Boys and girls can be led to enjoy such classics as Andersen's and Grimm's fairy tales, *Alice in Wonderland,* and for those who prefer, Bible stories. It will be fun for parents to reread these stories and relive their own childhood days. At the same time the child will become familiar with constantly quoted literature, acquire a love for reading, and automatically build up a vocabulary.

There is nothing wrong with children who prefer blood-and-thunder stories and the gory versions of fairy tales; they, like adults, enjoy the excitement of a story vivid in details about justice meted out to the wicked.

I said to my granddaughter Mary, age eight, "Why do you like gruesome fairy stories better than those that turn out happily for everybody?" Her answer was, "They are more fun to read and they don't scare me because I know they aren't real—just fairy stories." When I was her age and exposed primarily to Bible stories my favorites were those of David who killed the giant, Goliath, with a slingshot and of Samson, the superman, who killed a thousand Philistines with the "jawbone of an ass."

Even though you read the accepted stories to your children, they are bound to go through the comic book phase. For a time they will be engrossed with this less desirable reading. Suddenly, it loses fascination and they settle for a few favorite comics in the daily newspapers.

Reading stories to children purely for pleasure slowly instills into their minds a love for literature—the basis of education.

Watching Television.   Television is the greatest medium for entertainment ever invented. The question is, "What programs shall I allow my children to watch?" Certainly, during preschool years impressionable minds should not be exposed to horror and violence. A child may love the story of "Snow White and the Seven Dwarfs" and not be at all disturbed by the actions of the wicked witch but scream with fear when seeing the witch on a screen. Frightening episodes displayed before a child's eyes are very real; when heard in the telling of a story they are only vaguely imagined.

Some control of TV watching is necessary through the school years. The seven- to ten-year-old child who becomes so stirred up after seeing a show depicting violence that he can't sleep or has nightmares, simply has to be denied such programs. However, I doubt that children old enough to know that what is seen on the screen is only make-believe are harmed by the average "Shooty Bang" show. After all, the "gooders" always win out over the "badders."

One should be concerned about the child who on beautiful days would rather watch TV than play outside. He needs help in finding friends and other interests.

Too much television viewing acts as a hypnotic and dulls the imagination. Even during high school years some control must be exercised. Ideally, homework comes first, reading second, and TV third. I am not criticizing TV. The general public gets the kind of programs it wants. It's up to parents to help select programs worth watching. Here is a knotty problem: The five year old wants to watch Mickey Mouse, the teen-ager a movie, and father a ballgame. Who wins?

FAMILY VACATIONS

A long automobile trip with the family can be fun but is bound to be interrupted from time to time by small crises in the back seat where the children are riding. After the first hundred miles—that is about as long as children's good nature holds out under the strain of too much togetherness—arguments are bound to arise. In fact, a long automobile trip with two or three active children in the back seat without a fair number of arguments and a few real fights is unheard of. Unfortunately, parents are human and can tolerate only so much bickering before they fly off the handle and squelch rear seat uprisings.

Prevention is the best treatment of children's quarrels in the car:

Stop frequently and have all the youngsters pile out for a soft drink or inspection of some interesting view or landmark.

Rotation of seating avoids the arguments about who shall sit in the front seat and who shall sit next to which window in the back seat. If father is doing the driving, mother and children change seats after each stop.

Bribery is probably not the most laudable means to an end but is effective in promoting peace and providing for the general welfare. At the beginning of a trip, I used to give each of our three children twenty nickels—dimes would be more appreciable today —with this stipulation: Whoever said a cross word or started a fight had to give each person in the car a nickel. My wife and I also had the same supply of nickels and the rules applied equally to us.

The effects were amazing. All of a sudden in a moment of forgetfulness a cross word would pop out and be immediately covered with honeyed words to avoid penalty. Nothing gave the children more pleasure than to have one of us make a slip—occasionally planned—and have to pay up.

Have fun, tell stories, don't get overtired by driving too far, and drive carefully. We don't want to see any of you in the hospital emergency room.

Minor illnesses and accidents are bound to occur on vacations. Here is a list of a few supplies and remedies to tuck away in a box in the luggage compartment.

Clinical thermometer. An illness without fever is not apt to be urgent.

Box of 5 grain aspirin tablets for aches, pains, sleeplessness, and crankiness.

Four ounce bottle of calamine lotion for rashes and itches.

Two ounce bottle of bismuth and paregoric. In some states you can't buy this without a doctor's prescription. This is not to be used for stomachache but for simple acute diarrhea so common on vacations. A five-year-old child may have a teaspoonful.

Box of BANDAIDS or CURADS.

Two rolls of sterile gauze; one inch and two inch.

Roll of ½ inch wide adhesive tape.

Bottle of suntan lotion.

Bottle of soothing spray for those who get sunburned.

Box of antacid tablets or soda bicarbonate for parents who eat too much greasy food.

Large can full of patience and good humor to be kept within easy reach.

PRAISE STIMULATES CHILDREN'S EFFORTS

For best results in raising children give a maximum of praise and a minimum of criticism. Everybody loves praise. Children especially thrive on this ego-nourishing pablum and are stimulated by it to greater efforts in anticipation of another serving. On the contrary, belittling criticism engenders a feeling of, "Oh, what's the use; I can't do anything right," and leads to anticipation of failure.

A child is stimulated to new ventures when his castle of awkwardly placed blocks is praised. He has done his best. The bizarre-colored drawings of the schoolchild mean something to him. Take time to see the pictures through his eyes and you'll find something worthy of acclaim.

When children go to school, competition between brothers and sisters is broadened to include contemporaries. If you want children to love school and develop a desire for learning, seek out and comment favorably upon the things they do well. You can't fool a child by falsely praising sloppy work but you can say, "A smart one like you can do better." Praise, not criticism, will stimulate him to do better.

The athletically inclined boy blessed with muscle coordination is apt to be popular in school in this age of sport worship. It's the boy who can't throw a ball who needs help. Praise his writing, drawing, reading, memory, anything—there is bound to be something he does well. Don't push the child to do what he can't do. Frustration will be the result.

Never ridicule a child. Think back to your own childhood and you will recall how crushed you were when some one thoughtlessly made fun of your best efforts.

And another thing, children, during the awkward preadolescent years, need support for their egos, especially the "ugly ducklings."

I said to a dejected, pimply-faced, twelve-year-old girl with bands on her teeth, protruding ears, and straight hair skinned back in a pony tail, "My, you have pretty brown eyes." She looked at me in disbelief. "You do, your eyes are really beautiful." When she saw that I meant it, her entire appearance changed; she straightened up, smiled, her whole face lighted up and her eyes—they truly were pretty—literally sparkled with delight.

A boost with honest praise is the greatest tonic in the world; it's as effective at age thirty as at three and still appreciated at eighty.

GOOD MANNERS

Good manners are an expression of friendliness, good will, and consideration for others. No child is born with these characteristics; they are slowly attained primarily by imitation and in a small measure by teaching. Ill manners signify maladjustment and rebellion toward the accepted ways of living.

Good manners develop easily in a well-adjusted child living in a home where mutual respect toward one another is routine; ill manners arise in the frustrated child exposed to an atmosphere of discord, harsh words, and disregard of hurt feelings.

Table manners are actually a small part of good manners learned almost entirely by imitation. Yet children have to be taught to come to the table with clean hands and faces, how to hold a knife and fork, not to snatch the biggest piece of cake or demand the choice portion of meat, to say please when asking that something be passed, to ask to be excused if leaving the table before others have finished. Don't expect too much too soon. Such refinements as drawing out a chair to seat a guest and passing dishes to others before serving oneself are not apt to be acquired before early teen age.

It takes a long time to teach children to stand up when elders or guests enter the room, to greet your friends with a pleasant "hello," not rudely to interrupt adult conversation, not always to demand the center of the stage, to quietly say "pardon me, do you know where my roller skates are" instead of bursting into the room and rudely shouting, "Where did you put my roller skates?"

An eight-year-old boy's manners at home may be atrocious but quite acceptable when he is a guest in a friend's home. You will be more than surprised when the hostess later comments about the fine manners of your boy and says, "How do you do it?" You have no answer. That is the way of children; they feel that to conform at home means loss of status, that to be on their best behavior away from home adds status. Slowly it sinks into a child's consciousness that his world runs more smoothly when rudeness and ingratitude are replaced by a smile or a thank you.

Gratitude, like all other desirable traits which distinguish man from animal, can be taught during early childhood. It is as easy to teach a child to say thank you as to teach him to say mommy, daddy, candy, or ice cream.

A hostess who after giving a party for children in the neighborhood gets a thank you from each as he leaves is more than rewarded for the effort she spent.

As children grow up they have to be taught to write thank-you notes to friends, grandmas, and aunties. In answer to the child's comment, "I don't know what to say," the answer is simply, "Just say 'thank you. I liked your present' or anything else you think of." If the child adds to his note, "It's my birthday next week," let it stand; grandma will chuckle and take the hint.

A sincere thank-you note is hidden praise. The giver knows that his effort was appreciated.

Good manners are a sign of self-respect and respect for others, the first step toward learning how to get along with people. Good manners are a sign of an educated heart.

ADOPTION

Before thinking of adopting a baby, both prospective parents must be sure they want a child. Adopting a baby is a most gratifying experience—admittedly not quite the equivalent of having one's own child—but thrilling and altogether satisfactory. The couple who adopt a child—preferably two for the sake of later childhood companionship—are responding to the finest of human impulses: the desire to share their love and to make their home complete.

When to apply for a baby is determined by many factors. Couples married in their early or mid-twenties usually wait about five years unless they have learned earlier through medical consultation that it is impossible for them to have children. Childless couples should not wait too long; at age thirty-five, certainly when nearing forty, it is very difficult for people to adjust easily to the great changes which a first baby brings to a home.

The most satisfactory way of adopting a baby is through a registered agency where trained workers will answer your questions, put your names on the waiting list for boy or girl, and will comply with your wishes about the child's nationality and religious background. In turn, representatives of the agency will thoroughly investigate you, your home, finances and standing in the community and, in general, will assess your potentialities as good parents.

Babies are preferably given out for adoption at about age two months. Early contact with the prospective mother is important. During infancy care of an adopted child is no different from that of one's own baby.

As adopted children grow up parents are inclined to be over-zealous in their attempts to raise model children. It can't be done.

All children are distinct individuals whether adopted or one's own. There is no such thing as a near-perfect child or parent. Accept adopted children as you would have to accept your own.

Talk with your neighbors and you will learn that everybody's children are a mixture of angel and demon, cooperation and rebellion. Some are easy to manage; some exhaust the patience of a saint. So long as an adopted child lives in an atmosphere of relaxed but sincere interest in his well-being, is loved and feels that he is wanted, he has as good a chance of turning out all right as one's own child.

It is impossible to keep a child from finding out that he was adopted. It's unfortunate that this is true but so it is and those who have attempted to conceal adoption have come to grief. Before a child learns from playmates that he is adopted, his mother must tell him. At a convenient time, take him on your lap and tell him this story with suitable variations: "Once upon a time there was a mommy and a daddy who had no children. They were very sad because they wanted a little boy very much. One day they went to a place where there were many babies. They looked and looked and all of a sudden they saw a little boy. (At this point a detailed description of the child himself.) They brought him home and here he is. You know what, he is going to live with us always." Later when the child asks, "Was I borned or 'dopted?" the story will have to be embellished. Imagination may be allowed to run wild in details—the essence must be true.

Over the years these questions will be asked, "Who were my real parents?" "What were they like?" "Why didn't they keep me?" "Will I always stay here?" You can answer truthfully that the agency told you that his real parents were good but unable to care for him, that he is just as much yours as though he had been born to you, that he will never be given up, and that this will always be his home.

FATHER IS IMPORTANT TOO

Little has been said in this book about father, not because his importance is unrecognized but because mother is the one who brings up the children. She cares for their daily needs, shares their sorrows and joys, and creates the environment of a happy home. But she doesn't do this alone. The cooperative attitude of a loving husband is the catalyst that transforms mother's menial tasks into a zestful occupation. To the young impressionable child, father is the hero who can go out into the world each day in any kind of weather, a man who can do everything. When a child brags, "My daddy can lick anyone in the block," he is only expressing his conception of how wonderful and all-powerful he thinks his daddy is. Children look to father as head of the family.

When children reach high school age they may begin to question father's infallibility, but no matter. By this age the basic traits of character have been firmly ingrained. The importance of the first ten years cannot be overemphasized; it is during this time that father plays an important role.

Children—and don't forget wives—respond to the slightest expression of love and to interest in the routine affairs of their day. It requires so little effort when coming home from work to kiss your wife, pat your boy on the head, and cheerily say, "And how is my big boy this evening?" or to pick up your little girl and say, "How is my darling daughter?" Of course, the children will answer, "Fine," and think you are the most wonderful daddy in the world.

Friendly greetings are powerful antidotes to the poisons of frustrations of everyday life. When men come home from work tired, after a trying day in which everything has gone wrong and the boss has seemed unreasonable, it's quite natural to "blow off steam" at home, the only place they feel free to let go their feelings. A slammed door and a growl frighten children and set the scene for fights at the dinner table. A smile and a hug pay tremendous dividends, bigger even than an increase in the paycheck. When your wife has gone to the effort of changing to a fresh dress, putting on some lipstick, and a ribbon in her hair in anticipation of your coming home, tell her how cute she looks and in that moment she will see you again as the gallant knight she married seven years ago.

To indicate that two human beings, man and wife, can always radiate sweetness and light is unrealistic. Parents are going to have misunderstandings—verbal battles with no holds barred. Outbursts of angry words are normal but let them be in private. Nothing is more frightening to children than a quarrel between parents. Karen, five years old, heard harsh words exchanged between her parents at the breakfast table. Her father got up and without kissing mother good-bye, put on his hat and walked out of the house slamming the door. Later Karen was found crying on the bed. When asked what the trouble was she sobbed, "I'm scared that daddy will never come back." He did.

The lashing words of oft-repeated quarrels before your children will surely tear away the supporting structures of love and security built in your home.

SEX EDUCATION

There should be no more self-consciousness in answering questions about sex than in answering other questions children ask from day to day. Yet there is, for the simple reason that all matters pertaining to sex are rather private. Close parent-child relationships in everyday life lead to acceptance of straightforward explanations about sex. Appropriate knowledge is slowly acquired by answering each question as it arises in words suitable to the child's age and ability to understand.

The difference between boys and girls intrigues children. Where there are children of both sexes in the family questions are easily answered by a simple statement, "A boy is a boy and a girl is a girl. The boy grows up to be a daddy and the girl grows up to be a mommy." When the subject is later brought up again, explain that a boy has a penis and a girl a vagina and be sure to add that both are normal. A girl may think that she is misshapen because she doesn't have a penis like her brother. When all the children in a family are of the same sex it is wise, in fact, essential, that they see members of the opposite sex early in life. Arrange to have your boy

or girl present when a neighbor gives a bath to a baby of the opposite sex. It is far better for children to see the difference early than
that they later conjure up in their minds distorted images.

"Mommy, where did I come from," is going to be asked by
every child before he is three to five years old. He will usually be
satisfied with, "From Mommy" or "Mommy and Daddy wanted
you," or "You were born at the hospital." Any simple answer will
satisfy at age three or four. At age five to seven the question will
come up again and if your answer to his question, "Where did I
come from?" is the standard one—"You grew inside of me," then
these inevitable questions will follow. "How did I get inside?" "How
did I get out?" "Can I have a baby?" That is the time you will
have to answer questions in a straightforward manner lest you give
the idea that there is something mysterious and taboo about sex.

In a happy home where children live in a friendly atmosphere
of mutual trust, explanations about sex will be accepted simply
because "That's what mommy told me." Children are stirred to
questions about sex by no other motive than pure natural curiosity.
Answer their questions in the spirit in which they are asked.

Children vary greatly in curiosity about the details of sex and
in their ability to comprehend. However, well before children are
ten years old they are going to get the answers to sex somewhere.
Far better that they get them straight from you than that they get
distorted ideas from other children. Tell them that a woman has
tiny eggs in her ovaries and that from time to time an egg matures
and is fertilized.

You needn't go into the details of the sexual act unless questions demand it. Explain that the baby grows in the womb for nine
months and then comes out of a special opening called the vagina.
Actually, it is not difficult to satisfy a child about the union of egg
and sperm. The entire story of love, marriage, and a desire for
children is woven into the explanation. A lovely picture will be
formed in the child's mind by adding the personal touch of including the child, his or her growing up, choosing a mate, establishing
a home, and also having children.

The Facts Of Life. When adolescence arrives, the story of sex changes to one of vivid reality. Then is the time for parents to give warning of the tragedy of premarital pregnancy and of the dangers of venereal disease.

This conclusion, call it puritanical if you wish, is based on years of medical practice during which I have listened again and again to the sorrowful tales of unwed mothers: I think it should be made crystal clear in sympathetic, understanding terms to every girl and boy as he or she enters puberty, that premarital sex relations should be avoided. As you sound the warning about exercising restraint, tell them you remember how thrilling it was on a lovely evening to date, to kiss and be kissed. Your children will appreciate your understanding attitude and will not label you "an old stick in the mud."

When you, mother, are talking to your daughter admit that the unfair but double standard of morals exists and that she is the one who will pay the penalty for premarital sex relations. Explain to her that nature has played a mean trick on us by making the sexual urge strong years before we are ready or able to care for children. Emphasize that we are above animals who, without restraint, reproduce as soon as they are mature. Underscore that falling in love is the most thrilling experience of life not to be marred or totally wrecked by the consequences of promiscuous sexual intercourse. Sex is beautiful; keep it so. Have fun, my darling daughter, enjoy your association with boys, but remember always to keep your guard up and stop short of the sexual act.

And another thing: It's considered smart and grown up to go along with the crowd on a drinking party. Absolutely no beer or alcoholic drinks of any kind so long as you are in high school, and preferably, not until you are twenty-one. The law in many states rules that no one shall purchase alcoholic beverages before age twenty-one. Observe the law and the spirit of the law in refusing drinks before age twenty-one. Remember, alcohol lessens inhibitions.

Be proud to be called a "square." Pay no attention to the false notion that to be popular you should "go all the way." It is a fact that the better boys who later are most apt to be fine husbands and considerate fathers marry the "squares." You are a wonderful daughter. Your happiness means more to us than anything else. Don't take a chance.

Father, talk frankly with your adolescent boy about sex. Tell him that he will meet boys who consider it smart and grown up to to have sexual experiences with promiscuous girls. It isn't smart—it's just plain stupid. Such girls are carriers of venereal disease—gonorrhea and syphilis. Remember, the sex urge is overpowering unless kept under control. No matter how much in love you are, one mistake may ruin the life of the girl you love as well as your own. You're still in high school and too young to take over the responsibility of marriage. Go with lots of girls but don't get so involved with one that you can think of nothing else but how wonderful it would be to get married. Wait, get your education first. For the sake of your future, my boy, wait.

Your mother has warned your sister about the dangers of alcohol. The same advice applies to you—no beer or drinking parties while you are in high school. After that I trust you will exercise good judgment.

There are those in this modern world who instruct their high-school children in the use of pills and other contraceptive devices. Maybe they are just being practical in not fighting what is often a losing battle.

Being a "square" can be interpreted as playing the game of life according to the best known rule—square.

THAT WONDERFUL BABY GROWS UP

Immediately after your baby was born, the cord was cut. From that moment on he was a new individual, totally dependent upon you but nevertheless a person different from all others who preceded him. Through the long period of infancy and childhood you nourished and guided him until now he is a mature individual, the finished product of your best efforts. Again the time has come to "cut the cord," and to relinquish all holds on your child; this is no easy task.

We want our grown children to be independent, self-reliant, and successful in whatever they choose to do. From the time a baby puts one block on top another, we stimulate the development of these characteristics by nurturing freedom of expression balanced with restrictive discipline, by giving judicious praise for accomplishments, and a minimum of criticism for failures.

To stand by and say nothing when our mature boy or girl makes what to us seems a mistake in the choice of life work or mate requires the utmost in restraint. Advice asked for and thoughtfully given may be accepted. Advice handed out with finality, without whole-hearted consideration of the mature child's wishes is worse than useless; if reluctantly followed it may lead to frustration and unhappiness; if not followed, to a rift in family relations.

Everybody makes mistakes. We made them; our children will make them. We can only comfort ourselves with the fact that we have done our best in rearing our children and pray, as they go out into the world, that those efforts have not been in vain.

When our children have married and have children of their own, then is the time we must doublecheck to be sure that the "cord has been cut."

Grandma and grandpa, you have finished your job; you have graduated from parenthood. Nevertheless, in your inmost souls you will never cease to be parents to your children. But stand in the background, cheer their successes, sympathize with their failures, be ready to give help when needed, and you will find that added to the pleasant years of happy parent-child relationship will be the priceless gift of mutual respect and friendship.

INDEX

About the Author:

WILLIS J. POTTS was born in Sheboygan, Wisconsin and received his B.A. at Hope College, in Michigan. After serving in World War I as a Sergeant in the Chemical Warfare Service, he attended the University of Chicago where he received his B.S. degree and his M.D. from Rush Medical College of the University of Chicago. He then did postgraduate study in Germany. Settling in Chicago, he became Assistant Associate Attending Surgeon at Presbyterian Hospital, professor at Rush Medical College, Surgeon-in-Chief at Children's Memorial Hospital, and professor of surgery at Northwestern University. Dr. Potts held the rank of colonel in World War II, serving as Surgical Consultant, Armed Services of the Orient. With Dr. Sidney Smith and Dr. Stanley Gibson, Dr. Potts was the originator of an operation for tetralogy of Fallot (blue baby). He also developed a number of instruments for cardiac surgery. Dr. Potts is the author of *The Surgeon and The Child,* and a syndicated column, "The Doctor and Your Child." He now lives in Florida with his wife, Henrietta. They have two sons and a daughter.

PRINTED IN THE U.S.A.